ICT
LAW BOOK

A Source Book for
Information and Communication Technologies &
Cyber law in Tanzania & East African Community

Adam J. Mambi

Mkuki na Nyota
DAR-ES-SALAAM

Published by:

Mkuki na Nyota Publishers Ltd.

Nyerere Road, Quality Plaza Building

P. O. Box 4246

Dar es Salaam, Tanzania

Website: www.mkukinanyota.com

ISBN 978-9987-08-074-8

CONTENTS

CHAPTER 7 Technology and Intellectual Property Rights 197

Acknowledgements

I would like to express my sincere gratitude to the following colleagues for their contributions which helped me to accomplish writing of this text book:

Dr Majamba (Senior Lecturer at the University of Dar Es Salaam UDSM) who edited this work and my beloved wife, Zainab C. Mambi for her tireless support and encouragement from the beginning of this project. I am also indebted to my Lecturer of Computer Law/ICT Law and Intellectual Property Law (Dr T. Hays) at the University of Aberdeen, UK. The knowledge I acquired from him paved the way for me to understand this subject better. My further appreciation goes to Professor John S. Nkoma, Director General of (TCRA), who read the final draft of the work and wrote its Preface.

There are a number of people whose ideas were very useful in the process of preparing this textbook. I am indebted to all of them. I would also like to thank and acknowledge the following authors whose works encouraged and helped me in understanding some legal uncertainties under the cyberspace; David Bainbridge,[1] Ian Lloyd[2] and Turban on E. (E-Commerce).

Lastly but not least, this work is dedicated to my parents, my wife and my children Abdul and Harith, not forgetting Several others who form part of my close family.

[1] *Introduction to Computer Law*, Longman 4th Edition. 2000.

[2] *Information Technology Law*, Lexis Nexis, UK 3rd Edition. 2000.

Preface

There is no doubt that computer technology specifically Information and Communication Technologies (ICT) which paved way for e-commerce and cyber crimes is growing dramatically. This growth has brought dramatic changes by revolutionising our customs and traditional methods of conducting business, communication and other activities that are based on paper methods. Technology is forcing most people to depart from old postal rule of communication to Internet communication or Electronic Data Interchange (EDI). Postal services and other related communication technologies are being greatly affected by the development of digital technology. The development of ICT has introduced new methods of banking and other financial transactions under the e-banking system. In addition to that, a new way of identification and verification under cyberspace has brought in digital or e-signatures using cryptography technology (PKI) as opposed to paper-based signatures (handwritten signatures). Technology convergence is growing very fast while changes in the legal system are slow. The days of analogy system with terrestrial transmitters are being rapidly overtaken by digital technology with satellite technology.

The impact of digital technology can also be observed in intellectual property rights specifically copyright and trademarks. While technology has facilitated access to and infringement of copyrighted works on-line, the introduction of Internet domain names has threatened trademark owners by creating illegal activities known as cyber-squatting. Many things are always happening due to the impact of technology and the world is peering to the new horizon or "new media".[3] It is believed that the technology has been further shifting "bricks and mortar companies" (physical world) to the Dotcom or Internet companies.[4] The development of digital technology has further facilitated the committing of e-commerce crimes or cyber crimes and other related illegal activities conducted under cyberspace.

While these new issues brought by the development of technologies under cyberspace have legal implications, the legal regime in some countries like Tanzania has not been changed to keep pace with these changes and regulate all activities that are happening under cyberspace. Most laws seem to be off-line designed to facilitate paper-based methods of transactions and communication which require writing, physical authentication, postal

---

3 Mambi Adam, The legal implications of the New Media/ICT, Paper presented at the Australasian Law Reform Commissions Conference, Sydney April 2006.

4 See Alister Kelman in Turban E., *E-Commerce* 2002. The argument here is that there are no physical goods and services apart from information or data based or digitised goods and services.

rule, best evidence rule, etc. All these no longer fit under this new media or digital technology. There are some initiatives that have been put in place in an effort to bridge the gap between the law and ICT in Tanzania. For instance in 2004, the Faculty of Law of the University of Dar Es Salaam introduced Computer Law/ICT Law as a subject for the first time.[5] Furthermore, the Law Reform Commission of Tanzania undertook a review and research on "off-line laws" under the e-commerce and cyber crime project in 2004[6] to see whether the existing laws were in tune with the developments of digital technology. The recommendations from the Law Reform Commission together with the decision of the court on the admissibility of e-evidence led to the amendment of the Evidence Act that now recognizes the admissibility of electronic evidence in the court. However, more still needs to be done as far as cyber laws are concerned.

I hope you will enjoy reading this textbook and benefit from the topical issues discussed here.

Professor John S. Nkoma
Director General
Tanzania Communications Regulatory Authority (TCRA)

---

5 The author of this textbook was the first lecturer on this subject. The author has also taught the subject on Professional Computing, Ethics, Law and Software/computer programmes protection and marketing for the computer science students, Computer Science Department, University of Dar Es Salaam under the African Virtual Learning University, organized by the Royal Melbourne Institute of Technology (RMIT), the World Bank Programme.

6 The author of this book was an initiator and pioneer of this project by writing a position paper that justified the field research. The author was also the first lecturer on Computer Law/ICT/Cyber Law at the Faculty of Law, University of Dar Es salaam in 2004.

List of Cases

1. Adams v. Lindsell (1818) 1 B & Ald.681
2. A & M Recordings, Inc. v. Napster No.00-16401, No.00-16403, U.S. Court of Appeals for the Ninth Circuit. 239 F.3d 1004; (2001) U.S.
3. Apple Computer Inc. v. Computer Edge Pty Ltd (1984) FSR 481
4. Badger Co. v. Application, (1970) RPC 36
5. Barclays Bank Ltd v. W J Sims Son and Cooke (1980) QB at 699
6. Beta Computers (Europe) Ltd v. Adobe System (Europe) Ltd (1996)
7. Byrne v.Van Tienhoven (1880) 5 CPD 344
8. Carlill v. Carbolic Smoke Ball Co. Ltd (1892) 2 Q.B 484, affd (1893) Q.B 1
9. Circuit Systems Ltd & Basten v. Zuken Redec UK Ltd (1995) Const. LJ, 201
10. Coco v. AN Clark (Engineers) Ltd (1969) RPC 41
11. Derby & Co. Ltd .v. Weldon (1991) 1.W.L.R 652
12. Enterprises, Inc. v. Frena 839 F. Supp 1552(1993).
13. Express Newspapers plc v. Liverpool Daily Post & Echo plc [1985] 1 WLR 1089
14. Faccenda Chicken Ltd v. Fowler [1986] 1 ALL ER 617
15. Feist Publications Inc. v. Rural Telephone Service Co Inc (1991) 111 S Ct 1228
16. Fisher v. Bell (1961) 1 QB 394
17. Finance Ltd v. Crown Financial management (1994)
18. Firstpost Homes v. Johnson (1995) 4 ALL ER 355
19. Hawley v. Whipple 48 N.H.487 (1869)
20. Gandy v. Casper Air Charters Limited, 23 E.A.C.A.
21. Grainger & Son v. Gouh (1896) A.C.
22. Harrods Ltd .v. UK Network Services Ltd (19980 FSR 265.
23. Hawley .v. Whipple 48 N.H.487 (1869)
24. House Fire & Carriage Accident Insurance Co. Ltd v. Grand (1878-79) L.R. Ex.D.216, CA

25. IBCOS Computers Ltd .v. Barclays Mercantile Highland Finance Ltd (1994) FSR 275
26. Joyce v. Sengupta (1993) 1 ALL ER 897.
27. Julian v. Crago, The Times in 1991
28. Lansing Linde Ltd v. Kerr (1991) 1 WLR 251
29. MBNA v. Freeman (1997) ESRF 797
30. Marks & Spencer plc and others v. One In A Million Ltd (1998) FSR 265
31. Mercantile Union Guarantee Co. v. Ball (1937) ALL ER 1
32. Mehta C., Limited v. The Baron Verheyen, 2 T.L.R. (R) 300
33. M. Witmark & Sons v. Pastime Amusement Co 298 F.470 E.D.SC. (1924)
34. New York Times Company, inc. al., Petitioners v. Jonathan Tasini Et Al Supreme Court of the United States 121 S.Ct.2381 2001
35. Nissan Motor Co .v. Nissan Computer Cop (1998) FSR 265 Supreme Court of the United States 121 S.Ct.2381 2001.
36. Northern Office Microcomputer (Pty) Ltd v. Rosenstein (1982) FSR 124
37. Quante Ltd v. Spaceward Microsystems (1990) RPC 83
38. Partridge v. Critenden (1968) 2 ALL ER 421
39. Pharmaceutical Society of Great Britain v. Boots Cash Chemists Ltd (1951) 2 Q.B.
40. Panavision International LP .v Toeppen case no. 97-554679th Cir, April (1998)
41. Pitman Training Ltd v. Nominet UK (1997) FSR 797 130
42. Prince Pl v. Prince Sportswear Group Inc (1998) FSR 21
43. R v. Governor (1989) 3 ALL ER 701.
44. Religious Technology Centre v. Netcom On-Line Communications Service 907 F.Supp.1361 (N.D. Cal. 1995).
45. Shetland Times Ltd. v. Dr Jonathan Wills (1997) FSR 604
46. Springsteen v. Flute International (2001)
47. St Albans City and District Council v. International Computer Ltd (1996) ALL ER 481

48. State Farm Mutual Auto Ins. Co. v. Brockhurst 453f.2d 533, 10th Cir. (1972)
49. The salvage Associate v. CAP Financial Services Ltd (1995) FSR 654
50. The Sega Enterprises v. Richards (1983) FSR 73
51. Tanzania Cotton Marketing Board v. Cogecot Cotton Company SA [1997] TLR 165 (CA)
52. Thomas Marshall (Export) Ltd v. Guinle (1976) FSR 345
53. Thorp v. Holdsworth, (1876) 3 Ch. D. 637
54. Thornton v. Shoe Lane Parking (1971) 2 QB 163, (1971)2 WL, (1971 1 ALL ER 686
55. Total Information Processing Systems Ltd v. Daman Ltd (1992) FSR 171
56. Trust Bank Ltd v. Le-marsh Enterprises Ltd, Joseph Mbui Magari, Lawrence Macharia, The High Court of Tanzania (Commercial Division) at Dar Es Salaam Commercial case no.4 of 2000 (Unreported)
57. University Press of London v. University Tutorial Press Ltd (1916) 2 Ch 601

List of Legislation

1. The Anti-cybersquatting Consumer Protection Act (ACPA) 1999, USA
2. The Australian Evidence Act 1995
3. The Arbitration Act [CAP 15 R.E.2002]
4. The Australian Electronic Transaction Act 1998
5. The Australian Corporations Act 2001
6. The Banking and Financial Institutions Act (Act No. 12 of 1991) [CAP 342 R.E.2002]
7. The Banking and Financial Institutions Act (Act No. 5 of 2006)
8. The Banking and Financial Institutions Act (BAFIA) 1989 of Malaysia
9. The Bill of Exchange Act
10. The Business Licensing Act (Act No. 25 of 1972) [CAP 273 R.E.2002]
11. The Business Names (Registration) Act (Ordinance No. 1 of 1930) [CAP 213 R.E. 2002]
12. The Capital Markets and Securities Act (Act No. 5 of 1994) [CAP 79 R.E.2002]
13. The Carriage of Goods by Sea Act (Ordinance No. 6 of 1927 [CAP 164 R.E.2002]
14. The Civil Procedure Code (Act No. 49 of 1966) [CAP 33 R.E.2002]
15. The Communication and Multimedia Act of Malaysia 1998 (Act 588)
16. The Computer Crimes Act of Malaysia 1997
17. The Computer Enhancement Act (2000), US
18. The Computer Fraud and Abuse Act (1986), US
19. The Copyright and Neighbouring Rights Act (Act No. 7 of 1999) [CAP 33 R.E.2002]
20. The Copyright and Rights in Databases Regulations (1997), UK
21. The Cyberspace Electronic Security Act (2000), USA

22. The Digital Millennium Copyright Act (DMCA) 2000, USA
23. The Digital Signature Act of Malaysia 1997
24. The Electronic Commerce Act, CAP 426, Malta
25. The Electronic Communications (Regulation) CAP 399, Malta
26. The Electronic Communications Privacy Act (1986), US
27. The Electronic Signature in Global and National Commerce Act (the "E-Sign Law") (2000), US
28. The Electronic Transactions Act (2000) Mauritius
29. The Employment and Labour Relations Act, No. 6 of 2004, Tanzania
30. The Evidence Act (1967) [CAP R.E 2002]
31. The Homeland Security Act (2002), US
32. The Income Tax Act of Tanzania, Act No.11 2004 as amended
33. The Information Technology Act, 2000, India
34. The Information Technologies (Misc) Act 1998 (Mauritius)
35. The Interpretation of Laws Act of Tanzania [CAP 1 R.E.2002]
36. The Labour Institutions Act, No. 7 of 2004, Tanzania
37. The Law of Contract Act [CAP 345 R.E.2002]
38. The Malaysian Communications and Multimedia Act of 1998 (Act 589)
39. The National Information Infrastructure Protection Act (1996), US
40. The Patents (Registration) Act (Ordinance No. 25 of 1936 and Act No. 1 of 1987) [CAP 217 R.E.2002]
41. The Patriot Act (2002), US
42. The Sale of Goods Act (Ordinance No. 18 of 1931) [CAP 214 R.E.2002]
43. The Sale of Goods Act (1979), UK
44. The Slovenian E-Commerce and E-Signatures Act (ESA) 200
45. The Supply of Goods and Services Act (UK)
46. The Tanzania Communications Regulatory Authority Act, 2003

47. The Tanzania Communications (Consumer Protection) Regulations, 2005 made under The Tanzania Communications Regulatory Authority Act 2003
48. The Trade and Service Marks Act (Act No. 12 of 1986) [CAP 326 R.E.2002]
49. The US Uniform Electronic Transaction Act (1999), USA
50. The UK Copyright, Design and Patents Act (1998), UK
51. The Written Laws (Miscellaneous Amendment) Act No.15 (2007), Tanzania

International Legal Instruments

1. Agreed Statements concerning the WIPO Performers and Phonogram Treaty 1996
2. The Berne Convention 1886, as amended in 1979
3. The Rome Convention for the Protection of Performers, producers of Phonograms and Broadcasting Organisations 1961
4. The TRIPS Agreement 1994
5. The Treaty on Intellectual Property in Respect of Integrated Circuits 1989
6. The Universal Copyright Convention 1952 as revised in1971
7. The EU Copyright (Computer Programs) Council Directive, 14/05/1991, No.91/250
8. The E.U. Copyright (Databases) Directive, 11/03/1996, No.96/9
9. The EU E-commerce Directive, OJ 2000 L 178/1
10. The EU Unfair Terms Directive Council Directive, 93/13/EEC, OJ L 95, April 1993
11. The Unfair Terms Directive Council Directive, 93/13/EEC, OJ L 95, 1993
12. The EU Directive 1994/EC on the Sale of Consumer Goods and Associated Guarantees
13. The Distance Selling Directive, 97/7/EC
14. The EU E-commerce Directive, 2003/31/EC
15. The EU Council Directive, 93/83/EEC of 1993
16. The EU Council Directive, 93/98/EEC
17. The Rules for Uniform Domain Name Dispute Resolution Policy 1999
18. The Uniform Domain Name Dispute Resolution Policy 1999
19. The WIPO Copyright Treaty 1996
20. The WIPO Performances and Phonograms Treaty 1996
21. The UN Convention on Electronic Communications 2001
22. The Convention on the Limitation Period in the International Sale of Goods ("Limitation Convention")

23. The United Nations Convention on Contracts for the International Sale of Goods ("United Nations Sales Convention")
24. The United Nations Convention on the Liability of Operators of Transport Terminals in International Trade ("Terminal Operators Convention")
25. The United Nations Convention on Independent Guarantees and Stand-by Letters of Credit ("Guarantees Convention")
26. The United Nations Convention on the Assignment of Receivables in International Trade ("Receivables Convention")
27. The Convention on the Recognition and Enforcement of Foreign Arbitral Awards ("New York Convention")
28. The Convention on the Limitation Period in the International Sale of Goods Vienna, 11 April 1980)
29. The United Nations Convention on Independent Guarantees and Stand-by
30. The United Nations Convention on the Assignment of Receivables in International Trade (New York, 12 December 2001)

ABBREVIATIONS

AC	Appeal Cases
ACPA	The Anti-cyber-squatting Protections Act
ADRP	Automated Dispute Resolution Processes
ALL ER	All England Law Reports
ASEAN	Association of South-East Asian Nations
ATM	Automated Teller Machine
Ch	Chancery
CMA	Commission for Mediation and Arbitration
DANIDA	Danish International Development Agency
e-ADR	Electronic Alternative Dispute Resolution
E-commerce	Electronic Commerce
e-crime	electronic crime
e-evidence	electronic evidence
e-document	electronic document
e-government	electronic government
e-mobile	electronic mobile
e-signatures	electronic Signatures
e-security	electronic security
EDI	Electronic Data Interchange
EFTPOS	Electronic Funds Transfer at Point of Sale
EU	European Union
FSR	Fleet Street Reports
G2B	Government to Business
G2C	Government to Citizens
G2G	Government to Government
GPO	General Periodicals On Disc
ICANN	The Internet Corporation for Assigned Names and Numbers

ICT	Information and Communication Technologies
IP	Intellectual Property
IPRs	Intellectual Property Rights
ISP	Internet Service Provider
ITU	International Telecommunication Union
IT	Information Technology
ITV	Independent Television
LDCs	Least Development Countries
M-pesa	Mobile Pesa
m-commerce	Mobile Commerce
OECD	Organization for Economic Co-operative and Development
PAYE	Pay As You Earn
PKI	Public Key Infrastructure
QB	Queen's Bench
RPC	Reports of Patents, Designs and Trade Marks Cases
SCORE	Standardized Corporate Environment
SIM	Subscriber Identity Module
SWIFT	Society for Worldwide Inter-bank Financial Transfer
TLR	Times Law Reports
TRIPS Agreement	Agreement on Trade Related Aspects of Intellectual Property Rights
TVT	Television ya Taifa, now Tanzania Broadcasting Corporation (TBC)
UDRP	Uniform Dispute Resolution Policy
UK	United Kingdom
UMI	University Microfilms International
UN	United Nations
UNCITRAL	United Nations Commission on International Trade Law

UNCTAD	United Nations Conference on Trade and Development
US	United States of America
WIPO	World Intellectual Property Organization
WPPT	WIPO Performances and Phonograms Treaty
WLR	Weekly Law Reports

KEY NOTES UNDER THE PREAMBLE

- *"[The customer] was committed at the moment when he put his money into the machine. The contract was concluded at that time.... the offer is made when the proprietor of the machine holds it ... the acceptance takes place when the customer puts his money into the slot. The contract was concluded at that time. The offer is made when the proprietor of the machine holds it out as being ready to recover the money. The acceptance takes place when the customer puts his money into the slot* (***Denning L.J in Thornton v. Shoe Lane Parking** [1971]2 QB 163, [1971]2 WLR, [1971] 1* **ALL ER 686**).
- *"In the context of contract formation, unless otherwise agreed by the parties, an offer and acceptance of an offer may be expressed by means of data message (online). Where a data message is used in the formation of a contract, that contract shall not be denied validity or enforceability on the sole ground that a data message for that purpose was stored* ***electronically [Article 11, UNCITRAL Model Law on E-Commerce(emphasis added)]****.*

CHAPTER ONE

The Development of Information and Communication Technologies and The Law

1.1 *Introduction*

What is Cyber Law, Computer Law or Information and Communication Technology Law (ICT/IT Law)? There is no clear definition of Cyber Law, Computer Law or Information and Communication Technology Law. However the subject can be briefly defined as the legal subject that emanated from the development of technologies, the innovation of computers and other related devices, the use of Internet and Electronic Data Interchange (EDI), etc.

The ICT Law observatory of the Swedish ICT Commission argues that one way of describing these hurdles in the area of technology or cyber law is to focus on 'the paradoxes of ICT law'.[1] The Swedish ICT Commission highlights the following explanations of ICT Law:

- ICT law includes almost all branches of law, but in order to be meaningful it must nevertheless be narrowed down and delimited;
- ICT law must be independent of technology, i.e. be technologically neutral. At the same time it must be able to regulate and steer technology and its various uses;
- The development of ICT law often requires broad as well as deep understanding of machinery and methods, but the legal solutions must be simple to understand and apply;[2]
- ICT law requires foresight but it is very difficult to predict future developments, situations, applications, issues, etc. in ICT;
- ICT law demands 'new laws', which must be based on inherited legal views and existing legal concepts and regulations; and
- There is no consensus on what to call ICT Law. Some people still regard ICT Law as 'Information Law', i.e. as a general law of information

1 See the Swedish ICT Commission Report Stockholm 2002.

2 Ibid.

handling, others call it 'Computer Law', 'Internet Law', 'Cyberspace Law', 'Software Law', 'the new media law,' etc.[3]

The ICT Policy in Tanzania highlights that the development of ICT applications in the world has been increasing at a very fast rate thus boosting the economy of some countries while changing society's behaviour.[4] ICT advances since the end of the 20th century have led to multiple convergences of content, computing, telecommunications and broadcasting. ICT advances have also brought about changes in other areas, particularly in knowledge management and human resources development.

The policy further states that the increasing capacity of ICT has further been empowered by the growth of a global network of computer networks known as the Internet.[5] It has changed the way business is done, facilitated learning and knowledge sharing, generated global information flow, empowered citizens and communities in ways that have redefined governance, and have created significant wealth and economic growth resulting in a global information society.

There is sufficient evidence that in Tanzania several large organizations and companies make extensive use of networked computers, some with Internet access. The banking sector makes heavy use of ICT to provide improved customer service with some banks using Very Small Aperture Terminal (VSATs) or public leased lines to interconnect their branches and cash dispensing Automatic Teller Machines (ATMs).[6]

Generally the rapid pace of innovations in the ICT sector is believed to have considerably reduced the costs of access to ICT, while generating new services in the forms of e-commerce, e-finance, e-government, m-commerce and other related e-transactions which contribute to greater economic efficiency.[7] The revolution in information technologies has fundamentally changed society and will probably continue to do so in the future. It is now easier to do many tasks.[8] It has been further argued that people should note that a conspicuous feature of information technology is the impact it has and will have on the evolution of telecommunications technology.[9] In this case, one can observe that classical telephony, involving the transmission of human voice, has been overtaken by the exchange of vast amounts of data, comprising voice, text, music and static and moving

---

3 Ibid.
4 See the National Information Communications Technologies policy, 2003.
5 Ibid.
6 Ibid.
7 UNCTAD Information Economy Report, 2008, at page 2.
8 See EU Council Explanatory Report to the Convention on Cyber Crime at http://conventions.coe.int accessed on 8 September 2008.
9 Ibid.

pictures. Obviously, this exchange no longer occurs only between human beings, but also between human beings and computers, and between computers themselves.

ICT has created new transactions, production and consumption forms resulting in cost-saving transactions and faster and better communication among users. As noted by the United Nations (UN), there is no doubt that the increased use of electronic communication improves the efficiency of commercial activities, enhances trade connections and allows new access opportunities for previously remote parties and markets, thus playing a fundamental role in promoting trade and economic development of any country, both domestically and internationally.[10]

The use of cyberspace and technology has resulted in cyber transactions, cyber crimes, jurisdiction problems, etc. The world, therefore has to come up with the relevant legal framework that will bridge the gap between digital technology and the law. The legal implications brought by cyberspace have contributed to the fast growth of the subject of cyber law or ICT law. Having realized the challenges and impact brought by the technologies under the emerging information society, some people raised their concerns on the legal response to computers and other related devices. In line with this, the earliest stage in the evolving relationship between law and computer technology or information and communication technologies was witnessed between 1945 and 1970.[11]

Lloyd argues that the main aspect of the phenomenon of digitization which seems to carry a more considerable legal significance is that data becomes almost a totally pliable commodity with the expanding market for multimedia products whereby a single CD may contain recordings of sound, text, music and moving images that has legal implications on intellectual property rights.[12] Furthermore, an increasing number of transactions at national and international trade are being carried out by means of EDI and other means of communication commonly referred as electronic commerce. The use of alternatives to paper based methods of communication and storage of information including the legal value of computer records substantiated the need for a quick legal and policy response. There is also great concern on the impact of digital technology over intellectual property rights whereby Internet transfer of information in digital format is threatening owners of intellectual property rights as the transmission speed has been increasing. This has also led to more complex and substantial

[10] See Preamble 1 United Nations Convention on the Use of Electronic Communications in International Contracts.

[11] See Lloyd J.I., *Information Technology Law*, 3rd Edition, Butterworth, 2000 at page 2.

[12] Ibid at page 3.

data being transmitted and downloaded online leading to infringement of copyrighted works in most cases.

More importantly, MP3[13] software system which quickly allows music to be transmitted over the Internet in real time is cheaply accessible to many computer users. This is causing considerable concern to the owners of copyright in musical and other related works. On the other hand, the rise of dot.com (.com) with the Internet Domain names and cyber-squatting has also raised the concern over trademarks or service marks and domain name owners.

The great concern on the need of regulating cyberspace and the use of Internet has been there since the revolution of ICT. It is believed that German was the first country in the world to introduce computer specific legislation in 1970. The said computer specific statute which was enacted by the German State of Hase, was in the form of a Data Protection Act.[14] This was followed by the specific intellectual property provisions in Europe in mid 1980 followed by more statutes based on e-commerce and cyber crimes in the 20th century. This was the starting point of regulating the use of cyberspace by legislation.[15]

1.2 *An Overview of E-commerce and its Legal Implications at Global Level*

In the 19th century the world witnessed the development of railways which affected commerce by reducing the cost of shipping a ton of goods tenfold when compared to transportation by wagon or canal barge.[16] The so called new media in the 20th century has brought along fundamental changes that are likely to impact on peoples' lives and old laws that were made prior to the innovations of computers and advancement of technology. The 20th Century witnessed rapid and new innovative technologies in line with the use of Internet, bringing fundamental changes in the way things happen, e.g. the way we live, work and think in this world of digital technology whereby people are peering to the new horizon.[17] Internet use in Africa has been rapidly growing over the past few years which made the continent the world's fastest growing Internet market. For instance by May 2004, Africa had 12 million Internet users. The ratio between total populations and Internet users in the respective African countries shows that there are

13 An audio-specific format that was designed by the Moving Picture Experts Group (Wiki Pedia).

14 Ibid at page 4.

15 Ibid.

16 Turban E., on *E-Commerce*, 2002 at page 1.

17 See Mambi. A., "Peering to the New Horizon", The New Media, Paper presented in the Australasian and Asian Law Reform Commission Agencies Conference (ALARAC) Sydney, 2006.

6.8 users per 100 inhabitants in South Africa, 3.6 in Egypt, 3.7 in Morocco and 0.7 in Tanzania.[18]

The current rapid innovative technologies have brought fundamental changes on the way commerce and communication, take place. Traders and individuals are becoming more and more reliant on information technology to smooth the progress of international business transactions and many people believe that fully-fledged electronic commerce is nearing a reality.[19]

The use of modern means of communication such as electronic mail (e-mail) and EDI for conducting international trade has been increasing very fast and offers advantages such as security, low costs and quick and efficient access.

More reliable and convenient market places are being created and extended online beyond the traditional boundaries, where sales and shopping can take place anywhere within a short time. While the current digital technology allows personalization where messages are delivered to individuals and groups, the cost of information and communication is reduced at the same time raising its quality and accuracy.[20]

Indeed the use of computers and other related devices has resulted in fundamental changes in the way business, transactions and communication takes place in the world. Forms of agreements including other contractual documents are being created using computers and transmitted electronically in the world in real time. The technology on electronic banking has introduced ATMs and electronic funds transfer (EFTs) whereby transactions are made among financial institutions and more significantly at the point-of-sale. The recent mobile commerce (m-commerce) that facilitates payment and banking by mobile phones has been promoting the growth of m-commerce. The use of e-mail and EDI has been increasing rapidly over the world facilitating transactions and communication.

The development of ICT, the Internet and the World Wide Web has also radically changed our way of communicating, running business and doing research creating a new "business communication environment" has been described in symbolic language derived from the traditional physical world.[21] It is believed that the past decade has witnessed rapid and enormous growth in ICT-related trade and business flow and full recovery from the notable crisis in 2000, with growth in ICT goods equal to those in overall manufacturing trade and above the average growth of trade in

[18] See TCRA Journal No.7 2004, at page 18.

[19] See Farhan AL-Farhan on The Impact of the UNCITRAL Model Law on international legal systems Saudi Arabia information technology development from a legal perspective, 2002.

[20] Laudon K & Traver, *E-commerce* 3rd Edition, 2007, at page 13.

[21] See the Swedish ICT Commission Report 2002.

ICT services.[22] The research by United Nations Conference on Trade and Development (UNCTAD) indicates that in 2004, exports from developing countries such as South Africa exceeded those from developed countries. The successful deployment of ICT for e-commerce and other related e-transactions will be beneficial to the users and the growth of economy where there is an enabling regulatory environment. These technological developments will attract more people where the governments concerned are committed to frameworks, policies and laws that address the digital divide between the rich and poor.

The lack of legal guidance in the field of e-commerce, for example, may derive from the customary limitation to computer data as immaterial information. Electronic equivalents to physical places and objects, and the difference between rules and regulations applicable to immaterial information on the one hand and a person's protected custody of digital data and documentary evidence on the other hand are in most countries including Tanzania hardly mentioned. There is need to introduce effective cyber laws to regulate e–commerce and protect consumers.

Indeed the digital revolution brought by Information Technology (IT) or ICT has brought fundamental changes to communication or transactions which has fuelled dramatic developments for the new digital economy under the so called 'information society'.[23] Some scholars once argued that one day some social historian will look back with wonder at the havoc wrecked by the Internet.[24] Furthermore, there is no doubt that we are now living in an information society in which information in its many and various forms is becoming an important commodity and measurement of prosperity than physical objects bringing challenges as to how ICT will be regulated.[25]

Technological revolution has brought great changes, which have affected the way business is done, the way in which goods and services are ordered, marketed and the way in which contracts are made and fulfilled. This trend poses great challenges for the current off-line laws in Tanzania and other countries which must immediately respond to these developments on e-transactions that might boost the economy. The most significant aspect of this technological revolution is the marketing and supply of goods and services through electronic media or e-commerce.[26] Underpinning e-commerce, are the communications networks that allow computers and other related devices to exchange data on global networks under cyber

[22] UNCTAD Information Economy Report 2008, at page xxvii.

[23] Ibid.

[24] See Alistair Kelman in Turban E., on *E-Commerce*, 2002 at page 1.

[25] Lloyd J.I., *Information Technology Law*, 3rd Edition, Butterworth, 2000, at page 11.

[26] Bradgate R., *Commercial Law*, 3rd Edition, 2000, at page 21.

space. The Internet has dramatically changed the face of the physical world into a new cyberspace with little boundaries.[27]

1.3 *An Insight on the Concepts of E-commerce at a Global Level*

E-commerce has been growing at a very fast rate in the world starting from the developed countries to the developing countries. In the US it is believed that e-commerce has been significantly growing and expanding since 1995 from a standing start to a $172 billion retail business and approximately $1.5 trillion business to business (B2B) juggernaut in 2005.[28] This trend has indeed brought enormous changes in business firms, markets and more importantly even consumer behaviour. Laudon K & Traver highlight that the e-commerce revolution is just beginning and there was a notable increase of online consumers by more than 23% worth $142-$172 billion in the US by 2005.[29] In addition, the number of individuals online in the US increased to 175 million in 2005 as compared to 170 million in 2004. Another notable impact of e-commerce was the expansion of B2B by 30% in 2005.

The word e-commerce emanated from the evolution of digital technology. There is no English or legal dictionary that has attempted to define e-commerce to date. However various literature and practical experience indicates that e-commerce is an area with various and multi-dimensional definitions which might even change as technology changes.[30] Despite these definitions the term e-commerce can be simply defined as a commercial exchange system, which makes use of computers, and communication network advances. It is the use of information in electronic forms instead of paper, for business or government operations. This suggests that e-commerce means the use of technological advances to promote everything involving the exchange of business information among computers and humans or traders and customers.[31] While e-commerce is the use of the Internet and the Web to transact business or digitally enabled commercial transactions between and among organizations and individuals, e-business is the digital enablement of transactions and processes within a firm, involving information systems under the control of the firm.[32] It is equally important to note that e-commerce as a concept includes

---

27 Op cit at page v.

28 See Laudon K & Traver, *E-commerce*, 3rd Edition 2007.

29 Ibid.

30 WIPO report caries a 4 page Annexure compiling 10 different definitions.

31 Kaetzel L.J., *E-commerce and IP on the Internet* 1996 at page 186. http://fire.nist.gov/bfrlpubs/build96/art 033.html 26/2/03.

32 Laudon K & Traver, E-commerce, 3rd Edition 2007 at page 10.

commercial activities undertaken online, including international trade transactions, advertising and domestic business–to-consumer (B2C) and B2B transactions to mention a few.[33]

As a network, e-commerce has been further defined as sale or purchase of goods or services conducted over computer-mediated networks. In this way the goods and services are ordered online but payment and ultimate delivery of the goods/services may be conducted on-or offline.[34] No wonder e-commerce might become m-commerce and many other related words depending on the development of technology. The most important thing is to create policies and legal framework on cyberspace activities that are dynamic to cope with any technological changes.

Moreover e-commerce can be termed commercial transactions[35] over digital networks (whether open[36] or closed networks[37]) that increase delivery speed and reduce operational costs through computer-to-computer transactions and web-enabled mobile phone communications.[38] Presently e-commerce may be classified into several main parts depending, of course, mainly on the nature of the transaction. If a transaction is done between businesses, it is called B2B e-commerce whereby the customer is another enterprise or another department within the same enterprise.[39] It is the largest form of online business whereby businesses focus on selling to other businesses. A good example from the US is the ChemConnect.com which is the chemical industry that creates an electronic market for chemical producers and users.

The second type of e-commerce is termed as business-to-customer e-commerce (B2C) which refers to the placing of finished goods/services to end-users, i.e. customers who can be corporate entities or individuals whereby online businesses sell their goods or services to individual consumers. The most common example is Amazon.com website which is a merchandiser that sells consumer products to retail consumers.[40] The development of e-commerce has simplified the means and modes for consumers to sell to each other under the consumer to consumer (C2C). In r C2C, individuals purchase and sell from one another, for instance in

33 Mackenzie P.D., *E-commerce Law-China.* http://www.perkinscoie.com/resource/ecomm/prc.htm 26/02/2003.

34 OECD defined e-commerce i.e. the 'Networks' over which relevant activities are carried out; the 'Processes' that ought to be included within the general domain of e-commerce. See UNCTAD 2001: 6.

35 Commercial transactions may comprise but not limited to selling and purchase.

36 The term 'open network' means a network, such as the Internet, using non-proprietary protocols.

37 An illustration of 'closed network' is electronic data interchange (EDI).

38 In what is now referred to as m-commerce where commercial transactions are done through mobile electronic facilities such as mobile telephones.

39 It is also referred to as B2B e-commerce.

40 Laudon & Traver C., *E-commerce*, 3rd Edition 2007 at page 17.

auctions such as eBay.com which provide a market place where consumers can easily auction or even prepare the market, place the product or goods and sell directly to other consumers. In line with this, there is also the so called consumer-to-business (C2B) where consumers post prices at which they are willing to buy goods and services from businesses.[41]

The development of digital technology has also come up with other types of e-commerce that is Peer-to-Peer (P2P) e.g. Kazaa.com and Mobile Commerce (M-Commerce) e.g. eBay. Whereas the former technology (P2P) enables Internet users to share files and computer resources directly, the later enables the transactions on the web using wireless digital devices. The impact of these technologies is discussed in depth in the following chapters.

1.4 *Benefits of E-commerce*

Generally, e-commerce is believed to be the result of the development of Internet and the World Wide Web which has created enormous expansion of cheap digital services and market places worldwide competing with physical world services.

E-commerce, which is a product of digital revolution, has a number of advantages in comparison to traditional commerce, which is based on paper use. Firstly, under e-commerce information flows more quickly and in more directions than in the orthodox commerce giving businesses opportunities to access more markets at low cost and with minimal capital investment and few staff. In this way, the information flow improves competitiveness and customer services, reduces transaction costs and overheads while avoiding traditional limitations of restricted access to information.[42] A large proportion of information between organizations or individuals may be easily handled electronically including quoting or submitting of tenders, ordering, etc.

Secondly, E-commerce saves time and money[43] and the risk of lost or damaged documents is reduced when documents are transmitted electronically in a form of data message or attachments. The innovation and the use of EDI facilitate the placing and dispatching of orders between commercial undertakings.[44]

Thirdly, e-commerce offers great opportunities to both business and consumers at a cheap rate.[45] Business persons cannot necessarily meet with

---

41 UNCTAD 2001:84.

42 WIPO, paragraph 207.

43 Kaetzel I.J., *E-commerce and IP on the Internet* page 186, NIST Gaithersburg.

44 Lloyd I., *Information Technology Law*, 3rd Edition 2001 at page xliv.

45 Bradgate R., on *Commercial Law*, 3rd Edition 2000 at page 21.

their consumers when transacting business electronically thus saving both time and transport costs. It offers businesses access to a wider, potentially global physical outlet. It enables customers of both goods and services to choose from a wider range of suppliers electronically than is possible using traditional means.

Some research and studies such as the E. Global (1999)[46] reported that the number of people online more than doubled from 44 million in 1997 to 95.4 million in 1998, that is in the space of a year and over the same period the total global revenue from e-commerce tripled, from $10.8 billion to $37.6 billion. The revenue figures include both business-to-business (B2B) and business-to-consumer (B2C) depending on the Internet. This study predicted that global E-Commerce Revenue (ECR) has the potential to grow beyond $1.6 trillion by 2003 if illegal activity on the web can be controlled.

Transaction under cyber space is making geographical distance to cease thus creating jurisdiction problems. Likewise, ordering goods and services, carrying out banking transactions, making travel and other ticket reservations, collecting and passing on information, etc. can be done through one medium, from the same position, without the parties involved needing to move from point A to B or meet face to face is likely to create legal issues like disputes.[47]

Under this era of e-commerce, computers are creating automation of tasks, which previously required human involvement and were time consuming.[48] E-commerce is also believed to create more new jobs for graduates and young managers in all fields, e.g. marketing, management, entrepreneur studies and information systems.

It is now possible for computers and other related devices to receive orders, form contracts online in some Electronic Data Interchange systems (EDI). This raises important legal issues for Tanzania and other East African countries that lack effective legal framework to regulate transactions on cyberspace. For instance can a computer accept an offer and create a contract? For example, when a person wishes to buy goods or services and makes an offer to an online supplier, can the merchant's web server accept the offer and create a valid contract? Indeed the growth of e-commerce in most cases will depend on, among other things, the quality of the legal rules and enforcement in ensuring that transaction data is protected and secured from

---

46 http://www.fdih.dk/site_dir/fdih/uploads/3a6f164f5bb80_eeurope_exec_summ_sales.pdf. See also Farhan Al-farhan on The Impact of the UNCITRAL Model Law on international legal systems Saudi Arabia information technology development from a legal perspective 2002.

47 The Swedish ICT Commission Report 2002.

48 Turban E., *Electronic Commerce* 2002 at page 84.

electronic misuse worldwide. These arguments show some interesting legal issues which might be difficult to answer given the lack of legal framework on cyberspace in Tanzania. Case laws and other online laws from other jurisdictions can be useful in solving these legal issues.

Turban E. points out that English law and most other legal systems have a tradition of attributing the actions of a machine to the person who instructs it to execute a particular routine. This argument can be supported by the courts' decisions in various cases.[49] For instance in the United States, the court once ruled in the case of *State Farm Mutual Auto.Ins. Co. v. Brockhurst,*[50] that since the computer only operated as programmed by the insurance company, it was bound by the contract formed (in this case, an insurance renewal). Using these landmark precedents, the judiciary in common law countries like Tanzania would probably decide that a web server, as an agent of the online business, can both make offers and accept offers in order to create contracts or conduct transactions electronically.

There might be disadvantages of e-commerce as well depending on the nature of existing policies and legal framework. One should bear in mind that e-commerce is not only about business and technology but this vital area of technology supported by Internet has also socio-economic consequences if not taken care of. The great challenge can be seen on the whole question of privacy and intellectual property rights. Online shoppers are always visiting various websites such as Amazon, Google, eBay, etc. which advertise and facilitate business online under unregulated cyberspace.

The question of verification and authentication of e-documents and more importantly identification of parties to the transaction electronically might pose a great challenge. The question of e-security and privacy can be a great concern to the development of e-commerce. Hackers and other related e-culprits might be a threat to the parties who are doing business online as they might be able to illegally intercept the transaction and direct the money to their accounts if there is no effective electronic security supported by cyber laws. This is the challenge to the governments in place. They need to come up with effective institutional policy and legal framework to regulate this area rather than just assuming that the Internet has no boundaries beyond social and regulatory control. There is no doubt that the bright future of e-commerce will highly demand the creation of effective regulatory framework worldwide disregarding the fear and assumption that cyberspace is self-regulatory and self-governing phenomena.

---

49 In *Thornton v. Shoe Lane Parking* (1971) 2 QB 163, (1971) 2 WL, (1971) 1 ALL E R 686 the court ruled that a customer contracted with a car park machine (representing the owner) when he fed in his money and received a claim ticket. See also arguments by Denning L.J. at page 686.

50 453f.2d 533, 10th Cir. (1972).

1.5 *ICT Policy Statements on Legal Implications of ICT in Tanzania*

The ICT Policy highlights that globalisation and the pervasiveness of ICT and especially the Internet have given rise to new types of needs, rights and vulnerabilities.[51] For secure electronic transactions to occur, an environment of trust must be created and sustained through the legal and regulatory apparatus. Cyber-criminals around the world are constantly seeking loopholes through which to perform illegal or illicit businesses. Any country that has inadequate cyber-law is essentially offering a safe-haven for cyber-criminals to act with impunity. Tanzania needs to create and sustain a secure cyber-law environment, in addition to already existing legislation, before any significant new developments can emerge in ICT related services.

In terms of legal framework, the ICT Policy clearly states that:

1. The Government will review existing laws and regulations in order to repeal or adjust those that are not conducive to the healthy growth of the ICT industry and enact new ones that take account of issues associated with Internet Governance and the convergence of telecommunication, broadcasting and information systems.
2. The Government will set-up legal regulatory frameworks that are appropriate to the ICT sector taking into account that electronic transactions are also susceptible to electronic criminality.
3. The Government will have compelling interest in shielding contents inappropriate for minors or those that promote behaviour that might endanger minors and society.
4. The Government will promote business in electronic form in a secure environment and put in place a legal framework to provide the guiding principles, rules and legislation.
5. The Government will regularly carry out a review of policies and/or legislation in order to foster introduction of new services and technological innovation that will add value to the providers and end-customers of ICT enabled services.[52]

[51] See The National ICT Policy of Tanzania, 2003 at page 4.

[52] Ibid at page 4.

CHAPTER TWO

The Impact of E-Commerce and The Law in Tanzania in a Comparative Perspective

2.1 *Introductory Remarks*

Tanzania is among commonwealth countries located within the East African Region among the Member States of the East African Community. The country is also among the SADC Members. In 1961 Tanzania attained independence from the British. Tanzania inherited the British Common Law System. Most of the laws that were enacted during the British colonial system were still applicable 25 years after independence. The country has been slowly changing her legal system to cope with globalization, economical and political reforms. The development and innovation of technology that has brought in the application of Information and Communication Technologies in the world is greatly impacting Tanzania.

2.2 *The Legal Implications of E-commerce in Tanzania*

The rapid growth of e-commerce over the world has brought challenges and affects Tanzania's commercial offline laws and other related laws and the society at large given the nature of paper based transactions.

Generally the legal system in Tanzania is mainly based on common law principles. Regulatory steps to secure electronic transactions such as digital signatures, reforms to business laws, dispute settlement and others have not yet been promulgated.[1]

The basic Commercial Laws in Tanzania are derived from the 19th Century and they are mainly based on the English Legal System. The laws were designed to facilitate paper-based transactions that require the use of documents, written notices and manuscript signatures. These laws are thus not tuned to technological changes. Most laws that deal with contracts provide for certain legal requirements which might only apply on the physical world environment. For instance where contracts are concerned, there are usually three different types of formalities that may be required namely writing, signature and some kind of third party authentication or

---

[1] Bwana J., *Challenges facing Regulation of e-commerce in Tanzania* at page 67. In 2007 the Government amended the Evidence Act to recognize the admissibility of electronic evidence via Act No.15 of 2007 (Written Miscellaneous Amendment Act).

involvement such as notarial execution. The rationale behind the requirements of these formalities are mainly based on two legal certainties (writing) and authentication (signature) and may be required either by statute or by the parties themselves. Most written contracts contain a standard clause which states that no amendments to the contract will be valid or binding unless reduced to writing and signed by both parties, which makes the use of those formalities mandatory.[2] However it seems that in the context of international sales contracts for movables only the first two requirements are relevant.[3]

These paper based method requirements can pose an obstacle to the development of e-commerce at national, regional and international level. As Professor Christopher Reed argued the laws in most countries were developed over a long time during which physical actors and physical media were the only, or at least the primary, mechanisms by which transactions with legal consequences could be effected.[4] The professor was referring to the traditional or physical transactions. The Internet environment has brought about a "new wine, old bottles" situation. Despite the changes and regulatory reforms made by the country since independence, most of the laws enacted since British Colonial rule before the 1960s are still in force.

The traditional requirement of writing and original documents can be observed under Section 80 of Income Tax Act[5] which provides that:

> unless otherwise authorized by the Commissioner by *notice in writing* every person shall maintain … such documents …[6]

The Commissioner is further by *notice in writing* empowered by the law to require a person to translate a document into an official language.

Subsection (4) reiterates the requirement of writing whereby a Commissioner is mandated by service of a *notice in writing* to require a person to retain documents described with reasonable certainty in the notice for such period may be specified in the notice.

On the other hand, the laws in South Africa such as Electronic Communications and Transactions provide functional equivalence between the requirements of writing under the paper based methods and a paperless

---

2 See Wright, *Electronic Commerce* §16.3.2; Fritzemeyer & Heun 1992 *CR* 131; Eiselen 1995 *SA Merc LJ* 10-11; Heinrich 1994 *CR* 120.

3 Ibid. See also the United Nations Convention on Contracts for the International Sale of Goods, Vienna 1980 (CISG).

4 Reed C., *Internet Law; Text and Materials* 2000 at page 148.

5 The Income Tax Act, No.11 of 2004. See also Income Tax Act 2006 as amended from time to time.

6 See Section 80 (3) of The Income Tax Act No.11 of 2004.

environment. For instance Section 12 clearly provides that "a requirement in law that a document or information must be in writing is met if the document or information is:

(a) in the form of a data message; and

(b) accessible in a manner usable for subsequent reference".

The development of e-commerce and e-government specifically the communication of legally significant information in the form of data are likely to be hindered by obstacles to the use of such data messages, or uncertainty messages as to their legal effect or validity. The current legislation governing transactions and communication including storage of information are inadequate and outdated as they do not reflect or contemplate the use of e-commerce and the implementation of e-government. Indeed the legal requirements prescribing the use of traditional paper based documentations and authentication in Tanzania constitute the main obstacle or impediment for the development and use of modern means of communication and electronic transactions.

There is no doubt that the current commercial laws are likely to be affected by these rapid e-commerce changes, inviting alternative regulatory approaches that would not impede e-commerce while advancing and ensuring consumer protection interests.[7] The significant challenge for the laws is thus to facilitate the use and development of e-commerce through creating an enabling and suitable environment in which it can develop. Suppliers and consumers need to be encouraged to use e-commerce while making some regulations that give the required degree of confidence. In this case, the challenge posed by e-commerce for the law is the challenge faced by commercial law generally to strike the balance between facilitation and regulation.[8] Some potential areas that might be affected by the use of e-commerce are copyright, data protection and confidentiality. The question is how to solve these legal implications that are likely to be brought by digital technology thus threatening the development of e-commerce in Tanzania and East African Community in general.

The issue that plagues one's mind is whether electronic documents should be equal to traditional paper documents. The other legal question is whether changes in the electronic environment in Tanzania can bring about factual situations that may or may not have been foreseen. Consequently, as the IT Law observatory of the Swedish ICT Commission (supra) argues that legal solutions that were well-situated at a certain

---

7 See the Final Report on E-Commerce and cyber crimes by the Law Reform Commission of Tanzania 2006.

8 Ibid.

stage may become uncertain or even disputed and in need of review. The practice in most countries shows that the law does not come into play until a societal phenomenon is threatened by the impact of ICT.

South Africa has enacted a law which is technology neutral and positions paper based requirements on an equal footing with e-documents or data message. This is reflected in the following provisions:

17 1) Subject to Section 28, where a law requires a person to produce a document or information, that requirement is met if the person produces, by means of a data message, an electronic form of that document or information, and if:

(a) considering all the relevant circumstances at the time that the data message was sent, the method of generating the electronic form of that document provided a reliable means of assuring the maintenance of the integrity of the information contained in that document; and

(b) at the time the data message was sent, it was reasonable to expect that the information contained therein would be readily accessible so as to be usable for subsequent reference.

18 1) Where a law requires a signature, statement or document to be notarized, acknowledged, verified or made under oath, that requirement is met if the advanced electronic signature of the person authorized to perform those acts is attached to, incorporated in or logically associated with the electronic signature or data message.

(2) Where a law requires or permits a person to provide a certified copy of a document and the document exists in electronic form, that requirement is met if the person provides a print-out certified to be a true reproduction of the document or information.[9] Malta is among the small countries using common laws. Some countries like Malta have gone further by enacting a law which is media and technologically neutral and positions the paper based requirements on an equal footing with e-documents or data message. This can be evidenced by the following provisions which must be considered and adopted by Tanzania;

"5. (1) If under any law in Malta a person is required or permitted to give information in writing, that requirement shall be deemed to have been satisfied if the person gives the

[9] See the Electronic Communications and Transactions Act.

information by means of an electronic communication: Provided that -

(*a*) at the time the information was given, it was reasonable to expect that the information would be readily accessible so as to be useable for subsequent reference; and

(*b*) if the information is required to be given to a person, or to another person on his behalf, and the first mentioned person requires that the information be given in accordance with particular information technology requirements, by means of a particular kind of electronic communication, that person's requirement has been met; and

(*c*) if the information is required to be given to a person who is neither a public body nor to a person acting on behalf of a public body, then the person to whom the information is required or permitted to be given, consents to the information being given by means of an electronic communication;

(*d*) if the information is required to be given to a person, or to another person on his behalf, and the first mentioned person requires that a particular action be taken by way of verifying the receipt of the information; that person's requirement has been met".[10]

India which is among the countries using common law principles has enacted an effective legal framework that has taken into account the development of digital technology by providing functional equivalence between the paper based method and electronic document. This can be reflected from just the following few provisions with added emphasis by the author;

[S.81A. Presumption as to Gazettes in electronic forms:

"The Court shall presume the genuineness of every electronic record purporting to be the *Official Gazette*, or purporting to *be electronic record* directed by any law to be kept by any person, if such electronic record is kept substantially in the form required by law and is produced from proper custody.]"[11]

[S.85A. Presumption as to electronic agreements:

"The Court shall presume that every *electronic record* purporting to be an agreement containing the digital signatures of the parties was so concluded by affixing the digital signature of the parties.]"

[10] See Electronic Commerce CAP 426.

[11] See the Information Technology Act; 2000. See also Sarkar, *Law of evidence*, 16 Edition, Volume 1, 2007 at page 1382.

[S.85B. Presumption as to electronic records and digital signatures:

"(1) In any proceedings involving a secure electronic record, the Court shall presume unless contrary is proved, that the secure *electronic record has not been altered* since the specific point of time to which the secure status relates."[12]

2.3 *An Insight on Model Laws and Other Cyber Laws from Other Jurisdictions in a Comparative Perspective with Tanzania*

The UNCITRAL Model Laws and other related Model Laws can be useful in seeking solutions to the above stated legal problems. For instance some of the core provisions of the UNCITRAL Model Law stipulate that "information shall not be denied legal effect, validity or enforceability solely on the grounds that it is in the form of a data message."[13] The subsequent article provides that legal requirements for writing[14] signature[15] and the use of originals[16] can be satisfied by the use of appropriate data messages and that rules of evidence should not deny the admissibility of data messages solely because of their form.[17] Ideally the Commonwealth Model Laws which are on an equal footing with UNCITRAL Model Laws were designed to assist common law countries and other countries in drafting or enacting their cyber laws. Countries with common law principles that lack cyber laws like Tanzania can create a legal framework that can take into account some relevant provisions of UNCITRAL Model Laws and other related cyber laws.

Furthermore, the 1980 Vienna Convention on the International Sale of Goods (hereafter referred to as "the Convention") deals with the sale of goods which have an international character and addresses the requirement of writing, originality and manuscript signatures in line with cyber transactions. For instance Article 11 of the Convention aims to rectify the situation in a number of jurisdictions where computer evidence would be excluded. The said Article provides that "a contract of sale need not be concluded in or evidenced by writing and is not subject to any requirements as to form. It may be proved by any means, including witnesses".

On the other hand, The Slovenia Electronic Commerce and Electronic Signature Act (ESA) 2000 provides for functional equivalence

12 Ibid.

13 Article 5 of UNCITRAL Model law, guide to enactment 1996.

14 Ibid, Article 6 .

15 Ibid, Article 7.

16 Ibid, Article 8.

17 Ibid, Article 9.

between paper based requirements and data message. For instance the said law provides that "where another statute requires a party to present a paper document or provides for a legal effect to be incurred, if a paper document is not presented, then presentation of an e- document will be deemed to place the party in compliance with a statutory requirement, with these proviso: the e-document must be accessible by its recipient for subsequent reference.

The law further positions the statutory requirement of original documents with e-documents or data message on an equal footing. To this effect, the law stipulates that if another statute requires that a paper document be presented or stored in its original form, this statute will be deemed to have been complied with by the presentation or storage of an e-document, if: (1) there is a reliable assurance that the e-document has not been modified since its creation, or that any alteration would be detectable; (2) after presentation to another person, that person is able to access and display the e-document; and (3) the e-document will be in the same format as the original, or will accurately convey the same information as the original.

Lastly, the Slovenia Electronic Commerce and Electronic Signature Act (ESA) 2000 has solved the traditional requirement of document retention under digital technology. This has been done by putting the provision under the law which provides that:

"if another statute mandates that a document that has been created, transmitted or accepted in paper or electronic form be stored, that statutory requirement may be satisfied by storing it as an e-document if: (1) the e-document has the same format in which the document was created, transmitted or accepted, or it can be shown that the information contained in the e-document is the same as when the document was created, transmitted or accepted; (2) the information in the e-document is accessible and can be subsequently displayed for reference in an understandable form; (3) if it was originally an e-document, it will be stored with an indication of its origin and destination and the time and place it was transmitted and accepted; and (4) it is stored in such a manner that the data contained in the e-document cannot be altered, or any alteration of the data can be easily ascertained; however, it is acceptable if the e-document includes communication data that is generated by the computer information system during the transmission or reception of the e-document."[18]

One can further observe how the cyber law in India has dealt with the traditional requirement of document retention under digital technology as seen under the statutory provision below:

[18] The Slovenia Electronic Commerce and Electronic Signature Act (ESA) 2000.

"S. 7. (1) Where any law provides that documents, records or information shall *be retained for any specific period,* then, that requirement shall be deemed to have been satisfied if such documents, records or information are retained in the *electronic form,* if—

(a) the information contained therein remains accessible so as to be usable for reference;

(b) the electronic record is retained in the format in which it was originally generated, sent or received or in a format which can be demonstrated to represent accurately the information originally generated, sent or received;

(c) the details which facilitate the identification of the origin, destination, date and time of dispatch or receipt of such electronic record are available in the electronic record."[19]

The traditional requirement of original documents is clearly solved under the South African statute as follows:

19 (1) Where a law requires information to be presented or retained in its original form, that requirement is met by a data message if:

a) the integrity of the information from the time when it was first generated in its final form as a data message or otherwise has passed assessment in terms of subsection (2); and

b) that information is capable of being displayed or produced to the person to whom it is to be presented.[20]

The traditional requirements of original documents are also addressed under the Malta Laws (supra) statute as follows:

7. "(1) Unless otherwise provided by or under this Act, if under any law in Malta, a person is required to produce *a document that is in the form of a paper*, or of any other substance or material, that requirement is deemed to have been satisfied if the person produces, by means of an electronic communication, an electronic form of that document (*emphasis added*)."[21]

8. "(1) If under any law in Malta, a person is required to record information in *writing,* that requirement is deemed to have been satisfied if the person records the information in electronic form (*emphasis added*)."[22]

19 See The Information Technology Act, 2000.

20 See Section 13 of the electronic communications and transactions Act.

21 See Electronic Commerce CAP 426.

22 Ibid.

To ensure the effective development and utilization of ICTs, LDCs governments like Tanzania, need to prioritize ICT development and establish the necessary regulatory framework that facilitate the implementing of e-government and specifically e-commerce to support ICT services and applications. Government intervention is also necessary to ensure and maintain fair competition in the ICT sector and prevent monopolies or collective dominance practices which certainly impact on accessibility.[23] On such a basis, legislative reforms should involve the enactment of laws relating to the telecommunications sector, consumer protection, e-commerce, e-signatures, intellectual property rights, and data protection. The policy reforms needed in Tanzania might not be very successful due to the nature of cyber space activities if there is no harmonization at the East African Community regional level. All countries within the region need to come up with uniform cyber laws that are dynamic. The countries can benchmark or borrow experience from other developing countries that have succeeded in creating harmonized cyber laws. The Association of South-East Asian (ASEAN) which is believed to be the first regional organization in the developing world to have set in motion the harmonization of its members' e-commerce legislation might be useful experience at EAC level.[24]

According to Mohamed S. Abdel Wahab,[25] the Egyptian government has been actively fostering legislative and regulatory reform to support the liberalization of the telecommunications sector. The government has enacted several laws that aim at supporting ICT development and diffusion such as Law No.82/2002 for the Protection of Intellectual Property Rights complying with the Trade-Related Aspects of Intellectual Property Rights (TRIPS) Agreement, Telecommunications Law[26] based on some fundamental principles amongst which are universal access, free competition, protection of users, and encouraging investment in the ICT sector.

2.4 *Traditional Contracts Vis-à-vis Cyberspace Contracts Under Common Law in a Comparative Perspective with Tanzania*

Generally a contract is any agreement that can be enforced by the law between two or more persons to do or abstain from doing some act or acts

---

[23] See Mohamed S. Abdel Wahab, on "Online Disputes resolution challenging the global digital divide" MCI Arb., LLM, is an Assistant Lecturer at the Faculty of Law, Cairo University, Egypt and a Researcher and Part-time Lecturer at the School of Law, Manchester University, UK. In Tanzania these can be done by Regulatory bodies such as the Fair Competition Commission, Tanzania Communications Regulatory Authority (TCRA), Energy and Water Utilities Authority (EWURA).

[24] See UNCTAD Economy Report, 2008 at page xxxv.

[25] Mohamed S. Abdel Wahab, "On-line Disputes resolution challenging the global digital divide" at pages 7-8.

[26] No. 10/2003.

with an intention of creating legal relations.[27] The laws governing contracts are one of the areas, which can be affected by the development, and use of e-commerce. Normally under English Law or Common Law the formation of a contract requires four main elements namely offer, acceptance, consideration and intention to create legal relations. These elements might be affected by the development and the use of e-commerce. Common Law countries like Tanzania have historically relied heavily on the transfer of written, signed and authenticated documents. Some statutory rules require that some contracts be made or evidenced in a particular way namely by deed, under seal and writing. They also have to be signed manually before a witness and be evidenced with original documents.

Undoubtedly the development of digital technology, for instance the use of electronic communication using computers represents a major challenge and opportunity in this respect. In this area problems are greater in connection with the legal requirements for writing and handwritten signature than in relation to offer and acceptance.[28]

Some countries like the UK have made great effort to solve legal issues and challenges brought by electronic commerce challenges by passing the Electronic Communications Act 2000 which give the "appropriate Minister" efficient powers to make orders carrying this process forward. Apart from providing functional equivalence between electronic documents and paper based documents or data message the law recognizes that requirements for writing and manuscript signatures may hamper the use of e-commerce. Other developing countries like Mauritius, Singapore, India, Malaysia, Seychelles, etc. have not been left behind in creating legal framework that regulate cyberspace.

It is unfortunate to see the laws governing contracts and other related transactions in some countries including Tanzania that strictly apply traditional postal rules for the communication and revocation of offer and acceptance as[29] laid down in the earliest landmark case of *Adams v. Lindsell*[30] and *House Fire Insurance v. Grand* respectively.

2.5 *Contractual Communications of Offer and Acceptance Online*

Generally, for an acceptance to be legally valid it must be communicated to the person who has the authority to accept (offeror himself).[31] An

[27] See Smith & Keens, *Law for Business*, 13th edition, 2006 at page 85.

[28] Ibid.

[29] (1879) L.R.4EX.DN.26.

[30] (1818) 1 B & Ald.681.

[31] See [Felthouse v. Bindley (1863)] and Steel Authority of India v. Salem Stainless Steel Suppliers (1994) 1 SCC 247. See also Gogna, on A Text Book of Mercantile Law, 2005 at page 25.

acceptance of an offer has no legal effect unless it is communicated to the other part, like an offer, the acceptance can be communicated by any act or omission of the acceptance by which he intends to communicate it or by any act or omission which has the effect of communicating it. As a matter of fact the communication of an acceptance is complete at different times for the offeror and acceptor. For the offeror the communication of an acceptance is complete when it is put in the course of transmission to him and the offeror becomes bound by the acceptance as soon as the letter of acceptance is posted by the acceptor. Likewise, the communication of an acceptance is complete when it comes to the knowledge of an offeror and the acceptor becomes bound by his acceptance only when it comes to the knowledge of an offeror.[32]

It is a cardinal principle of contract laws under common law that the revocation of an offer or acceptance is said to be effective only if it is communicated. In this way, the communication of revocation is complete at different times for the person who makes it, and also for the person to whom it is made. In other words, for the person who makes the revocation, the communication of revocation is complete when it is put into a course of transmission to the person to whom it is made. And for the person to whom revocation is made, the communication of revocation is complete when it comes to his knowledge.[33]

The general position of Common Law is that where the communication is made by post the contract arises on the date the letter of acceptance is posted, that is when an offer made by one party is accepted unconditionally by the other. This rule is found in Tanzania under the principal law which governs most contracts in Tanzania.[34]

On the above later case Signer L.J. argued that:

> "*the acceptor in posting the letter has put it out of his control and done an extraneous act the matter, and shows beyond all doubt that each side is bound.*"[35]

In *Adams v. Lindsell*[36] the plaintiffs were wool manufacturers in Bromsgrove, Worcestershire. The defendants were wool-dealers at St. Ives in Huntingdon. On the 2nd of September 1817, the defendants wrote to the plaintiffs, offering a quantity of wool on certain terms and requiring an answer

32 Gogna, *A Text Book of Mercantile Law*, 2005 at pages 25-27.

33 Ibid.

34 Section 4 of the law of Contract Act CAP 345 [RE.2292] which provides as to when communication of offer, acceptance and revocation is complete.

35 Ibid.

36 Ibid.

"in course of post". The defendants misdirected their letter, which did not reach the plaintiffs until the evening of 5th September. That same night the plaintiffs posted a letter of acceptance, which was delivered to the defendants on 9th September. If the original offer had been properly addressed, a reply could have been expected by the 7th September, and meanwhile, on 8th September, not having received such a reply, the defendants sold the wool to other parties. As an academic problem, three possible answers were available in this case. An offer made through the post might be regarded as accepted in the eyes of the law basing on the following scenarios.

(a) As soon as the letter of acceptance is put into the post; or

(b) When the letter of acceptance is delivered to the offeror's address; or

(c) When the letter of acceptance is brought to the actual notice of the offeror.

The above scenario raises some legal problems under the digital technology era with the rapid growth of e-commerce. Out of the above three legal issues, the Court of King's Bench in *Adams v. Lindsell* preferred the first solution and decided that the contract was concluded when the letter of acceptance was posted on 5th September.[37]

One might compare the position in the above case with the case of *Byrne v. Van Tienhoven*[38] whereby his Lordship Lindley J laid down an important rule. The question of determining time and place under cyberspace contracts has always been a problem due to the fact that cyberspace does not recognize boundaries whereby parties can communicate and form their contracts electronically anywhere. The legal issues here will be the determination of the place of solving disputes among the parties who might be located and reside in different jurisdictions with different laws.

Reference can be made to various case laws and cyber laws from other countries. For instance the following provisions from South African Law might be useful;

"22. (1) An agreement is not without legal force and effect merely because it was concluded partly or in whole by means of data message

(2) An agreement concluded between parties by means of data messages is concluded at the time when and place where the acceptance of the offer was received by the offeror".

---

[37] See Cheshire, Fifoot & Furmston's, *Law of Contract,* 4th Edition 2001 at pages 56-57.

[38] (1880) 5 CPD 344.

"23. A data message:

(a) used in the conclusion or performance of an agreement must be regarded as having been sent by the originator when it enters an information system outside the control of the originator or, if the originator and addressee are in the same information system, when it is capable of being retrieved by the addressee:

(b) must be regarded as having been received by the addressee when the complete data message enters an information system designated or used for that purpose by the addressee and is capable of being retrieved and processed by the addressee; and

(c) must be regarded as having been sent from the originator's usual place of business or residence and as having been received at the addressee's usual place of business or residence."

2.6 *Judicial and Legal Considerations*

Various judicial and legal provisions can be considered to see how the courts deem the effectiveness of communication of offer and acceptance under cyberspace. Case laws and various legislation indicate that an offer and acceptance of offer are complete only when they are properly communicated to the other parties.

In the *House Fire Insurance v. Grand* the Court through his Lordship Thesiger (sic) LJ made the following landmark rule which can be compared with cyberspace contracts and communication of offer and acceptance:

> "*An acceptance which only remains in the breast of the acceptor without being actually and by legal implication communicated to the offeror, is no binding acceptance … But if the post be treated as the agent of both parties, then as soon as the letter of acceptance is delivered to the post office, the contract is made as complete and final and absolutely binding as if the acceptor had put his letter into the hands of a messenger sent by the offeror himself as his agent to deliver the offer and to receive the acceptance … The acceptor, in posting the letter has put it out of control and done an extraneous act which clinches the matter, and shows beyond all doubt that each side is bound. How then, can a causality in the post office, whether resulting in delay, which in commercial transactions is often as bad as no delivery, unbind the parties or unmake the contract.*"[39]

The court went further in cementing the above principle and came up with the final binding rule as follows:

[39] See Singh A., *Law of Contract*, 2005 at page 29.

> "*It may be taken as now settled that, where an offer is made and accepted by letters sent through the post, the contract is made the moment the letter accepting the offer is posted, even though it never reaches its destination.*"[40]

The legal position in India which is paramateria with Tanzania is to the effect that, the communication of an offer is complete when it comes to the knowledge of the person to whom it is made.[41] As a matter of fact, an offer cannot be accepted unless and until it is brought to the knowledge of the offeree whereby the offeror becomes bound by it (i.e. if it is accepted by the offeree, then the offeror cannot retract it). It may be noted that an offer, accepted without its complete knowledge does not create any legal relation. This means that when the offer is made by post its communication will be complete when the letter containing the offer reaches the offeree. The term "reaching of letter" means, when the letter reaches and comes to the knowledge of an offeree. However the situation might be complicated when it comes to cyberspace contracts. The current laws are only clear on the communication of offer and acceptance under the physical world using postal means of service leaving cyber contracts unresolved.

The impact of e-commerce can further be observed in the way communication takes place under digital technology given the lack of laws to regulate cyberspace. Things could be complicated where parties have chosen their contractual communication to be by way of e-mails but have not stated whether to apply the postal rule or the telex mode of communication taking into account that an e-mail message does not show a signal on its arrival compared to other methods of communication. The situation is further complicated by the problematic requirements of writings, original sealed documents and manuscript signatures.

There are a considerable number of traditional statutory rules in countries that apply Common Law principles like Tanzania about particular types of contracts requiring them to be made or evidenced in a particular way. These requirements which are contrary to electronic contracts can be briefly categorized as follows:

(1) The contract must be under seal. This is a legal requirement for a valid contract.

(2) The contract must be in writing.

(3) The contract must be evidenced in writing and signed before a witness.

---

[40] Ibid.

[41] Compare section 4 of the Indian Contract Act with the Law of Contract in Tanzania. See also Gogna, in *A Text Book of Mercantile Law*, 2005 at page 25.

The definition of writing and signature under the current laws does not involve data message. In addition to that it is impossible for both parties entering into contract to use other parties to witness their transactions under cyberspace.

In the UK, examples of contracts that must be made in writing can be found under the marine insurance contracts, regulated consumer credit agreements, hire purchase agreements where the credit does not exceed 25,000 pounds, contracts for sale or dispositions of land.[42] This is just an exception to the general rule as there are other laws that give equal status to the requirement of writing with data message.

In Tanzania a good example of such contract requirement is found under Section 9 of the Sale of Goods Act[43] which provides that "a contract for the sale of any goods … shall not be enforceable by action unless the buyer accepts part of the goods so sold, and actually receives, the goods, or gives something in earnest to bind the contract or in part payment, or unless some note or *memorandum in writing* of the contract is made and *signed* by the party to be charged or by his agent in that behalf".

These legal requirements under the so called offline laws presuppose legal problems and barriers to e-commerce development. It might be difficult to implement e-governance on other related e-transactions if effective cyber laws are not promulgated in Tanzania and East African Community in general.

2.7 *Suggested Legal Solutions for Facilitating E-contracts*

Indeed UNCITRAL Model Laws and Common Wealth Model Laws are the best solutions for the implementation of online contracts with regard to the above traditional requirements. Specifically Article 6 and 7 of UNCITRAL Model Laws redefine the aspects of writing and signature to fit into the digital world and provide certainty to cyber contracts and promote e-commerce in general.

Article 6 of UNCITRAL Model Laws on E-commerce, which provides for the functional equivalent approach between data message or e-documents and paper based documents, reads as follows:

"Where the law requires information to be in writing, that requirement is met by a data message if the information contained therein is accessible so as to be usable for subsequent reference".

---

[42] See the Law of Property (Miscellaneous Provisions) Act 1989. See also Smith & Keenan's, *Law for Business 2006* at pages 138-140.

[43] The Sale of Goods Act [CAP 214 R..002].

Article 6 is in fact related to Article 5 whereby the former recognizes the enforceability of data message as the same with a paper based document that is original.

The EU E-Commerce Directive provides that "Member States shall ensure their legislation allow contracts to be concluded electronically".

The Directive goes further to oblige Member States "to ensure that the legal requirements applicable to the contractual process neither prevent the effective use of e-contracts nor result in such contracts being deprived of legal effect and validity on account of their having been on-line."[44]

It is not surprising that most countries like Tanzania and other countries in East Africa whose legal systems are based on common law principles have historically relied heavily on the transfer of written, signed and authenticated documents. Undoubtedly the invention of computers and development of electronic communication presents a major challenge and opportunity in this respect. There is need to amend repeal or enact new laws that will provide functional equivalence between e-documents and paper based documents. Efforts geared to achieve this have been started by the Law Reform Commission of Tanzania which has recommended for the reforms of business laws.[45]

2.8 *On-line or Distance Contracts*

Unlike face to face transactions under the physical world, Internet and the use of computers have simplified transactions such as buying and selling of goods or services electronically. Underpinning such buying and selling are commercial contracts conducted electronically between the parties within one country or from different jurisdictions which can pose a considerable challenge on the existing offline laws, let alone the jurisdiction problem. Prior to the digital revolution and Internet, most on-line contracts were conducted using Electronic Data Interchange (EDI).[46] The development of technology and the use of Internet brought e-commerce in place, whereby people can conduct on-line contracts on cyberspace which do not necessarily need parties to be in a continuing relationship or come face to face and sign their agreement manually. In other words e-commerce mainly deals with real time, once-off transactions between parties who have never met. There is no statute in Tanzania that regulates and provides guidance on e-transaction.

---

44 OJ 2000 L 178/1.

45 The Author of this book was the pioneer of this landmark project namely The Legal Framework for E-commerce and Cyber Crimes in Tanzania, 2005.

46 Turban E., *Electronic Commerce*, Sweet and Maxwell Publishers, London 2002 at page 67.

The Icfai Journal of Cyber Law reveals that enforceability of the so called clickwrap contracts has always been critical and debatable when it comes to online transactions.[47] It is further argued that whether it is a written contract or an online one, 'consensus ad idem' i.e. 'meeting of minds' is essential in the formation of an enforceable contract. The position in the US was first clarified by the Court in *Specht v. Netscape Communications Corporation,* whereby the second circuit held that the integrity and credibility of electronic contracts particularly clickwrap contracts depends on a two-tier requirements, i.e. "reasonably conspicuous notice" and "unambiguous manifestation of assent".

The Court went further in another case by providing that "the other criterion for validity of an online contract could be the ability to reject". This was extensively discussed in *Register.com, Inc. v. Verio, Inc*, whereby the plaintiff failed to utilize the standard clickwrap agreement whereby access to its services will be withheld until a party affirmatively assents to its terms. The second circuit unanimously held that "assent now-terms later" contracts were not enforceable because they eliminated the user's necessary ability to reject the agreement.

With e-commerce, it is common to observe many people being involved in what is commonly referred to as distance selling and buying contracts using distance communication through the Internet. A distance selling contract has been defined as any contract concerning goods and services concluded between a supplier and a consumer under an organized distance sales or service provision scheme run by the supplier, who for the purposes of the contract, makes exclusive use of one or more means of distance communication up to the moment at which the contract is concluded.[48] This is a contract where the supplier and the consumer do not come face to face prior to the conclusion of the contract. They may communicate through the use of telephone sales, mail order, m-commerce, telescoping, e-mail, facsimile or e-commerce. The question is how to determine as to when and where the contract is concluded online. The determination of time and place of cyberspace contracts under the current contract laws which advocate for physical world contracts might be difficult. The situation might be more difficult in case of dispute as to the performance of contract.

The legal position is that where no time is specified with regard to the performance of the promise, the promise must be performed within a reasonable time. The term 'reasonable time' in each particular case is a question of fact as it depends upon the customs of the trade, special

[47] See The Icfai Journal of Cyber Law, Vol vi No. 4 of 2007.

[48] Bainbridge D., *Introduction to Computer Law*, 4th Edition 2000 at page 272.

circumstances of the case or the intention of the parties at the time of making the contract. Where the contract provides for the time of performance, the promise may be performed at any time during the usual hours of business on the specified day and the promise should be performed at the place where it was required to be performed.[49] For instance X promised to deliver goods at Y's warehouse on the 1st of January. On the agreed day, X brought the goods to Y's warehouse, but after the usual working hours. The goods were thus not received at the warehouse. In this case, X has not fulfilled his promise as the goods were not delivered during the usual hours of business.

The challenge here is how to avoid dealing electronically with minors (people who have not attained the age of majority)[50] who are not legally eligible to make a contract. It is the general principle that the enforceability of an agreement to contract depends on the competency (capacity of parties to contract) of parties concerned to enter into an agreement among other things. This is admittedly a big challenge to the legislators and law enforcers.

All these kind of contracts are not in line with the myth often held by the general public under Common Law that contracts must be in writing and have signatures.

2.9 *Determination of Jurisdiction, Time and Place of Formation and Performance of E-contracts at International Level*

2.9.1 The position at regional and national level

As highlighted in the last paragraphs, distance contracts under e-commerce pose legal challenges such as determination of time and place. Some jurisdictions have developed legal mechanisms to solve such legal issues. For instance in Europe, the EU Electronic Commerce Directive attempts to solve the problem of the place and time of the formation of electronic or distance contracts. Article 11 of the said Directive stipulates as that:

...except when otherwise agreed by the parties who are not consumers, that in cases where the recipient of the services places his order through technological means, the following principle applies-

---

[49] See Sections 46 and 47 of The Law Contract of Tanzania [CAP 345 R.E 2002] and the Law Contract Act of India.

[50] In most legal systems the age of majority of a person is above 18 years old. That means persons who are under 18 are regarded as minors or young persons who are presumably not able to enter into contracts. The agreements with minors are voidable at the option of the minor save for the necessary needs.

"the Service Provider has to acknowledge the receipt of the recipient's order without undue delay and by electronic means. The order and the acknowledgement of the receipt are deemed to be received when the parties to whom they are addressed are able to access them."[51]

A good example at national level can be drawn from Malaysia, Singapore, India and other countries with effective legal frameworks on cyber laws. For instance the Slovenian law on E-Commerce and Digital Signature solves the problem of determining time and place of transmission and reception. To determine the question of time of dispatch, the law provides that, an e-message will be assumed to have been sent when it enters a computer information system outside the control of the sender or his agent. Likewise, the place of transmission and reception is determined by the principle that an e-message is assumed to have been sent from the sender's place of business or his permanent residence at the time of transmission. The law further provides that "an e- message is assumed to have been received by the receiver's place of business or his permanent residence at the time of the receipt".[52]

Malta laws on the other hand provide for transmission of electronic communication by solving the problem of determining time of dispatch, time of receipt, place of dispatch and receipt as follows:

"12. (1) If an electronic communication enters a single information system outside of the control of the originator, then, save as otherwise agreed between the originator and the addressee of the electronic communication, the dispatch of the electronic communication occurs at the time when it enters the information system.

(2) If an electronic communication enters successively two or more information systems outside of the control of the originator, then, unless otherwise agreed between the originator and the addressee of the electronic communication, the dispatch of the electronic communication occurs when it enters the first of those information systems."[53]

"13. (1) If the addressee of an electronic communication has designated an information system for the purpose of receiving electronic communications, then, save as otherwise agreed between the originator and the addressee of the electronic communication, the time of receipt of the electronic

[51] See Turban E., on *E-commerce* at pages 92-93.

[52] See Slovenian ESA 2000.

[53] See Electronic Commerce, CAP 426.

communication is the time when the electronic communication enters the information system.

(2) If the addressee of an electronic communication has not designated an information system for the purpose of receiving electronic communications, then, save as otherwise agreed between the originator and the addressee of the electronic communication, the time of receipt of the electronic communication is the time when the electronic communication comes to the attention of the addressee."[54]

"14. (1) Save as otherwise agreed between the originator and the addressee of an electronic communication -

(*a*) the electronic communication is deemed to have been dispatched at the originator's place of business; and

(*b*) the electronic communication is deemed to have been received at the addressee's place of business."[55]

2.9.2 The position at regional and international level

In the 18 years since the contents of the United Nations Convention on Contracts for the International Sale of Goods, Vienna 1980 was agreed; the face of business communications has changed radically by the introduction of newer technologies and applications such as fax, electronic data interchange (EDI) and the internet posing challenges and legal problems.[56]

Problems created by uncertainty as to the legal value of the use of electronic communications in international contracts constitute an obstacle to international trade. In 2005 the UN General Assembly adopted the remarkable Convention on the Use of Electronic Communications in International Contracts. The UN was of the view that the Convention will provide a common solution to remove legal obstacles to the use of electronic communications in a manner acceptable to States with different legal, social and economic systems.[57]

This UN Convention on contracts contains a series of inter-related provisions directed at different aspects of the contract formation process,

---

54 Ibid.

55 Ibid.

56 See *Siegfried Eiselen,* Potchefstroom University for CHE, Potchefstroom, South Africa. The research for this article was made possible by a grant from the Max Planck Institut für ausländisches und internationales Privatrecht, Hamburg which is hereby gratefully acknowledged. See also http://www.cisg.law.pace.edu/cisg/biblio/eiselen1.html).

57 See Explanatory note by the UNCITRAL secretariat on the United Nations Convention on the Use of Electronic Communications in International Contracts at page 13.

including the time and place of dispatch and receipt of messages, which impacts on the moment of contract creation.[58] One of the major aims of the said "e-Convention" is to enhance legal certainty and commercial predictability where the parties use e-communication in making contracts at international arena.[59] The Convention further facilitates business to business (b2b) contracts under cyber space. More importantly, the Convention compliments with the UNCITRAL Model Law on E-commerce by solving the problem of determining a party's location in an electronic environment; the time and place of dispatch and receipt of electronic communications; and the use of automated message systems for contract formation.

The Convention recognizes the importance of functional equivalence as highlighted by the UNCITRAL Model Laws (Articles 6, 7 and 8) by providing for the criteria to establish functional equivalence between electronic communications and paper based documents – including "original" paper documents – as well as between electronic authentication methods and hand-written signatures.[60] Arguably, the Convention makes sure that certainty and validity of and enforceability of e-contracts are equivalent with paper based transactions. By 2008 nothing had been done in legally recognizing the importance of this Convention in Tanzania and EAC in general, but the Convention was highly recognized and accepted at EU level. This is reflected from the EU Commissioners who vehemently stated that:

These provisions of the 2005 UN Convention clarify that the rules of electronic contracting do not replace the traditional contract requirements. For example, the use of electronic contracting to exchange an offer and acceptance would not result in an enforceable contract if applicable contract law requires consideration that is still lacking. This means that, a country adopting the provisions of the 1996 Model Law or the 2005 Convention can merge these provisions easily with its existing contract law, whether such country is a common law, civil law or any other system of contract law. The best alternative would be to adapt the traditional form requirement to electronic contracts by providing a rule that electronic contracts may, in principle, be sufficient to satisfy the writing, signature or other forms requirement. The 2005 Convention adopts this more flexible alternative, under Article 9(2). Consequently, any legal requirement that an "original: be produced or retained is an insurmountable burden on e-commerce, unless that requirement is adapted for electronic messages".

[58] See Article 10 on invitations to make offers Article 11, and Article 13.

[59] See the Report of OUT-LAW.COM at http://www.out-law.com/page-6394 accessed on 9 August 2008.

[60] Ibid.

The question of determination of means and modes of communication in making e-contracts is another issue that creates uncertainty. As noted earlier the common law principle of communication is based on the use of postal rule *(Adams v. Lindsel)*. Uncertainty as to the legal value of the use of electronic communications in international contracts constitute an obstacle to international trade. In 2001, the United Nations through its Commission (UNCITRAL) decided to prepare an international instrument (United Nations Convention on the Use of Electronic Communications in International Contracts) which deals with issues of electronic contracting. This instrument also aims to remove obstacles to electronic commerce in existing uniform law conventions and trade agreements.

The UN Commission was responding to the increased use of electronic communication that improves the efficiency of commercial activities, enhances trade connections while allowing new access opportunities for previously remote parties and markets, thus playing a fundamental role in promoting trade and economic development, both domestically and internationally.[61]

This Convention mainly applies to the use of electronic communications in connection with the formation or performance of a contract between parties whose places of business are in different states. The Convention also provides a common solution to remove legal obstacles to the use of electronic communications in a manner acceptable to States with different legal, social and economic systems. However the Convention does not apply to negotiable instruments such as bills of exchange, promissory notes, consignment notes, bills of lading, warehouse receipts or any transferable document or instrument that entitles the bearer or beneficiary to claim the delivery of goods or the payment of a sum of money. There should be no disparity of treatment between electronic communications and paper documents, but is not intended to override any of the requirements contained in Article 9 of the Convention.[62] The Convention further reflects and complements with the UNCITRAL Model Laws on the question of non discrimination between e-transactions or data and paper based transactions by clearly stating that information "shall not be denied validity or enforceability on the sole ground that it is in the form of an electronic communication.[63]

---

[61] See the United Nations Convention on the Use of Electronic Communications in International Contracts.

[62] Ibid.

[63] Compare Article 8 of the UN Convention on e-communications and Article 5 of UNCITRAL Model Laws. See also the Report of the UN Working Group on the above Convention.

2.9.3 Relevant provisions of the UN Convention on the use of electronic communications in international contracts

Some relevant provisions of this Convention that are worth mentioning as far as electronic communications and digital signatures are concerned are:

Legal recognition of electronic communications is dealt with by Article 8 which provides as follows:

"1. A communication or a contract shall not be denied validity or enforceability on the sole ground that it is in the form of an electronic communication."

The question of electronic evidence as compared to physical world evidence is stipulated under Article 9 as follows:

"1. Nothing in this Convention requires a communication or a contract to be made or evidenced in any particular form.

2. Where the law requires that a communication or a contract should be in writing, or provides consequences for the absence of writing, that requirement is met by an electronic communication if the information contained therein is accessible so as to be usable for subsequent reference.

3. Where the law requires that a communication or a contract should be signed by a party, or provides consequences for the absence of a signature, that requirement is met in relation to an electronic communication if:

   (a) A method is used to identify the party and to indicate that party's intention in respect of the information contained in the electronic communication; and

   (b) The method used is either:

      (i) As reliable as appropriate for the purpose for which the electronic communication was generated or communicated, in the light of all the circumstances, including any relevant agreement; or

      (ii) Proven in fact to have fulfilled the functions described in subparagraph (a) above, by itself or together with further evidence.

4. Where the law requires that a communication or a contract should be made available or retained in its original form, or provides consequences

for the absence of an original, that requirement is met in relation to an electronic communication if:

(a) There exists a reliable assurance as to the integrity of the information it contains from the time when it was first generated in its final form, as an electronic communication or otherwise; and

(b) Where it is required that the information it contains be made available, that information is capable of being displayed to the person to whom it is to be made available.[64]

On the other hand, legal issues and uncertainties as to the determination of time and place of dispatch and receipt of electronic communications are also covered under this Convention as follows:

"1. The time of dispatch of an electronic communication is the time when it leaves an information system under the control of the originator or of the party who sent it on behalf of the originator or, if the electronic communication has not left an information system under the control of the originator or of the party who sent it on behalf of the originator, the time when the electronic communication is received.

2. The time of receipt of an electronic communication is the time when it becomes capable of being retrieved by the addressee at an electronic address designated by the addressee. The time of receipt of an electronic communication at another electronic address of the addressee is the time when it becomes capable of being retrieved by the addressee at that address and the addressee becomes aware that the electronic communication has been sent to that address. An electronic communication is presumed to be capable of being retrieved by the addressee when it reaches the addressee's electronic address."

3. An electronic communication is deemed to be dispatched at the originator's place of business and is deemed to be received at the addressee's place of business, as determined in accordance with Article 6.

4. Paragraph 2 of this article applies notwithstanding that the place where the information system supporting an electronic address is located may be different from the place where the electronic communication is deemed to be received under paragraph 3 of this article.

Article 6. Location of the parties

1. For the purposes of this Convention, a party's place of business is presumed to be the location indicated by that party, unless another

[64] See Article 10.

party demonstrates that the party making the indication does not have a place of business at that location.

2. If a party has not indicated a place of business and has more than one place of business, then the place of business for the purposes of this Convention is that which has the closest relationship to the relevant contract, having regard to the circumstances known to or contemplated by the parties at any time before or at the conclusion of the contract.

3. If a natural person does not have a place of business, reference is to be made to the person's habitual residence.

Article 8. Legal recognition of electronic communications

1. A communication or a contract shall not be denied validity or enforceability on the sole ground that it is in the form of an electronic communication.

Article 10. Time and place of dispatch and receipt of electronic communications

1. The time of dispatch of an electronic communication is the time when it leaves an information system under the control of the originator or of the party who sent it on behalf of the originator or, if the electronic communication has not left an information system under the control of the originator or of the party who sent it on behalf of the originator, the time when the electronic communication is received.[65]

2. The time of receipt of an electronic communication is the time when it becomes capable of being retrieved by the addressee at an electronic address designated by the addressee. The time of receipt of an electronic communication at another electronic address of the addressee is the time when it becomes capable of being retrieved by the addressee at that address and the addressee becomes aware that the electronic communication has been sent to that address. An electronic communication is presumed to be capable of being retrieved by the addressee when it reaches the addressee's electronic address.

3. An electronic communication is deemed to be dispatched at the place where the originator has its place of business and is deemed to be received at the place where the addressee has its place of business, as determined in accordance with Article 6.

Article 11. Invitations to make offers

A proposal to conclude a contract made through one or more electronic communications which is not addressed to one or more specific parties, but is generally accessible to parties making use of information systems, including proposals that make use of interactive applications for the placement of

[65] Op cit.

orders through such information systems, is to be considered as an invitation to make offers, unless it clearly indicates the intention of the party making the proposal to be bound in case of acceptance.[66]

However there are certain remarkable exceptions on the applicability of the Convention for the purposes of recognizing the importance of physical world transactions in certain circumstances given the difference in legal regimes among the countries in the world.

These exceptions are reproduced below for easy reference:

Article 2. Exclusions

1. This Convention does not apply to electronic communications relating to any of the following:
   (a) Contracts concluded for personal, family or household purposes;
   (b) (i) Transactions on a regulated exchange;
   (ii) foreign exchange transactions;
   (iii) inter-bank payment systems, inter-bank payment agreements or clearance and settlement systems relating to securities or other financial assets or instruments;
   (iv) the transfer of security rights in sale, loan or holding of or agreement to repurchase securities or other financial assets or instruments held with an intermediary.
2. This Convention does not apply to bills of exchange, promissory notes, consignment notes, bills of lading, warehouse receipts or any transferable document or instrument that entitles the bearer or beneficiary to claim the delivery of goods or the payment of a sum of money.[67] According to UN Working Group, the exclusion of negotiable instruments and similar documents was done because of the potential consequences of unauthorized duplication of documents of title and negotiable instruments including any transferable instrument that entitles the bearer or beneficiary to claim the delivery of goods or the payment of a sum of money and make it necessary to develop mechanisms to ensure the singularity of those instruments.[68] The exclusion was also based on the need for ensuring their uniqueness of negotiable instruments and title deeds or contracts that created or transferred rights in real estate.

[66] Op cit.

[67] See Explanatory note by the UNCITRAL secretariat on the United Nations Convention on the Use of Electronic Communications in International Contracts at page 13.

[68] Ibid.

The Convention applies to international contracts, that is, contracts between parties located in two different States, but it is not necessary for both of those States to be contracting States of the Convention. However, the Convention only applies when the law of a contracting State is the law applicable to the dealings between the parties, which is to be determined by the rules on private international law of the forum State, if the parties have not validly chosen the applicable law.[69] The Convention does not contemplate a duty for the parties to disclose their places of business, but establishes a certain number of presumptions and default rules aimed at facilitating a determination of a party's location. The Convention does not venture into determining when offers and acceptances of offers become effective for purposes of contract formation.

2.9.4 The legal implication of the UN Convention on e-communication to other international legal instruments

There are considerable number of UN Conventions, Treaties and Agreements that are recognized by this Convention whereby upon signing and ratifying parties are bound by other Conventions mentioned below. This can be reflected from paragraphs 1 and 2 of article 20 of the Electronic Communications Convention whereby, by the provisions state that upon ratifying the Convention, and except as otherwise declared, a State would automatically undertake to apply the provisions of the Convention to electronic communications exchanged in connection with any of the conventions listed in paragraph 1 or any other convention, Treaty or Agreement to which a State is or may become a contracting State.[70]

These UN legal instruments include:

1. The Convention on the Limitation Period in the International Sale of Goods ("Limitation Convention");[71]
2. The United Nations Convention on Contracts for the International Sale of Goods ("United Nations Sales Convention");[72]
3. The United Nations Convention on the Liability of Operators of Transport Terminals in International Trade ("Terminal Operators Convention");[73]

---

[69] Ibid.
[70] Ibid. See also Article 20 of the Electronic Communications Convention.
[71] United Nations publication, Sales No. E.95.V.15.
[72] General Assembly resolution 50/48, annex (Vienna, 11 April 1980).
[73] General Assembly resolution 56/81, annex.

4. The United Nations Convention on Independent Guarantees and Stand-by Letters of Credit ("Guarantees Convention");[74]
5. The United Nations Convention on the Assignment of Receivables in International Trade ("Receivables Convention");[75]
6. The Convention on the Recognition and Enforcement of Foreign Arbitral Awards ("New York Convention");[76]
7. The Convention on the Limitation Period in the International Sale of Goods Vienna, 11 April 1980);
8. The United Nations Convention on Independent Guarantees and Stand-by;
9. The United Nations Convention on the Assignment of Receivables in International Trade (New York, 12 December 2001).

Tanzania and other East African Community members including EAC itself need to consider this important Convention and see the possibility of signing and ratifying for the development of economy through electronic transactions.

2.10 *Electronic Contracts in Other Jurisdictions*

Some countries and Model Laws provide for the legal recognition of electronic contracts under e-commerce. For instance the United Nations Commission on International Trade Law (UNCITRAL) on Electronic Commerce with Guide to Enactment 1996 provides that:

> "*In the context of contract formation, unless otherwise agreed by the parties, an offer and acceptance of an offer may be expressed by means of data message. Where a data message is used in the formation of a contract, that contract shall not be denied validity or enforceability on the sole ground that a data message for that purpose or stored electronically…*"[77]

The UNCITRAL Model Laws are aimed at creating electronic equivalence of written, original documents and signatures to create equal balance between paper-based methods and electronic methods such as data message. Notably Article 6 places writing and original documents on equal footing with a data message.

---

[74] United Nations, *Treaty Series*, vol. 330, No. 4739 (New York, 11 December 1995).
[75] General Assembly resolution 43/165, annex.
[76] United Nations, *Treaty Series*, vol. 1695, No. 29215 (New York, 10 June 1958).
[77] See Article 11 UNCITRAL Model Law on E-Commerce.

On the other hand, the EU adopted the Distance Selling Contract Directive or Electronic Commerce Directive[78] which contains provisions that highlight the legal recognition of electronic contracts in the situation where domestic laws require that contracts be made in certain forms under paper based methods. The requirements of writing and manuscript signatures in physical transactions or communications are met by this Article when it comes to cyberspace transaction or communication.

The Directive defines the term "distance contract" as:

> "*Any contract concerning goods or services concluded between a supplier and a consumer under an organized distance sales or services provision scheme run by the supplier, who, for the purpose of the contract, makes exclusive use of one or more means of distance communication up to including the moment at which the contract is concluded.*"[79]

Likewise, Article 11 of the E-Commerce Directive seems to solve the problem of uncertainty as to when and where the e-contract or distance selling contract is concluded as follows:

> *...except when otherwise agreed by the parties who are not consumers, that in cases where the recipient of the services places his order through technological means, the following principles apply:*
>
> *-the service provider has to acknowledge the receipt of the recipient's order without undue delay and by electronic means,*
>
> *-the order acknowledgement of receipt are deemed to be received when the parties to whom they are addressed are able to access them.*[80]

The Electronic Commerce Directive is aimed at solving the traditional requirements for paper-based documents. The said Directive stipulates that:

"Member States shall ensure that their legislation allows contracts to be concluded electronically. Member States shall in particular ensure that the legal requirements applicable to the contractual process neither prevent the effective use of electronic contracts nor result in such contracts being deprived of legal effect and validity on account of their having been made electronically."[81]

---

[78] See Directive 97/7, OJ 1997 L 144 and OJ 1999 C 30. For the Definition of Distance Selling Contract, see Article 2 of the EU Directive.

[79] Article 10.

[80] See also Turban E, *on E-Commerce* at pages 92-93.

[81] See Article 9 of OJ 2000 L 178/1.

On-line consumers are well protected under these Directives which apply to all forms of distance selling contracts and on-line communications. The Directive also highlights and addresses issues as to where the contract is formed under cyberspace including choice of Law[82] as equally indicated by judicial decisions in *Entores v. Miles Far East Corp*[83] and *Brinkibon Ltd v. Stahag S. S. GMBH.*[84] These Directives have to be read together with the Brussels[85] and Rome[86] Conventions which makes remarkable provisions that protect consumers on-line.

Some countries that use Common Law such as Australia, South Africa, Malta, Singapore, etc. have effective legal framework that provide for the recognition and use of electronic contracts and other related electronic transactions. This can be reflected from Malta law provisions on e-contracts as follows:

"9. (1) An electronic contract shall not be denied legal effect, validity or enforceability solely on the grounds that it is wholly or partly in electronic form or has been entered into wholly or partly by way of electronic communications or otherwise.

(2) For the purposes of any law relating to contracts, an offer, an acceptance of an offer and any related communication, including any subsequent amendment, cancellation or revocation of the offer, the acceptance of the contract may, unless otherwise agreed by the contracting parties, be communicated by means of electronic communications."[87]

"10. (1) Unless otherwise agreed by parties who are not consumers, where the recipient of the service places his order through technological means:

(*a*) an electronic contract is concluded when after placing his order; the recipient of the service has received from the service provider an acknowledgement of receipt of the order made by the recipient:

Provided that the service provider must acknowledge receipt of the order made by the recipient without undue delay and by electronic means; and

(*b*) the order made by the recipient and the acknowledgement of receipt are deemed to have been received when the parties to whom they are addressed are able to access them.

---

82 Article 11.
83 [1955] 2 ALL ER 493.
84 [1982] ALL ER 293 at 296.
85 C 189 of 28//07/90.
86 OJ 180 L 266/1.
87 See Electronic Commerce CAP 426.

(2) Unless otherwise agreed by parties who are not consumers, the service provider shall provide the recipient of the service with effective and accessible technical means to identify and correct handling and input errors and accidental transactions prior to the conclusion of the contract.

(3) The provisions of sub article (1) (*a*) and of sub article (2) shall not apply to contracts concluded exclusively."[88]

Indeed most laws (off-line laws) in some countries that regulate transactions at physical world are structured in such a way that they are able to equally protect all consumers dealing under cyberspace and physical world. The laws and regulations provide important rights to consumers by providing a mandatory requirement that all goods be of satisfactory quality, certain standards, and fit the intended purposes.[89] More importantly, consumers are offered legal remedies in case of defective products which cause personal injury and property damage. These laws include among others;

- The Sale of Goods Act of 1979. Tanzania has the same law though it has never been amended to cope with technological changes.
- The Supply of Goods and Services Act 1982.
- The Consumer Protection Act 1987.
- The Unfair Contract Terms Regulations Act 1999[90]
- The Unfair Contract Terms Consumer Protection Regulations[91]
- The Consumer transactions (Restriction on Statements) Order, 1976.

2.11 *Online Contracts for the Transaction of Physical goods in a Comparative Perspective*

Unlike physical world contracts, cyberspace has facilitated transactions that involve physical goods online. Normally these types of contracts arise where a Web page is being used in conjunction with more traditional advertising as an alternative shop window, e.g. for the sale of alcohol, books or compact disks. Although the contract is formed over the Internet, the performance by the supplier is constituted by the dispatch of goods to the ultimate purchaser. Thus the question of advertisements and promotion of goods online arises.

88 Ibid.

89 See The Sale of Goods Act of 1979, The Supply of Goods and Services Act 1982 and The Consumer Protection Act. See also Turban E., *on E-Commerce* at pages 30-31.

90 These Regulations require certain exclusion clauses with consumers to satisfy a reasonable test.

91 This Law regulates exclusion clauses and limitations on liabilities in contracts with consumers.

Generally, traditional or off-line contracts by nature are bilateral where both parties are bound and there is the exchange of promise. This argument can be substantiated by some court cases from the UK courts as shown below. On the other hand, online advertisements can create unilateral contracts for example an announcement that offers money or reward for the performance of an action, which does not necessarily oblige the accepting party to notify the advertiser apart from doing the act. In this case on-line advertisements therefore need to be carefully drafted to ensure that customers and lawyers interpret them as advertisement and not unilateral contracts to avoid what happened in the case of *Carlill v. Carbolic Smoke Ball Co. Ltd* which concerned unilateral contracts.[92] In this case the defendants were proprietors of a medical preparation called The Carbolic Smoke Ball. Through their advertisement, they offered to pay £100 to any person who contracted influenza after using the ball. The claimant who sued them for recovery of £100 for using the ball as directed succeeded in her claim. The issue was whether there was an offer or just an invitation to treat.

The main facts of this case can be summarized as follows:

Carbolic Smoke Ball Co. advertised in the newspaper that anyone who would take, according to the printed directions, the "Smoke Balls" manufactured by it would not contract the increasing epidemic influenza or colds. A reward of £100 was offered by the company to anyone who contracted influenza or a cold after using the Smoke Balls according to the printed directions. It was also added that £1,000 had been deposited with the Alliance Bank showing the sincerity of the company.

Mrs Carlill used the Smoke Balls according to the printed directions, but she subsequently suffered from influenza. In this case, it was decided that she was entitled to the reward.

To avoid liability in this case Carbolic Smoke Ball Co. forwarded the following contentions[93]:

(a) That there was no intention on the part of the company to enter into legal relations as the advertisement was merely a puff.

(b) That the offer was not made to any particular person.

(c) That Mrs Carlill had not communicated her intention to accept.

With regard to the first argument it was said by His Lordship that the advertisement said that £1,000 had been deposited in the bank, therefore it cannot be said that the "£100 would be paid" was intended to be a mere puff.

[92] [1892] 2 Q.B 484.

[93] See Gogna, *A Text Book of Mercantile Law*, 2005 at pages 25-30.

With regard to the second argument, it was decided that an offer need not be made to a specific person but it can also be made to the world at large. In such cases, a contract is made only when a person comes forward and performs the conditions of an offer.

With regard to the third argument, it was decided that in cases like this, communication of an acceptance is not necessary. Performance of the conditions is sufficient acceptance.

From the above two examples it is very clear that an offer may be made to the world at large. But the contract is made only with any ascertained person, who having the knowledge of the offer, comes forward and performs the conditions of offer or acts according to the conditions mentioned in the offer.

It may be noted here that where the general offer is of continuing nature as in the case of Smoke Balls case, it can accepted by any number of persons until it is retracted. But where the offer needs the finding of a missing thing or some information as in Har Bhajan Lal's case, it is closed as soon as the first information is received by the offeror.[94]

In an Indian case (*Harbhajan Lal v. Harcharan Lal*)[95] a young boy absconded from his father's house. The father offered a reward in a pamphlet stating that anybody who traces the missing boy and brings him home will be given Rs. 500. One Mr Har Bhajan Lal, who knew about the reward saw the boy at Dharamsala Railway Station and took him to the police station. Har Bhajan Lal sent a telegram to the boy's father that he has found his son. In this case, it was decided that an offer through hand bill (pamphlet) was made to the whole world and could be accepted by anyone who fulfilled the conditions of the offer. Mr Har Bhajan Lal, by tracing the missing boy, had substantially performed the conditions of the offer; therefore it was held that he was entitled to receive the reward. The above two cases indicate that an offer may be made to the world at large meaning that it is not necessary for an offer to be made to a specific person.[96]

Online merchants are also advised to observe the clear distinction between an offer and invitation to treat in order to protect them from making unintentional offers which might lead to more complaints.[97] The Common Law principle[98] that shop displays and price lists are invitation

---

94 Ibid.

95 [AIR 1925 All 539].

96 See Gogna, *A Text Book of Mercantile Law*, 2005 at pages 25-30.

97 Turban C., *E-commerce* 2002 at pages 79-85.

98 *Pharmaceutical Society of Great Britain v. Boots Cash Chemists Ltd [1951]* 2 Q.B. See also Fisher v. Bell [1961] 1 QB 394 at 399. For more details see Turban C., E-commerce 2002 at pages 82-83.

to treat is also likely to apply to e-mail price lists and websites, which are electronic analogy of shop windows.

In the *Pharmaceutical Society of Great Britain v. Boots Cash Chemists*[99] goods were displayed in A's shop with price chits attached to the articles. B, a customer entered the shop and picked up a bottle of medicine from the shelves. This will not amount to an acceptance of an offer to sell. It is merely an offer by the customer to buy, and there will be no acceptance of the offer until the price is accepted by A, the shopkeeper. The issue before the court was whether there was a contract between A and B the moment B picked up a bottle of medicine from the shelves. The Court held that:

> "*it is a well established principle that the mere exposure of goods for sale by the shopkeeper indicates to the public that he is willing to treat but does not amount to an offer.*"

It was further held in the above case that the display of goods in this way did not constitute an offer.[100] In *Grainger & Son v. Gouh*[101] it was further argued by the court that

> "*The transmission of a price-list does not amount to an offer to supply an unlimited quantity of the wine described at the price named, so that as soon as an order is given there is a binding contract to supply that quantity. If it were so, the merchant might find himself involved in any number of contractual obligations to supply wine of a particular description which he would be quite unable to carry out, his stock of wine of that description being necessarily limited.*"

These principles equally apply to online advertisements through websites or online databases. Online advertisements and display of goods electronically need to be carefully done to avoid confusion to customers.

In another landmark case,[102] X advertised that "Cocks and hens 25s each". Y accepted it and agreed to buy cocks and hens for 25s each. It was held by the court that such classified advertisements are merely an invitation to receive offer and not offer to sell.

---

[99] *[1951]* 2 Q.B. at 801 as cited by Turban E., *E-commerce* 2002 at page 82.

[100] See also *Esso Petroleum Ltd v. Customs and Excise Commissioners [1976] 1 ALL ER* 117.

[101] [1896] A.C. See also the citation in Turban C., *E-commerce* 2002 at page 83.

[102] *Partridge v. Critenrden (1968) ALL ER 421].* See also *Travellion v. Minck, 32 ALJ 43* whereby it was argued that the opening of the shop is mere invitation to the public to come into the shop. It is voluntary and without consideration. Apart from special legislation, it is open to a shopkeeper, at any time, to refuse to deal with any member of the public. It is not necessary for the shopkeeper to give any reasons for his refusal. For fuller discussion, see Turban E. on E-commerce, 2002 at pages 98-105.

2.12 *Online advertisements*

There is no doubt that cyberspace and the use of Internet has facilitated merchants and suppliers to advertise their goods and services cheaply and more efficiently worldwide online. Various websites with crucial advertisements such as information about a person or business, the services offered are now available and may be viewed and used for free by anybody using Internet search engines or simply using Google search. At the same time, advertising content is displayed for which the site operator receives a payment.

Generally advertisement under the physical world is regulated in various ways. Cyber advertisements need also to be regulated to protect online consumers against misleading advertisements and unfair terms competition. Online advertisements need to be carefully construed so that they are only invitation to treat not offers. In other words website owners who intend to deal with their goods and services electronically, are required to observe and make clear that they are not intending to make offers to sell or supply but making a mere invitation to treat or inviting offers from their customers, this is regarded as a mere shop window under the law.[103]

It gives the on-line business the option to accept or refuse dealings with particular customers. On-line advertisements can create a unilateral contract where one party only is bound. Compare online advertisements with the judicial rule laid down in the case of *Partridge v. Critenden.*[104] Some Judicial decisions have indicated that the problem faced by on-line physical advertisements which create unilateral contracts whereby one party only is bound can also be faced under on-line advertisements as highlighted in *Carlill v. Carbolic Smoke Ball Co. Ltd*[105] which concerned unilateral contracts. Indeed online advertisement can create legal implications to both consumers and suppliers or website owners. All these e-transactions need to be well addressed under the current and proposed laws. Alternatively Web Merchants are advised to use disclaimers clearly indicating that the "web-advertisement" is only invitation to treat contrary to offer or unilateral contracts. [106]

It has been clearly argued that to avoid confusion and legal technicalities, the offer should be distinguished from mere statements of intention. The terms of an offer should be clear so that there is no confusion whether it is a valid offer or a mere statement of intention. Sometimes, a person declares that he has the intention to do something; this does not amount to an offer. Such statements merely indicate the intentions that an offer will be made in future or an offer will be invited in future.[107]

[103] See Smith & Keenan's, *Law for Business,* 2006.
[104] [1968] 2 ALL ER 421.
[105] 1892] 2 Q.B 484, affd [1893] Q.B 1, 156.
[106] See Turban C., *E-commerce* 2002 at pages 72-73.
[107] Gogna, *A Text Book of Mercantile Law,* 2005 at pages 25-30.

2.13 *E-transactions and Contracts for the Supply of Digitized products and Services*

Digital technology has necessitated certain goods and services to be ordered and supplied on-line very cheaply and faster than offline transactions under the physical world. Likewise, it is possible for consumers to order their products and services and make payments electronically but delivery can be done physically due to the nature of goods which cannot be digitized. These types of cyberspace contracts normally involve the on-line supply of data, such as software, text or multimedia products and often involve the granting of license of any copyrighted material comprised within the products. These computer related goods and services can easily be digitized and transferred electronically.

Through the Internet, certain products such as software, videos, books, music, newspapers, magazines, and films no longer have to be physically delivered in hard copy format only to the purchaser. Suppliers can instead send the products or services in digital form over the Internet providing both time and cost savings.

The probable legal question here is whether these are goods for the purposes of Sale of Goods Act and other related laws.

Reference can be made to Section 61 of the UK Sale of Goods Act which provides that goods include all personal chattels but exclude all things in action (e.g. cheques and share certificates) and money, although a coin which is a curio piece is a good for the purposes of a contract of sale.[108] The term also includes *emblements*, i.e. crops to be severed before soil are generally sold with a view to severance and though they may sometimes be of the nature of land for the purposes of the Law of Property (Miscellaneous Provisions) Act 1989, they are usually goods within the meaning of the Act of 1979.[109]

In Tanzania for example Section 2 of the Sale of Goods Act (supra) provides that:

> *"goods" "includes all chattels personal other than things in action and money, emblements, industrial growing crops, and things attached to or forming part of the land, which are agreed to be severed before sale or under the contract of sale".*

This definition of goods does not accommodate goods sold online or digitized goods.

[108] Mass v Hancock [1899] 2 QB 211 as cited in Smith & Keenan's, in Law for Business 2006 at page 280.

[109] See Smith & Keenan's, *Law for Business*, 2006 at page 280.

Some judicial decisions from various jurisdictions have attempted to define digitized goods.[110] The UK Sale of Goods Act had the same definition with Tanzania but it has now been amended by The Sale and Supply of Goods Act 1994 to accommodate digital technology. In *St Albans City and District Council v. International Computer Ltd*[111] the court tried to interpret Section 61 of the UK Sale of Goods Act 1979 and Section 18 of the Supply of Goods and Service Act to find out whether the definitions of software and computer programs fit under these laws. Sir Lain Glidewell came out with a clear interpretation and decided that while software and computer programs are not goods a computer program "*per se*" in diskettes are goods.[112] This decision is very important in determining the legal status of software and software contracts specifically in case of determining contractual liability for defective software. The difficulties in making the distinction between goods and services with regard to software was first considered in the case of *Robinson v. Graves*[113] whereby the court was trying to determine whether there was a contract of goods or service.

The UK courts have done more in trying to define whether computer programs or digitized software are goods. The US courts have also not been left behind in determining whether software are goods under the law. This is reflected from *Advent System Limited v. Unisys Corporation*[114] as cited by Turban in his book *E-commerce* on page 70 which indicates that computer programs are the product of an intellectual process, but once implemented in a medium are widely distributed to computer owners and in this case they can be treated as merchantable commodities.

The Sale of Goods Act of Tanzania[115] which is an example of typical offline law derived from English legal systems defines goods as "all personal chattel other than things in action or money". This definition does not definitely suit the sale and supply of digitized goods and services. While in the UK the sale of goods over the Internet is governed by the Sale of Goods Act 1979, in Tanzania there is no legal framework that regulate e-transactions. Furthermore in the UK services which include online banking, financial services, insurance, and gambling are regulated under the Supply of Goods and Services Act 1982.

Due to the nature of the current laws and probably limited computer legal knowledge for our courts, the courts are likely to face a dilemma in answering the following legal issues.

---

110 See the Scottish case; *Beta Computers (Europe) Ltd v. Adobe System (Europe) Ltd [1996] S.L.T.604.*

111 *[1996] All E.R 481.*

112 Ibid.

113 [1935] 1 KB 579.

114 (1991) 925 F.2d 670, US CA.

115 CAP 214 [R.E.2002].

Under cyberspace contracts, where and how is the contract actually formed? In what ways can acceptance be communicated and where do transactions really happen? Can a computer or web server accept an offer and form a contract? What type of a contract is likely to be created; is it unilateral or bilateral? And how can the terms be honoured? If a person wishes to buy a book through the web for instance, Amazon. Com and makes an offer online, who will be the parties that will be bound by the contract?

When "X" sends an email to "Z", the following questions will arise: when is the contract really formed, and who forms it, the sender or the receiver bind under what terms? In case of breach, how can the contract be enforced before the court of law given the boundary-less nature of Internet?

Some scholars have argued that the moment the merchant sends back the e-mail to the buyer; the contract is formed on the merchant's side.[116] *In Thornton v. Shoe Lane Parking,*[117] Denning L.J. suggested that:

> *"[The customer] was committed at the moment when he put his money into the machine. The contract was concluded at that time … the offer is made when the proprietor of the machine holds it ... the acceptance takes place when the customer puts his money into the slot. The contract was concluded at that time. The offer is made when the proprietor of the machine holds it out as being ready to recover the money. The acceptance takes place when the customer puts his money into the slot."*[118]

The decision of the US Court in *State Farm Mutual l Auto Ins. Co. v. Brockhurs*[119] which seems to be very relevant in our discussion is worth referring to. In this case the Court ruled that since the computer only operates as programmed by the insurance company, it was bound by the contract formed. All these decided cases can be very useful in Tanzania in addressing some legal issues that are likely to arise under cyberspace.

The South African e-law provides for the determination of time and place of communications, dispatch and receipt as follows:

"23. A data message:

(a) used in the conclusion or performance of an agreement must be regarded as having been sent by the originator when it enters an information system outside the control of the originator or,

---

[116] Turban C., *E-commerce*, 2002 at page 80.
[117] [1971] 2 QB 163, [1971] 2 WL, [1971] 1 ALL ER 686.
[118] Ibid at page 689.
[119] Cir (1972) 453 F.2d 533, 10th Circuit.

if the originator and addressee are in the same information system, when it is capable of being retrieved by the addressee:

(b) must be regarded as having been received by the addressee when the complete data message enters an information system designated or used for that purpose by the addressee and is capable of being retrieved and processed by the addressee; and

(c) must be regarded as having been sent from the originator's usual place of business or residence and as having been received at the addressee's usual place of business or residence."

In India, the whole question of e-contracts attribution, acknowledgment and dispatch of electronic records, acknowledgement of receipt, time and place of dispatch and receipt of electronic record are clearly covered under Sections 11, 12 and 13 of the Information Technology Act 2000.[120]

2.14 *The Legal Implication of Technology on the Communication Sector*

2.14.1 Introductory remarks

The development of digital technology has brought a great impact on the communication or telecommunication sector. While in the past technology development one could observe separate technologies such as voice, data and video that can now share resources and interact with one another creating the so called new efficiencies known as, the current trend under the ICT there various emerging networks, services, firms, and devices creating different types of convergence.[121] In the past one could see different services with different networks and providers but the present has moved towards everything on everything (convergence). With the development of digital technology, the market is seeing an increased technological convergence of the hitherto distinct sectors of telecommunications, media and information

[120] For instance Section 11 and 13 of the Information Technology Act 2000, provides as follows: "An electronic record shall be attributed to the originator—

(a) if it was sent by the originator himself;

(b) by a person who had the authority to act on behalf of the originator in respect of that electronic record; or

(c) by an information system programmed by or on behalf of the originator to operate automatically."

"13. (1) Save as otherwise agreed between the originator and the addressee, the dispatch of an electronic record occurs when it enters a computer resource outside the control of the originator."

[121] See Stefano Briffa, "Technological Developments as a driver for Regulatory Policy Changes." Convergence, a Paper presented at the COMMNET-IT Legal framework for ICTs Programme, Malta June 2008.

technology.[122] These convergences among other things include networks whereby everything are on IP and services which allow access to various applications, programs and search engines. In other words, technological innovations are linking traditional telephony technologies with advanced IP-Based networks whereby the technological convergences is now raising technical, legal and policy implications for most countries.

While everything is put into devices provided by one undertaking, the billing can be done in one bill and everything can be available everywhere. It is no longer possible to regulate each technology separately as convergence services no longer depend on the technology used. Indeed convergence affects a multitude of businesses globally, telecommunications, transport, financial services as well as manufacturing, information services and other services. The converged technologies can further bring some legal implications on intellectual property rights especially copyright. This means that information services which were once delivered by distinct and separate technologies (such as paper, cassette tape, video and CD may now be delivered by the same or interchangeable technology. This new dimension of shifting from analogue to digital recording, is likely to come up with a convergence of radio, television, VCR, computer and digital recording technologies into a single living room Internet communication, information and entertainment unit through fibre optical and satellites or the so called broadband communications which pose challenges on IPR protection such as copyright and other related rights given the current ineffective laws.

While under the current broadcasting laws the emphasis is put on regulation of content the cyberspace is least regulated due to its nature of being boundary-less.

The impact of the current convergence of technologies and applications in Tanzania and other countries has led ICT operators to offer a bundle of traditional telecommunication, broadcasting and information services through the same network. One can observe the way this convergence of technologies has blurred the traditional distinction between telecommunication and broadcasting and between content and carriage. Indeed this trend has brought new legal and regulatory challenges, including re-orienting the licensing framework towards addressing the realities of convergence. This fundamental change calls for a new coherent regulatory framework which applies to all transmission infrastructures irrespective of types of services carried through them.[123] Many developing countries, including Tanzania, have moved to completely new regulatory frameworks.

---

[122] See *An Inventory of Policy Positions and Practical Guidance by ICC's Commission on E-Business, IT and Telecoms (EBITT)*, First edition 2007.

[123] See TCRA Journal No.7 2004, at page 1.

Tanzania has already introduced the Converged Licensing Framework (CLF) through Tanzania Communications Regulatory Authority irrespective of lack of clear legal framework that clearly address all legal issues related to the converged technologies. The initial move towards converged regulation was done through the Tanzania Communications Regulatory authority Act No. 12 of 2003 which merged the ten Tanzania Communications Commissions and the Tanzania Broadcasting Commission.[124]

The converged licensing system enables several service providers to apply for the Network Facility License (NFL), Network Services License (NSL), Application Services License (ASL) and Content Services License (CSL). While Network Service Licence (NSL) allows a licensee to operate and maintain public electronic communications networks with various technologies (like CDMA, GSM WCDMA, WILL, ASDL), the Application Service Licence (ASL) facilitates provision of electronic communications services to end users.[125]

The technology revolution has converged most things into a single media. Initially under the analogue system the broadcasting and other telecommunication systems were regulated differently using the licensing system. The major rationale behind licensing radio, television and cinematographic system has been to ration access to and use scarce resources.[126] Indeed before the evolution of the information society, the so called analogue broadcasting and other related communications highly justified the use of the licensing system because they were based on terrestrial transmitters with limitations on the whole range of frequencies.[127] A good example of the licensing system for broadcasting in Tanzania which does not suit the current digital technology that has brought the communication convergence and electronic communications through Internet can be drawn from the following provisions of The Broadcasting Act:[128]

S.9. *Prohibition on unlicensed broadcasting:*

"No person shall transmit or receive and transmit, or otherwise operate a broadcasting service, deal in broadcasting apparatus or do or permit anything to be done for which a licence is required under this Act, unless he is in possession of an appropriate licence."

---

[124] Ibid.

[125] Ibid.

[126] See Lloyd I., *Information Technology Law* at page 12.

[127] Ibid.

[128] The Broadcasting Services Act, 1993 [R.E. 2002 Chapter 306].

S.10. *Qualification and application for licence:*

"(1) An application for a licence under this Act may be made only by–

(a) a citizen of the United Republic;

(b) a company at least 51% of whose shareholding is beneficially owned by a citizen or citizens of the United Republic which is not, directly or indirectly, controlled by persons who are not citizens of the United Republic and whose principal place of business or registered office is in the United Republic." (Ibid)

11. *Issue of licence*

(1) Where the Commission is satisfied that a particular applicant meets the requirements of this Act for a licence holder it shall grant him a licence in the prescribed form and subject to payment of the prescribed fee.

(2) Upon the grant by the Commission of an application under Section 10, it shall cause notice of that decision to be published in the *Gazette* and in any newspaper published in the United Republic, as well as to be given to the applicant.

(3) Where the Commission decides to grant an application for a licence, it may attach conditions to the licence in relation to:

(a) the frequencies that may be used in the operation of a station, the power limitations in respect of a station, the technical servicing and inspection of a station and any other technical specifications;

(b) ...

(c) ...

(d) *the location* of a transmitter station, when applicable, and *the specific geographical area* to which the broadcast may be made (*emphasis added*). (Ibid)

On the other hand, the definitions under this law which are based on a single regulatory system for broadcasting and real world telecommunication system under the single or territorial regulatory system clearly indicate that the law did not contemplate the impact of ICT.

Some of the remarkable definition under the Broadcasting Act of Tanzania that might not suit broadcasting services under cyberspace are as follows:

"broadcasting apparatus" means an *apparatus*[129] for the reception of television broadcasts or for the reception of sound broadcasts, and where an apparatus is designed or constructed for the reception of *both television and sound broadcasts (other than those relating to television broadcasts)* such apparatus shall be deemed to comprise two sets of apparatus, one for the reception of television broadcasts and one for the reception of sound broadcasts, as the case may be (emphasis added);

"broadcasting service" means a radio communications service, in which the transmissions are intended for direct transmissory reception by members of the general public,

"radio communication service" means the *transmission of writing,* signs, signals, pictures and sounds of all descriptions of any kind, wholly or partly by means of electromagnetic waves of frequencies between *ten kilocycles per second and three million megacycles per second;(emphasis added)*. (Ibid)

Due to the development of ICT which has brought satellite technology, the era of licensing myth whereby broadcasting was confined within the particular national boundary has been highly defeated by the global operation posed by boundary-less Internet. As highlighted in the foregoing discussion, the legal framework for broadcasting in Tanzania which is mainly based on analogy with the sectoral approach regulatory system cannot regulate the convergence technology. There is no way countries can avoid the compulsory move from single or territorial regulatory system to a global regulatory system.[130]

On the other hand, most countries in the world have different restriction rules on content regulations specifically as to what should be broadcasted and what should not be broadcasted or televiewed. It is now very possible to observe cases arising out of the satellite broadcasts channels and station broadcasting and showing obscene materials which are legal in the country of origin but illegal in the country of destination. For instance, in the Netherlands or Dutch laws obscene materials such as pornography is legal, but in Tanzania they are strictly prohibited under the law. In such a situation, it might be difficult for countries like Tanzania to enforce such laws. Experience on these legal and enforcement difficulties can be drowned from the UK under the national and EU laws whereby using the national laws the UK has in a number of occasions failed to regulate the satellite broadcasting and televising of obscene materials such

[129] Does the word "apparatus" include computer PC or Mobile handset which receives all data, broadcasting services and other related services in a converged technology?

[130] Ibid.

as pornography. It has been reported that there was once a well-publicized case concerned a satellite channel 'Red Hot Dutch.[131] In this case an order was made under the provision of the Broadcasting Act 1990 which had the effect of prohibiting the supply of the decoders necessary to receive the offending signals.[132] In this situation, enforcement problems are clearly seen due to the fact that in most cases the UK's legal control seems to be more restrictive as compared to other state laws including EU members. For instance it is very possible to observe that according to the UK law some materials might be illegal but might be legal in the country of origin which makes enforcement difficult.

2.14.2 Omnibus legislation for convergence technologies?

Arguably, as technology develops it is becoming difficult to control and regulate the whole issue of convergence of telephones, broadcasting, television, cinema, etc. under the old sectoral laws and rules. It is advisable that developing countries like Tanzania should move fast to find the best way of integrating the regulatory system to cope with the convergence that is coming out of technology advancement. The operation of global networks under cyberspace through the Internet has opened unlimited boundaries, thus creating jurisdictional problems in terms of the regulatory system and enforcement mechanisms. In line with this, the use of Internet as a channel of voice telephony is defeating the radio, traditional land line and wireless line. It is now quite possible for any form of content such as sound, text, still or moving pictures or many radio programmes and TVs to be easily accessed through Internet or Satellite or any transmission medium at any time. These developments bring critical legal challenges.[133]

Unlike Tanzania, Malta reviewed and overhauled her regulatory framework for the electronic communications sector in 2004, with the enactment of ECRA, providing a technology neutral framework that caters for continued technological development. The ECRA, along with the related subsidiary legislation, is harmonized with the European Union framework for the sector and adequately regulates all the policy areas under consideration.

Furthermore, in Malta the Digital Terrestrial GIO transmissions have replaced analogue free to air transmissions after analogue turn-off. Digital Terrestrial GIO transmissions will take place in unencrypted form and are therefore receivable by anyone possessing a DTTV set-top box without any subscription being necessary. TV transmission services in Malta are

[131] The facts of this case are summarily cited by Lloyd I. in *Information Technology Law* at page 12.
[132] Ibid.
[133] See Lloyd I., *Information Technology Law* at page 18.

currently provided over Cable and Digital Terrestrial networks. The provisions of Section 51(1) of the ECNSR, as well as other relevant provisions of the Maltese Electronic Communications legislation, will apply to any other platform that eventually provides TV transmission services in Malta.

In particular Regulation 51(1) of the ECNSR clearly states that:

> "*The Authority may impose reasonable 'must carry' obligations for the transmission of specified radio and television broadcast channels and services, on undertakings providing electronic communications networks used for the distribution of radio or television broadcasts to the public where a significant number of end-users of such networks use them as the principal means to receive radio and television broadcasts: Provided that such obligations shall only be imposed where they are necessary to meet clearly defined general interest objectives...*"

Regulation 51(1) serves to give guidance as to the direction that needs to be followed in the assignment of the frequencies reserved for the purpose of carrying broadcast channels meeting GIOs.

On other hand, the EU Directive framework focuses on the need for a single regulatory framework for convergence technology as stated below:

> "*The convergence of the telecommunications, media and information technology sectors means all transmission networks and services should be covered by a single regulatory framework.*"[134]

2.15 *Negotiable Instruments Under Cyberspace Environment*

A negotiable instrument is like cash in the sense that the property in it is acquired by one who takes it bonafide and for value whereby the maxim *nemo data non habet* has no application.[135] Generally, there are many types of negotiable instruments that are used in various transactions. However the most common negotiable instruments include a promissory note, bill of exchange or cheque. In other words "a negotiable instrument means a promissory note, bill of exchange or cheque payable either to order or to the bearer. Briefly these instruments can be defined as follows:

1. Promissory note: It is a negotiable instrument, in writing which contains an unconditional promise by one person to pay a certain sum of money to a specified person.

[134] As cited by Stefano Briffà, COMMNET-IT Legal framework for ICTs, Malta June 2008.
[135] See Cheshire, Fifoot & Furmston, *Law of Contract*, 4th Edition 2001 at pages 577-578.

2. Bill of exchange: It is a negotiable instrument in writing which contains an unconditional order directing a certain person to pay a certain sum of money to the bearer of the instrument or to the specified person.
3. Cheque: It is a negotiable instrument, in writing which contains an unconditional order directing a specified banker to pay a certain sum of money to the bearer of the instrument or to a specified person.[136] The main essentials of negotiable instruments which might not be fulfilled using data message include:

   a) Must be in writing.

   b) Must contain an unconditional order to pay.

   c) Must contain an order to pay in terms of money only.

   d) Must contain an order to pay a definite amount of money.

   e) Must contain certain parties.

   f) Must be signed by the drawer.

Under normal circumstances for an instrument like a cheque to be valid and negotiable it must comply with the following legal requirements:

- It must be in such a state that nothing more than its delivery is required to transfer the right which it contains to a transferee.
- It must be one which is transferable by delivery by virtue of either a statute or of the law of merchant.[137]

The Laws governing negotiable instruments like cheques, bill of exchange, promissory notes, etc. in Tanzania do not reflect e-transactions which pose challenges to the growth and development of e-commerce. However the laws in India seem to accept electronic cheques like physical cheques as cited under the following provision of the Information Technology Act.

> "The provision of this Act, for the time being shall apply to, or in relation to, electronic cheques and the truncated cheques subject to such modifications and amendments AS may be necessary for carrying out the purposes of the Negotiable Instruments ACT 1881..."[138]

2.16 *Cyber Contracts or Invitation to Treaty?*

Under normal circumstances one needs to be careful in distinguishing an offer from an invitation to treaty or invitation to receive an offer. For

---

[136] See Gogna and Chand S., *A Text Book of Mercantile Law*, New Delhi, India 2005.

[137] Ibid.

[138] See Section 81A of the Information Technology Act, 2000. See also Sarkar, *Evidence Law*, 2007, Volume 2 at page 2574.

instance a shopkeeper's catalogue of prices is not an offer apart from just an invitation to the intending customers to offer to buy at the indicated price. Likewise the transmission of a price list of drinks or any goods does not amount to an offer to supply unlimited quantity of the wine described at the price named, so that as soon as an order is given there is a binding contract to supply that quantity.[139] The same reasoning was raised in *Pharmaceutical Society of Great Britain v. Boots Cash Chemists Ltd*[140] on the basis that a display of goods in a shop with a price list attached is not an offer even if there is a 'self-service system' in the shop. The Court further held in this landmark case that:

> "it is a well established principle that the mere exposure of goods for sale by a shopkeeper indicates to the public that he is willing to treat but does not amount to an offer for sale… the customer is informed that he may himself pick up an article and bring to the shopkeeper with a view to buying it and if, but only if, the shopkeeper expresses his willingness to sell is the sale completed."[141]

The development of digital technology has also brought legal implications on contracts, offers, invitation to treaty and advertisement. Under cyberspace it is possible to observe on-line advertisements whereby goods and services can be promoted and sold eventually on-line. Arguably, the shopkeeper's catalogue of prices or the transmission of a price list of drinks or any goods under physical world should equally be treated with the website advertising goods and service with price lists. Online merchants, therefore, need to observe the fine distinction between an offer and invitation to treat. Invitations to treat are advertisements that promote the sale of products but are not offers in themselves (no unilateral contract). Some notable legal issues to be considered here are whether these kinds of contracts are bilateral or unilateral. It should be remembered that online advertisements can create unilateral contracts whereby one party in this case the advertiser is bound while the acceptor does not need to notify the advertiser. It is advised that online advertisements must be carefully drafted to ensure that customers and lawyers interpret them as advertisements and not unilateral contracts to avoid what happened in the case of *Carlill v. Carbolic Smoke Ball Co. Ltd*[142] which concerned unilateral contracts.[143] In this case Bowens suggested that it was an offer made to all people in the world.

---

[139] See Singh A., *The Law of Contract*, 9th Edition 2005.

[140] (1952) 2 QB 795 at page 802. (1995) 1 ALL ER 482 (CA).

[141] *Pharmaceutical Society of Great Britain v. Boots Cash Chemists Ltd* at page 801 as cited by Turban E., *E-commerce*, 2002, at pages 82-83.

[142] [1892] 2 Q.B 484, affd [1893] Q.B 1, 156.

[143] See Turban C., *E-commerce*, 2002 at page 82.

Indeed the arguments of Lord Godard in *Pharmaceutical Society of Great Britain v. Boots Cash Chemists Ltd* (sic) cited by Singh A in his book *Law of Contract*, are very relevant as far as cyber transactions such as advertisements are concerned. His Lordship argued that:

> "It would be wrong to say that the shopkeeper (compare with web-merchant) is making an offer to sell every article in the shop to any person who might walk in and that person can insist on buying any article by saying 'I accept your offer'. In most bookshops customers are invited to go in and pick up books and look at them even if they do not actually buy them. There is no contract by the shopkeeper to sell until the customer has taken the book to the shopkeeper or his assistant and said 'I want to buy this book' and the shopkeeper says 'yes'. That would not prevent the shopkeeper, seeing the book picked up, saying 'I am sorry I cannot let you have that book; it is the only copy I have got and I have already promised it to another customer'. Therefore, I am of the opinion, that the mere fact that a customer picks up a bottle of medicine from the shelf in this case does not amount to an acceptance of an offer to sell. It is an offer by the customer to buy, and there is no sale effected until the buyer's offer to buy is accepted by the acceptance of the price." (*emphasis added*)[144]

2.17 *From Physical World Auctions to Cyber Auctions*

2.17.1 An overview of online auctions

There has been rapid growth in the development and use of online auctions aimed both at consumers and businesses. Computer technology has facilitated auction business to be carried on-line whereby buyers are not necessarily forced to come face to face with auctioneers and even other competing parties. The emergence and prevalence of websites conducting online auctions and other related e-business such as eBay has improved the shopping environment for consumers in terms of choices and prices. People can easily find a better deal or acquire a ceased-to-produce item on eBay where millions of items are available for sale.[145] However these websites dealing with the online C2C auctions might cause problems in most cases to the consumers given the borderless and anonymity characteristics of the Internet. Most laws in Tanzania and other countries dealing with consumer protection were formulated for the purposes of protecting consumers under physical world.

---

[144] (1952) 2 QB 795 at page 802. (1995) 1 ALL ER 482 (CA). See also Avtar Singh in *Law of Contract* 2005 at pages 18-19.

[145] See The Icfai Journal of CYBER LAW 2007, Vol. 4.

There has been an increase in online auction fraud and other related cyber crimes targeted at consumers. The National Consumer League's research indicated that online auction fraud has dominated the champion position among all online consumer threats since 1998.[146]

Unlike the traditional auction, the world of technology has now embarked on the so-called online-auction. Not surprisingly, there is no specific legislation dealing with on-line auctions but this trend raises interesting legal questions.[147] Some jurisdictions have introduced some laws that equally protect consumers under physical and digital world. The European Union, for example has promulgated the Distance Selling Directive 97/7/EC and e-Commerce Directive 00/31/EC after taking into account the different characteristics of e-Commerce. The UK and India have not been left behind in formulating effective legal framework that regulate and protect online auction consumers and other related e-consumers. For instance, the Consumer Protection (Distance Selling) Regulations 2000 was introduced to regulate business dealers online, for the purpose of the contract to provide the consumer with goods or services under an organized distance by making exclusive use of one or more means of distance communication. Some of the obligations to the suppliers can be highlighted as follows:

a) The supplier must give consumers clear information including details of the goods or services offered, delivery arrangements and payment, the suppliers details and the consumer's cancellation right before they buy (known as prior information),

b) The supplier must also provide the information in writing. The consumer has a cooling-off period of seven working days.

2.17.2 *A comparative analysis between physical and cyber auctions*

If one compares a traditional auction company such Sotheby's with cyber auction companies such as eBay, one can easily observe considerable differences in terms of the means and volume of auction activities. It has been argued that, unlike in the traditional auction, scenario such as trading at Sotheby's, where relevant parties could be in an identical venue with the specific item for auction, Online Auction Websites (OAWs) such as eBay merely use the Internet as a tool to create a virtual venue where no parties would meet and buyers even have no opportunity to examine the item they intend to purchase.[148]

---

[146] Ibid.

[147] Turban E., *Electronic Commerce,* Sweet and Maxwell Publishers, London 2002 at pages 45-46.

[148] For fuller discussion, see The Icfai Journal of CYBER LAW 2007, Vol. 4.

The clearest difference which seems to be another advantage of OAW is the large volume of online auctions and fast transactions on eBay, which are greater than that of Sotheby's. The other interesting difference is that, whereas traditional auction houses such as Sotheby's are seen physically storing goods for sale, OAWs like eBay do not take title to or handle the goods bought or sold using the medium of Internet.[149] In this case, consumers under eBay and other related websites are always exposed to a higher risk in respect of potential problems resulting from the anonymity and borderless features as facilitated by eBay than Sotheby's. Furthermore, unlike transacting with the traditional auction companies, online auction consumers are, to a certain extent, facing a more difficult situation when they come across problems when purchasing items. (Ibid)

2.17.3 Other legal uncertainties under cyber auctions as compared to physical auctions

Indeed some of the interesting fundamental legal issue is the question of the method of acceptance by the auctioneer. The general principle under current law in most countries like Tanzania stipulates that, "a sale by auction is completed on the fall of the auctioneer's hammer or in any other customary manner."[150] With online auctions there is the practical and even legal problem that there is no auctioneer's hammer. In practice, this problem seems to be resolved by setting a closing time on the website by which all bids must be placed. The highest bidder at the time the auction closes is bound to contract unless the reserved price has not been reached.[151] It should be noted that the law regulating sale of goods is part and parcel of the law of contract. In this case any reforms relating to contract laws should involve reforms to the sale of goods and consumer protection laws. The laws regulating this area need to provide for a closing time that is equivalent to "the fall of hummer" as the means of obtaining the last bidder or winner.

The development of e-commerce has gone further to the extent that airlines have moved to use of Internet sales and e-tickets as a means of reducing distribution costs and saving money in terms of ticketing paperwork and staffing. Customers can now make their bookings and payment online. The said traveling area needs to be regulated to protect the customers or consumers and other beneficiaries who are ordering and purchasing online tickets. Tanzania has not been left behind in exploring and exploiting this new mode of transaction online whereby some airline

[149] Ibid.

[150] See Section 59 (b) Sale of Goods Act of Tanzania Cap 215 and compare with the UK Sale of Goods Act, 1979.

[151] Ibid.

companies are now using e-ticketing. This can be evidenced by the Precision Air Services Limited which has embarked on interline electronic tickets.[152] The computerized ticketing service issues paperless documents that enable customers a single e-ticket to all destinations, which is convenient.

2.18 *The Impact of Technology on Gaming and Gambling*

2.18.1 Introductory remarks

One of the areas that seem to be highly impacted by the development of digital technology especially e-commerce is the famous play known as gaming or gambling which was common under the physical world. Due to the development of ICT, the mode of this play has been dramatically changed whereby more and more customers are being attracted to these lottery games. The world of online gaming is getting broader and better as distant gaming involves players who from the comfort of their homes can enjoy the thrill of the casino experience in real times as they play and communicate with real professional dealers.[153] All the necessary elements and information for gambling—transfer of funds, information about the game or lottery, and even information about who won or lost can easily be transmitted via the Internet.[154] The great challenge for most countries is how to monitor and control illegal online gambling.

Gaming and gambling are predicted to be among the real growth areas of e-commerce. By 2002 it was estimated that more than 6 billion pounds was gambled by bookmakers, casino operators and others online service providers.[155] Remote gaming is fast developing into a very profitable business as more people become accustomed to playing online. In Malta, the remote gaming industry took off in 2004 when Gaming Regulations were made. In line with this, for the past decades, the international remote online gaming industry has been eying Malta as an ideal centre from where it can conduct worldwide business operations.[156] Other countries like the UK, Italy, Spain, Germany and Caribbean countries have not been left behind in allowing and regulating online gaming. Since the introduction of the Remote Gaming Regulations in 2004, the Malta Lotteries and Gaming Authority has granted over two hundred remote gaming licenses which operate over 750 different online gaming sites.[157]

[152] See *The CITIZEN Newspaper*, Monday, 22 October, 2007 at page 25.

[153] See The Report by Malta Lotteries and Gaming Authority, 2008 at pages 30-31.

[154] See Reed C., *Internet Law*, 2000 at pages 246-247.

[155] See Turban E., *E-Commerce* at page 47.

[156] Op cit at 37.

[157] Ibid.

The most notable thing to be taken into consideration is to make online-players aware that they are not playing with their computers but rather accessing real games being played inside casinos. The effective policy and legal framework can assure players accessing such game sites rest easy in the knowledge that their results are highly authenticated and not being generated by a computer. This will also depend on the strictest measures to retain and ensure the highest security levels and best policies, code of ethics and rules that respect their privacy are adhered to.

Undoubtedly, there might be positive and negative consequences associated with gambling online. In this case, it might be difficult to control illegal electronic gaming under cyberspace due to lack of monitoring, controlling and enforcement mechanisms. This can be reflected from Greece whereby in 2000 spring, the media in Greece published claims that illegal electronic gaming had brought financial ruin to hundreds of families.[158] Outlets with gaming machines had sprung up everywhere in Greece in cafes, establishments that used to have pinball machines, and in public places. The publicity showed that more measures were needed, and led to the creation of a new law.[159]

In recent years, a great deal of attention has been devoted to studying and discussing the societal problems generally associated with casino gambling, such as addiction, diminished job performance, crime, money laundering, decreased investment, participation by minors, and a regressive effect on those with lower incomes.[160] However, very little is yet known about how the availability of gambling over the Internet will affect the society and the economy in general. Various studies have been done on assessment of the impact of gambling, and specifically electronic gambling, on individuals, families, businesses, social institutions and the economy.[161] To curb the problem of online illegal gambling, primary regulatory enforcement responsibility for gambling laws need to be developed.

In fact, in the US, there are more than forty-eight out of the fifty states that have legalized some form of gambling in their state. Although many of these states allow only state lotteries, and/or casino or bingo games for charitable purposes, an increasing number of states have legalized commercial casino gambling. The US Wire Communications Act (18 U.S.C.

---

[158] See Giorgos Lialios – Kathimerini Ban on electronic games sparks fierce opposition in Greece and abroad, Electronic games are an integral part of the Internet, say Internet cafe owners, some of whom have already gone out of business.

[159] Ibid.

[160] See Dan L. Burk: University of Minnesota Law School, 229 19th Avenue South, Minneapolis, MN, 55455 USA.

[161] Ibid. See also the Department of Justice of US and the National Gambling Impact Study Commission on the study of the scope and effect of Internet gambling before passing new legislation that would change the way in which Internet gambling is regulated or prohibited.

1084) currently prohibits someone in the business of betting and wagering from using a wire communication facility for the transmission in interstate or foreign commerce of bets or wagers on any sporting event or contest.[162] This law was originally enacted to assist the states and territories in enforcing their laws and to suppress organized crime involvement with gambling. Internet casinos are likely to be located abroad and beyond the easy reach of state authorities, the states are likely to seek federal assistance more frequently when foreign casinos offer gaming to local citizens in violation of local law.

Targeting has also been raised in the context of online gambling cases, where US courts have aggressively characterized offshore gambling sites as "targeting" local residents.[163] In *People v. World Interactive Gaming*[164] the court considered the targeting issue and stated:

> "A computer server cannot be permitted to function as a shield against liability, particularly in this case where respondents actively targeted New York as the location where they conducted many of their allegedly illegal activities." (Ibid)

Assisting states through enforcement of the Wire Communications Act, therefore, is fully consistent with the Department's law enforcement priorities. To be perfectly clear, however, the Department believes that many forms of Internet gambling can be effectively prosecuted under existing state and federal law. Because most methods of connecting to the Internet involve the use of "wire communication facilities" as defined in Section 1084, anyone in the business of betting or wagering who transmits or receives bets and wagers on sporting events via the Internet is acting in violation of the Wire Communications Act.[165]

In preparing and drafting legislation related to the transmission of information over the Internet such legislation needs to consider and provide for three important characteristics. First, the physical world activity and cyber activity should be equally treated in terms of prosecution and enforcement under the same laws. For instance, where a certain activity is prohibited in the physical world but not on the Internet, the Internet will become a safe haven for that criminal activity. All conduct that was previously deemed

[162] See statement of Kevin V. Di Gregory, Deputy Assistant Attorney General criminal division before the subcommittee on crime committee on the Judiciary US House of Representatives concerning gambling on the Internet presented on June 24, 1998.

[163] See Professor Michael Geist in his paper "Is there a there? Toward Greater Certainty for Internet Jurisdiction" at page 37.

[164] 714 N.Y.S. 2d 844 (N.Y.Sup. 1999), 1999 N.Y. Misc. LEXIS 425 (S.C. N.Y. 1999) [hereinafter World Interactive Gaming].

[165] Ibid.

illegal and criminal in the physical world under the off-line laws should become the same criminals when committed in cyberspace. This means that under any legal framework the legislative treatment of e-gambling should be consistent with the treatment of gambling via other wire and wireless methods of communication.[166]

2.18.2 E-gaming and intellectual property rights

There is great concern on the impact of e-gaming on intellectual property rights such as copyright as the activity might involve creation and development of software such as computer programs and other creative issues. For instance where the interests of a player and a publisher diverge, control over the use and development of the game will be an issue, which means that, ultimately ownership of the game will be an issue.[167] Undoubtedly, ownership of gaming scenaria and player gaming narratives will be largely governed by the intellectual property rights conferred under copyright law, and, in any conflict between game developers and game players, most particularly governed by the division of rights dictated under copyright doctrines addressing multiple authorship. Although there are no copyright cases to date that address the ownership of computer gaming scenaria, these principles are articulated in several cases.[168]

In most countries including Tanzania the laws governing intellectual property such as copyright law are unclear on the consideration and protection of the personal investment of game players in game characters and game narratives. It has been learnt that at the level of player perception, the output of the game typically constitutes a collection of sounds, images, and animation, and text, constituting an audiovisual work. Such works are protected under the law of copyright because copyright subsists in original works of authorship fixed for a perceptible duration in some tangible medium of expression. Since the audiovisual output of the game is fixed for some duration in computer hardware, copyright law will definitely apply. In addition to that, the computer code that controls and generates the game scenario will also fall under the system of copyright and in some cases patent rights where technical contribution is proved. The copyright laws and regulations need to be reformed to address all intellectual property rights issues arising from online gaming and gambling.

---

166 See www.law.umn.edu/facultyprofiles/burkd.htm.

167 See Dan l. Burk, electronic gaming and the ethics of information ownership, University of Minnesota Law School, Minneapolis, USA. See also Burk, D. (2004). Feminism and copyright in digital media. in Richard A. Spinello & Herman T. Tavani (eds.), Intellectual property rights in a networked world: theory and practice (161-181). Hershey, pa: idea group, inc.

168 Ibid.

2.18.3 Gaming and Gambling Activities in Tanzania

The activities of gaming and gambling in Tanzania are now becoming common to many people. There are so many gambling machines that are used in gaming play in most parts of the urban areas in the country. In 2003, the government of Tanzania passed a law to regulate gaming in Tanzania.[169] The Act provides for the Gaming Board of Tanzania – to provide for the control and licensing by the Board of gaming activities – to prohibit certain transactions and to provide for related matters.

However the Act is not user-friendly under the cyberspace. Most gaming activities that can be conducted electronically might not be well captured by this law. This means that, it might be difficult to control and prosecute remote, distance or online gaming. For instance the law provides for the obligation to pay taxes for the operators of gaming.[170] However it might be difficult to collect taxes from the people who conduct online activities electronically. The law further prohibits persons under the age of majority to be involved in gaming activities.[171] Again, under cyberspace it might be difficult to identify the ages of the parties involved in online gaming. This law needs to be amended to reflect the impact of digital technology and simplify the enforcement while protecting online consumers.

All casinos, charity casinos and slot operations at racetracks in Tanzania should be subject to regulatory requirements. Like other countries, the laws in Tanzania should provide for mandatory requirements such as registration of suppliers and employees, and approval of rules of play, gaming equipment, gaming management systems, slot machines, chips and tokens, internal control systems, surveillance and security systems, credit, record keeping, and recording of large cash transactions. All electronic gaming equipment must be tested, approved and inspected before it can be offered for patron play to ensure that it is not susceptible to cheating and meets acceptable standards of randomness, as well as hardware and software requirements.

However, there are some wordings on the part of definitions under the Gaming Act, which indicate to some extent that the law has taken into account the development of ICT though not effectively. These words include "credit card", "electronic transfer of money", and "slot machine" as indicated below:

The definitions of these relevant words under the Gaming Act are reproduced below:

[169] The Gaming Act, No.4 of 2003.

[170] See Sections 13 and 31.

[171] See Section 47.

- *"credit card"* means a card, code or other device with which a person may defer payment of debt, incur debt and defer its payment, or purchase property or services and defer payment, but does not include a card, code or other device used to activate a pre-existing agreement between a person and financial institution to extend credit when the person's account at the financial institution is overdrawn or to maintain a specified minimum balance in the person's account at the financial institution;
- *"electronic transfer of money"* means any transfer of money, other than a transaction initiated by a check, draft or other similar instrument, that is initiated through an electronic terminal, telephone, computer or magnetic tape for the purpose of ordering, instructing or authorizing a financial institution or person holding an account on behalf of another to debit or credit an account;[172]
- *"gaming activities"* means any game played with cards, dice, equipment or any mechanical electromechanical or electronic device or machine for money, property, checks, credit or credit card or any representative of value, including but without limiting the generality of the foregoing, bingo, wheel of fortune, baccarat, slot machine, horse race, lottery, wager or stake, any banking or percentage game or any other game.
- *"slot machine"* means any mechanical, electrical or other device, contrivance or machine which, upon insertion of a coin, token or similar object, or upon Payment Of any consideration, is available to play or operate, the play or operation of which, whether by reason of the skill of the operator in Playing a gambling game which is Presented for play by the machine or application of the element of chance, or both, may deliver or entitle the person Playing or operating the machine to receive cash, premiums, merchandise, tokens or anything of value, whether the payoff is made automatically from the machine or in any other form.

2.19 *Legal Challenges on E-gambling*

There are considerable technical, policy and legal challenges that are likely to be posed by the business activities of gaming and gambling online. It has been learnt that it is possible for gambling online to present an arbitrage opportunity for small countries and developing countries like Tanzania and other African Member States as unlicensed gambling are unlawful in most countries.[173] While an online gambling operation can make a conscious decision to commit crime in foreign jurisdiction by making sure

[172] See Gaming Act, No.4 of 2003.
[173] See Reed C., *Internet Law*, 2000.

they have no assets or management personnel in a certain country where its operations are unlawful, it can maneuver its activities to avoid going contrary to the laws of those countries.[174] Like Tanzania, the laws in UK[175] prohibit unlicensed gaming and unlicensed lotteries. What is interesting when looking at these UK Laws and the Gaming Act of Tanzania, is that an online casino or lottery located with their servers outside these countries, might not be caught by the law as committing offences.

2.20 *Jurisdiction Problems Under Cyberspace*

2.20.1 Introductory remarks

As e-commerce involves transactions over cyberspace or Internet, which is boundary less, contractual disputes and other related conflicts cannot be avoided. The problem here is how to answer some legal and other uncertainty issues that are likely to face the e-commerce environment. For instance where the dispute arises between two contracting parties from different countries it might be difficult to determine which law will apply and which country will have jurisdiction. Apart from legal uncertainties, it might also be hard to determine law enforcement agencies that can have power to exercise their jurisdiction on these cases.

Consider a consumer located in Tanzania or any country in East Africa or Africa generally who downloads an electronic book from Amazon.com, a leading e-commerce business located in Seattle, Washington. If the consumer is dissatisfied with the transaction – the downloaded e-book causes his computer system to crash and lose valuable data – and the parties are unable to negotiate a settlement. Where will consumer institute his suit?[176] Which law will be applicable? The consumer may decide to sue for the price of the book and resulting damages in a local courts in East Africa.

In this case there is no doubt that Amazon is likely to contest the action on jurisdictional grounds, arguing that the sales contract between the parties stipulates that any disputes should be brought into a court in Washington state. Should the local court in Tanzania or EAC dismiss the action by upholding the enforceability of the forum selection clause? Will doing so effectively eliminate the consumer's access to our consumer protection legislation? In 1999 in an Ontario case, a court dismissed a

---

[174] Ibid.

[175] See The UK Gaming Act 1968 and The Lotteries amusements Act 1976. Compare these Laws with Gaming Act, No.4 of 2003, Tanzania.

[176] See Professor Michael Geist in his paper "Is there a there? Toward Greater certainty for Internet Jurisdiction" at page 12. See also the argument in *Mendoza v. AOL*, Superior Ct. of Cal., County of Alameda, Dept. No. 22. (unreported, on file with the author) [hereinafter *Mendoza*].

class action lawsuit brought against Microsoft on the basis that a clickwrap agreement between the parties provided for the state of Washington law to govern any dispute.[177]

At European level the problem seems to be solved by the Brussels Convention 1968 on Jurisdiction and the enforcement of Judgments in Civil and Commercial matters. However the Rome Convention[178] seems to be more appropriate and up to date as far as e-commerce is concerned. According to this Convention, "contracts shall be governed by the law of the country with which it is most closely connected with, the country where the party who is to affect the performance ... at the time of concluding contract, his habitual residence or central administration."[179] See also Articles 4 and 5 of the Rome Convention.

2.20.2 How applicable are the territorial jurisdiction principles under international law on cyberspace world transactions?

The question of jurisdiction in solving disputes and identifying relevant laws has always been based on limited territorial principles. Thus, where someone commits an offence in a certain country while physically present in country A, then country A will have jurisdiction. Likewise where a dispute arises in a certain country, then the dispute will be solved in that country. Digital technology seems to diminish this notion as cyberspace transactions are not geographically based.[180]

However in 2000 a French trial court found jurisdiction over the Internet Service Provider (ISP) Yahoo located in California because its US auction did not prevent access to French residents to portions of the site on which persons offered to sell World War II memorabilia containing Nazi symbols.[181]

There is a limitation under International Law in exercising jurisdiction in a case which involves interests or activities of persons who are not resident in that particular country where cause of action arose.[182]

---

177 *Rudder v. Microsoft Corporation* (1999), 2 C.P.R. (4th) 474 (Ont. S.C.J.) as cited by Professor Michael Geist in his paper "is there a there? Toward Greater certainty for Internet Jurisdiction" at page 12.

178 1980 EEC Convention, Rome Convention 1980 (Articles 4 and 5).

179 See Article 3 Rome Convention 1980.

180 The Presentation by the Committee on Cyber law of Business law at the Annual meeting of California State Monterey, 2002.

181 *VEJF and LICRA v. Yahoo! Inc.*Ordonu, 2 May 2000.

182 RESTATEMENT (3RD) OF THE FOREIGN RELATIONS LAW OF THE U.S. ["RESTATEMENT"] & 401, comment a (1987) as cited in the Presentation by the Committee on Cyber law of Business law at the Annual meeting of California State Monterey at page 4.

For such a country to exercise its jurisdiction in dealing with disputes or cases involving non residents there must exist "jurisdiction to prescribe" or the applicable substantive laws of the form country to the particular persons and circumstances in order to adjudicate and enforce the decision. According to the Committee on Cyber law of Business law at the Annual meeting of California State Monterey chaired by Denis Rice argued that where a country has jurisdiction to prescribe, it can appropriately apply its legal norms to entertain dispute and enforce the decision.[183] In other words, a country is said to have jurisdiction to prescribe law with respect to the following issues; firstly the power to conduct issues on dispute can be wholly or in substantial part for cases which take place within its territory. Secondly, the jurisdictional power will also depend on the status of persons, or interests in things, present within its territory. Thirdly, the country can have power to conduct its jurisdictional mandate outside its territory that has or is intended to have substantial effect within its territory. Fourthly, the activities, interests, status, or relations of its nationals outside as well as within its territory has also to be taken into account.[184] Moreover the country can also have certain powers to conduct disputes and cases outside its territory by persons who are not its nationals that is directed against a limited class of other national interests.[185]

Jurisdiction to adjudicate means that the tribunals of a given country may resolve a dispute in respect to a person or thing where the country has jurisdiction to prescribe the law that is sought to be enforced.[186] However there are certain conditions that need to be met for a country to exercise its jurisdiction under international law whereby such exercise of jurisdiction is subject to the requirement of reasonability. States are required to exercise their jurisdiction to adjudicate on the basis of various links, including the defendant's presence, conduct, or, in some cases, ownership of property within the country, conduct outside the state having a "substantial, direct and foreseeable effect" within the country or the defendant's nationality, domicile, or residence in the country.[187]

[183] The Presentation Report by the Committee on Cyber law of Business law at the Annual meeting of California State Monterey, 2002 at page 2.

[184] Ibid.

[185] Ibid.

[186] RESTATEMENT (3RD) OF THE FOREIGN RELATIONS LAW OF THE U.S. ["RESTATEMENT"]. See also The Presentation Report by the Committee on Cyber law of Business law at the Annual meeting of California State Monterey, 2002 at page 3.

[187] Ibid.

2.20.3 *The use of fundamental jurisdictional principles under international law and the digital technology at EU level*

Fundamental jurisdiction principles within European countries are based on statute or regulation instead of case law interpreting constitutional due process limitations, as in the U.S case. The main legal instrument enforceable under the EU is The Brussels Convention which determines and controls jurisdictional issues within the EU. The Convention enshrines almost five major principles and rules that are applied in determining jurisdiction issues.

The first rule is found under Article 2 which states that "a person who is domiciled in an E.U. member country may be sued in that country". The second rule involves contract matters whereby the rule stipulates that a person may be sued in the place of performance of the obligation in question.[188]

On the other hand, the third rule is to the effect that where the dispute involves tort matters, a person may be sued in the place where the event causing harm occurred.[189] More importantly, the fourth rule provides that, a consumer may be sued only in the consumer's country of domicile.[190] Due to the inability of consumers to travel as compared to the suppliers, a consumer is given room to elect to bring an action in either his domicile or in the other party's domicile, so long as the consumer's was subject to a specific solicitation or advertising in the consumer's domicile. Finally, in all contracts that do not involve a consumer, the parties can agree on a forum for disputes.[191]

To address the advent of e-commerce in the context of the existing Brussels Convention, the E.U. Commission in 2000 recommended that jurisdiction should generally be based on the defendant's domicile, but that alternative jurisdictional grounds should be available if there were a "close link" between the court and the action or if the "sound administration of justice" would be facilitated.[192] In this scenario, the jurisdiction of the domiciliary country would continue and the place of performance would have jurisdiction over contract actions. In tort actions, jurisdiction would lie in the place "where the harmful event occurred or where there is a risk of it occurring." (Ibid)

---

[188] Article 5.

[189] Ibid.

[190] See Articles 13 and 14.

[191] Article 17. See also The Presentation by the Committee on Cyber law of Business law at the Annual meeting of California State Monterey, 2002 at page 4.

[192] See The Presentation Report by the Committee on Cyber law of Business law at the Annual meeting of California State Monterey, 2002.

The E.U. eventually issued the Brussels Regulation, with immediate enforcement in 2002. In contrast to a Convention or Directive, a "regulation" of the E.U. becomes binding in its adopted form without further implementation by the 15 member countries. The E.U. felt that the use of directives as means of preserving certainty and uniformity of jurisdiction was not effective, that is why the Commission opted for the effective Brussels Regulations. While the Brussels Regulation does not alter the main structure of the Brussels Convention, it effectuates certain changes that are intended to take account of new technological developments relating to e-commerce.[193] These regulations are very important as far as physical and digital world consumers' rights are concerned. Specifically, the regulation provides that "the courts of the consumer's domicile have jurisdiction over a foreign defendant if the latter pursues commercial or professional activities in the Member State of the consumer's domicile or, by any means, directs such activities to that Member State... and the contract falls within the scope of such activities". Both the Brussels Regulation and the Brussels Convention provide "that any pre-dispute choice of forum other than the consumer's domicile, if a consumer is dealing with a business, is null and void.[194]

The California State Committee on Cyber law of Business law in its report argues that in evaluating jurisdiction over an e-commerce dispute, it is important to determine at the onset whether there is any pre-dispute agreement on choice of forum.[195] Frequently there may be an agreement to have disputes settled by arbitration in a certain location, or an agreement that any litigation must be brought in courts of a certain state. In this way, where parties to the contract are presumed to have equal bargaining power and, therefore, an equal ability to accept or reject such clauses, the clauses are generally uncontroversial and enforced.[196]

Some countries have opted to have contractual choice of law and forum in solving e-commerce dispute where the problem arises with regard to jurisdictional issues. This is due to the fact that some disputes involving e-commerce might arise between parties from different jurisdiction who are bound by a contract determining the terms and conditions upon which they have agreed to interact. Frequently, the online contract itself may provide that any dispute concerning it s to be heard in the courts of a specified state ("choice of forum" clause or "forum selection" clause) and is to be determined under the substantive law of a specified state ("choice of law" clause).[197]

193 Ibid.

194 Ibid at pages 49-50.

195 Ibid.

196 Ibid.

197 Ibid at page 13.

The Rome Convention allows clauses stating the choice of laws and place of solving disputes. Indeed the Convention indicates that contractual choice of law clauses are generally enforceable, but not where the contract is entered into by a consumer or where only one country is connected to the issued in dispute; in the later situation, the contract will not preclude use of that country's mandatory rules.[198]

On the other hand, Article 5 of the Rome Convention does not enforce the waiver by the consumer of mandatory laws of their habitual residence designed for their protection, although a choice of law clause may apply different laws to other aspects of the contract and dispute. Where there is no choice of law clause, Article 5 provides that the law to be applied is that of the consumer's habitual residence, unless the contract is one for carriage or for provision of services exclusively in another forum.

2.20.4 The legal implications of digital technology on traditional principles of jurisdiction

Generally under the physical world the determination of jurisdiction is mainly based on principles of geographical location which has always been difficult to apply under the cyberspace which has no geographical boundary. Under digital technology it is now possible for a website to be viewed from different places in the world where there is access to the Internet. In this way, geographical location is becoming less significant in the context of jurisdiction. The cyberspace world or the information society age allows information over the Internet to easily pass through a network or networks linked to other computers or networks. Under cyberspace not only can messages between and among computers travel along different routes, but "packet switching" communication protocols allow individual messages to be subdivided into smaller "packets" which are then sent independently to a destination where they are automatically reassembled by the receiving computer.[199]

Under the digital world there is no doubt that the actual location of computers among which information is routed along the Internet is of no consequence to either the providers or recipients of information; hence there is no necessary connection between an Internet address and a physical jurisdiction. Moreover, websites can be interconnected, regardless of location, by the use of hyperlinks. Information that arrives on a website within a given jurisdiction may flow from a linked site entirely outside that jurisdiction. According to the Californian State Committee on Cyber law

[198] Ibid.

[199] Ibid.

of Business law, it is very possible for one pocket of an e-mail message sent from California to travel via telephone line through several different states and countries on its way to Italy whereby even the part of the "trip" may even go through a satellite in space.[200] Finally, notwithstanding the Internet's complex structure, the Internet is predominately a passive system; Internet communication only occurs when initiated by a user.[201]

There is a great possibility for the increase of e-disputes and conflict in future due to the rapid development and the use of ICT. As the use of Internet for e-commerce and other activities increases, the rate of e-disputes and other related conflicts is also increasing over the world without geographical or territorial limitation. The rules of jurisdiction over activities in e-commerce are evolving out of principles predating the Internet age. Repeatedly, courts and regulators have analogized the Internet to telephone or print media in analyzing jurisdictional issues. Whether this approach should continue in the future is a serious issue, because the Internet of today is but a glimmer of what lies ahead in digital communications.[202]

It is indisputable that the development of technology has been further diminishing the whole question of geographical territories. It has been argued that as the new global marketplace is becoming incredibly complex, the growth and pace of change in digital communications is accelerating. Each minute, millions of e-mail messages are being sent around the world. The wireless and other related technologies are dramatically facilitating the expansion of information-carrying capacity while changing the way networks are deployed.[203] The system for creating, distributing, selling and consuming products is already turning upside down. Advertising, ordering, billing and trading are being swept into networks in an accelerating and ever-widening fashion.

Electronic commerce in the world marketplace represented by the Internet inherently expands consumer choice, because it opens up every market to every buyer regardless of where the seller is located. In the same vein, electronic commerce gives buyers more advantages vis-à-vis sellers because buyers gain more possibilities. Thus, the implied concern that buyers will be taken advantage of by sellers to whom they are tied by geographic or other limitations is less appropriate in the e-commerce arena.

[200] Ibid.

[201] Ibid.

[202] See The Presentation by the Committee on Cyber law of Business law at the Annual meeting of California State Monterey, 2002.

[203] Ibid.

2.20.5 *Judicial consideration on the traditional jurisdiction principles to e-commerce in the US*

The first federal appellate court decision involving specific jurisdiction in cyberspace was *Cybersell, Inc. v. Cybersell, Inco ("Cybersell")* alluded to earlier as cited by the Californian State Committee on Cyber law of Business law.[204] In this case, the Ninth Circuit Court of Appeals rejected the notion that a home page "purposely avails" itself of the privilege of conducting activities within a jurisdiction merely because it can be accessed there. The plaintiff in Cybersell was an Arizona corporation that advertised its commercial services over the Internet. With reference to the Californian State Committee on Cyber law of Business law report, the defendant was a Florida corporation offering web page construction services over the Internet.[205] The Arizona plaintiff alleged that the alleged Florida trademark infringer should be subject to personal jurisdiction of the Federal court in Arizona because a website which advertises a product or service is necessarily intended for use on a worldwide basis. In finding an absence of jurisdiction the court articulated a three – part test for determining whether a district court may exercise specific jurisdiction over a non-resident defendant:

(1) The non-resident defendant must do some act or consummate some transactions with the forum or perform some act by which he purposefully avails himself of the privilege of conducting activities in the forum, thereby invoking the benefits and protections;

(2) The claim must be one which arises out of or results from the defendant's forum-related activities;

(3) Exercise of jurisdiction must be reasonable.

Applying the foregoing principles, the Ninth Circuit concluded that the Florida defendant had conducted no commercial activity over the Internet in Arizona. The Ninth Circuit found that posting an "essentially" passive home page on the Web using the name "Cybersell" was insufficient for personal jurisdiction.

In 1999, the US Congress made a remarkable decision by passing the Anti-cybersquatting Consumers Protections Act ("ACPA") which provides among other things "in rem proceedings" available in cases involving

[204] See The Presentation by the Committee on Cyber law of Business law at the Annual meeting of California State Monterey, 2002.

[205] See The Presentation by the Committee on Cyber law of Business law at the Annual meeting of California State Monterey, 2002.

cyber-squatting, where the owners of alleged infringing websites could not be found within the plaintiff's jurisdiction.

The US court further tested the ACPA in *Heathmount A. E. Corp. v. Technodome.com.*[206] In this case the federal court for the Eastern District of Virginia considered the application of the U.S. Anti-cyber-squatting Act to two Canadian litigants fighting over two domains: "Technodome.com" and "destination technodome.com." The plaintiff brought an action under the "in rem jurisdiction" provisions in the ACPA. The owner of the domain argued that the case should have been heard in the Canadian courts, citing as support forum non convenience and international comity. However there was an argument that a Canadian court would be less familiar with the provisions of the ACPA than the Virginia Court. On a more basic level, the plaintiff may not be able to assert the same rights in Canada, which lacks a body of law equivalent to the ACPA and whose enforcement of its trademark laws cannot extend into the United States.

While the development of digital technology has been increasing the number of Internet users, there has been rapid increase on the electronic disputes and litigations. Some countries like the US courts have been reluctant in assuming jurisdiction over foreign defendants based essentially on their operation of a website. As Internet use increases globally, so does the number of jurisdiction-related cases involving international litigations. A good example can be reflected from the case of *Ty Inc. v. Clerk,*[207] whereby the creator of Beanie Babies, sued defendants in the U.K. for trademark infringement, unfair competition, consumer fraud and deceptive trade practices. Defendants sold Beanie Babies and other products through a website registered under the domain name "beaniebabiesuk.com. The website, hosted by an ISP located in California, was accessible to viewers everywhere, including in Illinois. The defendants' website contained an e-mail link through which users could obtain product information, but they could not order merchandise directly through the site. To order, users had to print an order form from the website and either fax, phone, or mail it to the U.K.

The Illinois District Court dismissed the case for lack of jurisdiction, finding that although the defendants' website was not completely passive, because its e-mail link enabled customers to direct product – related and order – placement inquires to the defendants, the interactivity level was limited by the inability of customers to place orders over the Internet.

[206] Case No.CA-00-00714. See also The Presentation by the Committee on Cyber law of Business law at the Annual meeting of California State Monterey, 2002.

[207] 2000 U.S. Dis. LEXIS 383 (N.D.III). See also The Presentation by the Committee on Cyber law of Business law at the Annual meeting of California State Monterey Report at page 56.

The court stressed that defendants made it "extremely clear" on their website that they did not conduct online transactions.

On the other hand, the case of *Compuserve Inc. v. Patterson*[208] is among the earliest reported cases that seem to support online agreements or contracts based on clickwrap agreements and arbitrations. Using the clickwrap standards whereby the user typed the word "agree" to an online agreement whose choice of jurisdiction as one of several contacts to warrant holding the user subject to personal jurisdiction in service provider's home state. The Court held up a clickwrap choice of forum by an OAL subscriber where the subscriber could only enroll OAL by clicking the "I agree" button placed next to "the read me" button or the "I disagree" at the conclusion of the subscription agreement, which contained the forum selection clause.[209]

It has been further recently reported that The French-Defence Association sued Georgia Tech Lorraine, which is the European platform of the American Georgia Institution of Technology, because its home page is only presented in English.[210] This was due to the fact that the law as made in 1994 requires that public communications such as advertising and restaurant menus must be in French and if they are also translated, it must be into more than one language. It is also required that goods and services be offered in French in addition to any other language used.[211]

Likewise in December 1996, the Minnesota District Court ruled that the State of Minnesota had jurisdiction over Granite Gate Resorts Inc. and its President, who are based in Nevada. Granite Gate provided a commercial sports betting service which is illegal in Minnesota but represented that such a betting service was legal. Notably, the agreement between Granite Gate and its customers provided that all claims against Granite Gate must be commenced in Belize, whereas claims against customers could be brought in the customer's home state. In addressing the legal issues in hand, the Court used the five-factor test to determine whether Minnesota Courts had jurisdiction.[212] In another occasion observed in the US in 1981, Playboy Enterprises Inc obtained an injunction against Chuckleberry Publishing Inc and Tattilo Edtrice SpA to prevent them from selling

[208] 89 F.3d 1257 (6th Cir. 1996). See also The Presentation by the Committee on Cyber law of Business law at the Annual meeting of California State Monterey Report at page 44.

[209] See The Presentation by the Committee on Cyber law of Business law at the Annual meeting of California State Monterey, 2002 Report at page 44. See also Groff v. America Online, Inc., 1998WL 307001 (R.I.Super. May 27, 1998).

[210] Ibid.

[211] See White SW Computer Law presentation at www.computerlaw.com.au accessed on 8 September 2008.

[212] Ibid.

their magazine Playmen in the US.[213] The injunction prevented Tattilo from using the trade marks "Playboy" or "Playmen" or any other confusingly similar word in conjunction with the sale or distribution of English language publications and related products in the US.

The most notable instance on the jurisdictional territoriality problem under cyberspace involved the famous owner of Yahoo database which was alleged to conduct illegal activities electronically in France in 2000.[214] French courts took jurisdiction over Yahoo, a corporation located in Santa Clara Country with no presence in France, to adjudicate a complaint of French residents that they could access Yahoo's auction site on which Nazi memorabilia were being offered for sale. The complaint was also brought against Yahoo! France, which is Yahoo's French subsidiary, which is located in France, is in the French language and targets the French audience.

A spokesman for one of two plaintiffs, Ligue International centre le Racism, et I' Anti-Semitism ("LICRA"), alleged that there were more than 1,000 Nazi-related items (pictures, coins, flags, etc.) available on the auction site. When the Paris court first ruled on May, 22, 2000 that Yahoo was required to block access to such sites in France, where sales of such material are illegal, it gave Yahoo two months to develop a plan for such selective blocking. It subsequently extended this date in order to hear testimony from experts on the technical feasibility of such blocking. The French judge rejected Yahoo's argument that such screening technology does not exist; rather, the judge asserted, it merely does not work very well at present. Although links to the US auction site were then removed from the Yahoo! France site!,[215] Yahoo declined to block French access to its US web portal or put warning messages on its U.S. site. In November 2000, the French court ordered Yahoo to create a filtering system within three months that would prevent Internet surfers in France from accessing its online auctions. The Court imposed a fine of 100,000 francs ($13,000) per day for each day that Yahoo exceeded the deadline.[216]

---

[213] Ibid. See also Playboy Enterprises Inc v. Chuckleberry Publishing Inc & others as cited at www.computerlaw.com , whereby the Court found that by offering access to American customers via the Internet, Tattilo was in contempt of Court by breaching the injunction. Tattilo was ordered to:

- shut down its Internet site in Italy or refrain from taking new subscriptions from US residents.
- invalidate user names and passwords previously purchased by US residents and refund the remainder of their subscriptions.
- pay to Playboy, all gross profits earned from its Internet services provided to US residents.
- revise its Internet site to indicate that no subscriptions are available to US residents and pay Playboy's legal costs.

[214] INTL.HERALD-TRIBUNE (May 29, 2000). See also The Presentation by the Committee on Cyber law of Business law at the Annual meeting of California State Monterey, 2002 Report at pages 5-6 and 60.

[215] Ibid.

[216] Ibid.

2.20.6 International initiatives towards global online standards for cyber jurisdiction problems

As indicated earlier, e-commerce has brought a dilemma in the whole question of determining the jurisdiction in case of dispute or conflict arising between parties hailing from different jurisdictions. The world through various initiatives and projects has admitted that this is a critical issue that needs immediate international intervention. The Jurisdiction Project Report describes how critical it is to avoid uncertainties in e-commerce.[217] The report notes that the main question on the uncertainties with regard to jurisdiction under e-commerce is whether characteristics of Internet transactions necessitate new approaches to choice of law, which have not been adopted under the pressure of earlier forms of commerce.[218] Indeed the Internet makes things more complex. The argument over whether the law of the place of origin of the good or service or the law of the place of the consumer should be applied to e-commerce disputes involving consumers become fuzzy as to actual location of a commercial Internet transaction. The following questions arise: Where is a Web page located, where it is viewed, or on a client computer, or where the server transmitting the code is located? When is a transaction completed, when the server transmits a Web page, or when a client transmits the URL that automatically causes the page to be transmitted from a remote server?

There have been other global initiatives to find a solution to the jurisdictional problem over cyberspace to encourage confidence on the use of e-commerce. The most notable efforts include the proposals made by the American Bar Association (ABA) on empanelling a multinational Global Online Standards Commission (GOSC) to study jurisdiction issues and develop uniform principles and global protocol standards by a specific sunset date, working in conjunction with other international bodies considering similar issues. There some notable international organizations supported by the UN such as the Global Business Dialogue, Hague Conference on Private International Law, the Internet Law and Policy Forum, the International Chamber of Commerce, the UNCITRAL, the World Intellectual Property Organization (WIPO), the World Trade Organization (WTO) that have deliberately spent considerable time and effort studying and developing guidelines and principles on jurisdiction issues in cyberspace.[219] More importantly, the UNCITRAL has gone further by developing guidelines and uniform Model Laws that can be adopted

---

[217] See The Presentation Report by the Committee on Cyber law of Business law at the Annual meeting of California State Monterey, 2002.

[218] Ibid at page 73.

[219] See The Presentation Report by the Committee on Cyber law of Business law at the Annual meeting of California State Monterey, 2002 at pages 76-77.

by various countries in the world in solving cyberspace disputes and preparing their cyber laws.

On the other hand, The International Telecommunication Union (ITU) notes that due to the global, convergence nature most cases will require cross jurisdiction cooperation measures.[220] This is due to the fact that, it is possible for forensic evidence relating to botnet used to propagate spam or steal credit cards to be spread across several different countries. In this situation where countries need to create legal framework to cater for cyberspace cases, a primary consideration for legislation is to establish jurisdiction as done by Australia under The Australian Spam Act, 2003 which introduces the concept of country link to determine and decide what cases fall within the jurisdiction of the country implementing the law.

It has been noted that The Global Online Standards Commission in addition to the principles enumerated earlier has made some suggestions. The said Commission recommends among other things that, technological solutions, such as universal protocol standards, employed by intelligent electronic agents may be developed so that users and sponsors may electronically communicate jurisdiction information and rules (including rules relating to taxation), enabling such preprogrammed agents to facilitate the user's or sponsor's automated decision to do business with each other.[221]

2.21 *E-commerce and the Law of Property*

2.21.1 General overview

Generally, contracts or conveyances involving property laws such as real estate are made by deeds and other related documents. This is a mandatory requirement in most property laws. For instance in the UK the Law of Property Act provides that a lease of more than three years should be made by deed otherwise no legal estate can be created.[222] Section 2 (1) of the Law of Property (Miscellaneous) 1989 provides that a contract for the sale or disposition of an interest in land can only be made in *writing* and only by incorporating all the terms which the parties have expressly agreed in one *document* which must be *signed* (*emphasis added*). This requirement was also highlighted by the Court in *Julian v. Crago*, The Times in 1991. While in Tanzania property laws such as land laws and other related laws do not recognize e-transactions, e-conveyance and e-signatures, some countries like the UK have made some reforms on their property laws to cope with technology changes. For instance due to the development of digital

[220] See ITU Botnet Mitigating ToolKit Background information 2008 at pages 21, 82.
[221] Ibid.
[222] Sections 52 and 54. See also Smith and Keenan , *Law for Business*, 2006 at page 138.

technology, the Law of Property (miscellaneous provisions), UK Act 1989 has taken into account the impact of digital technology by recognising and allowing the use of electronic signatures in land deals.[223]

Unlike the UK, in Tanzania most laws do not recognize the validity of digital signatures hence there is no way deed or right of occupancies can be made electronically.

The UK Electronic Communication Act gives room for owners to conduct conveyance of right of occupancy or title deeds electronically.

2.21.2 E-commence and the real estate laws in Tanzania

2.21.2.1 The Land Act, 1999 [R.E 2002 CAP 113] Some of the provisions of the Land Act of Tanzania which do not allow dealing in land electronically such as disposition, transfer or conveyance can be observed and highlighted as follows:

Section 25 which stipulates for the procedure for application for right of occupancy provides that

"(1) An application for a right of occupancy shall be–

(a) submitted on a *prescribed form* and accompanied by a photograph;

(b) ...

(c) *signed* by the applicant or a duly authorized representative or agent of the applicant;" (*emphasis added*)

Section 27 further provides that "(1) The Commissioner shall, where it has been determined that a right of occupancy shall be granted to an applicant, make an offer in writing, hereinafter referred to as a "letter of offer" to that applicant setting out the terms and conditions upon which a grant may be made to that applicant. (See The Land Act, [R.E. 2002, CAP 113])

(2) A letter of offer shall–

(a) be in a prescribed form;

(b) contain all the terms and conditions subject to which a grant of a right of occupancy may be made;

(c) be signed by the Commissioner or an authorized officer;

(d) bear an official stamp;

[223] See Smith and Keenan's, *Law for Business*, 2006 at pages 101-102. Compare the UK laws with Laws in Tanzania such as Land Act and Village Land Act enacted in 1999.

(e) be delivered or sent by registered mail to the applicant or his duly authorized representative or agent.

(3) The Commissioner may withdraw a letter of offer after an affirmative reply to the offer has been received and shall be liable to compensate the applicant for any losses which the applicant has suffered by reason of the withdrawal of the letter of offer, unless within fourteen days of that withdrawal, he makes an alternative offer to the applicant which is in substantially the same terms as the offer which has been withdrawn.

Acceptance of offer of right of occupancy

Writing requirement can also be observed under this law in Section 28 which provides that "(1) An acceptance of offer of a right of *occupancy in writing shall–*

(a) *be in a prescribed form;*

(b) ....

(c) *be signed* by the applicant or his duly authorized representative or agent.

Subsection (2) is to the effect that a document which does not comply in every respect with the provisions of paragraphs (a) and (c) of subsection (1) and which is not accompanied by the necessary monies in one of the ways provided for in paragraph (b) of subsection (1), shall not be taken to be, and shall have no effect whatsoever as an *acceptance in writing.*

Part viii of the very law provides for the mode of disposition and dealings affecting land.

The relevant sections in our discussion under this part are Sections 64 and 65.

Section 64 which stipulates for execution of instruments in writing provides that:

"(1) Without prejudice to the provisions relating to attestations and execution under the Land Registration Act[224] and Registration of Documents Act[225] every instrument effecting any disposition under this Act shall, subject to the provisions of this Act, be executed in accordance with the provisions of this section by each of the parties consenting to it."

[224] Ordinance No. 36 of 1953 [2002 R.E. Cap. 334].
[225] Ordinance No. 14 of 1923 [R.E. Cap. 117].

(2) The execution of any *instrument referred to in subsection (1) by a person shall consist of his signing it or affixing a thumbprint* or other *mark* which shall evidence his personal acceptance of that instrument.

Furthermore, Section 64 which addresses the requirement of writing for enforcement of contracts relating to land provides that

"(1) A contract for the disposition of a right of occupancy or any derivative right in it or a mortgage is enforceable in a proceeding only if–

(a) the contract is in *writing or there is a written memorandum* of its terms;

(b) the contract or the written memorandum is signed by the party against whom the contract is sought to be enforced.

(2) A contract for a disposition referred to in subsection (1) may be made using a prescribed form".

Other relevant provisions are produced here below with words in italics for emphasis;

Section 35; Change of use

(1) An occupier of land under a right of occupancy may apply to the Commissioner for a change or variation to the conditions of that right of occupancy so as to enable him to undertake a development on or a use of that land or a disposal of the whole or a part of that land in connection with a development on or a use of that land which is not permitted by the conditions subject to which the right of occupancy was granted.

(2) An application under this section shall be–

(a) submitted on a prescribed form and be accompanied by a photograph;

(b) accompanied by the prescribed fee;

(c) *signed* by the applicant or his duly authorized representative or agent;

(d) sent or delivered to the Commissioner or an authorized officer;

(e) accompanied by any other information which may be prescribed or which the Commissioner may, in *writing*, require.

Application for grant of approval for disposition

(1) An application for a grant of approval for a disposition shall be–

(a) made on a prescribed form;

(b) *signed* by all the applicants;

(c) accompanied by any other information which is prescribed or which may be required by the Commissioner;

(d) accompanied by any fees which may be prescribed.[226]

Section 53; Validation of certain dispositions

(3) An application for a certificate of validation shall be made–

(a) on *a prescribed form;*

(b) accompanied by the prescribed fee;

(c) *signed* by the applicant or his duly appointed representative or agent;

(d) accompanied by any other information which may be prescribed or which the Commissioner may require.

Section 63; Execution of instruments in writing

"(1) ...

(2) The execution of any instrument referred to in subsection (1) by a person shall consist of his signing it or affixing a thumbprint or other mark which shall evidence his personal acceptance of that instrument".

The other laws that seem to apply offline principles contrary to e-transactions is the legislation regulating the registration of land and documents related to land transfer namely:

The Land Registration Act enacted in 1953 (as amended from time to time),[227] The Chatel Transfer Act[228] and the Registration of Documents Act 1924 [R.E 2002]. It is a fact that most transactions related to real property or estate are better suited to paper based methods for proper authenticity and evidential issues. However there are certain transactions such as preliminary applications, getting title deed and contracts related to transfer of such title deeds that might be made electronically. The main provisions of these

[226] Section 39.

[227] [R.E 2002, CAP 334].

[228] [R.E 2002 CAP 210].

laws that are purely made to suit physical transactions that are paper based methods are summarized below with some words put in italic to emphasise the impossibility of using this law under digital world transactions.

2.21.2.2 The Land Registration Act [R.E 2002, CAP 334]

The most relevant sections of this law that are likely to have an impact in e-commerce applications include Sections 10, 13, 41, 67, 78, 83, 85, 92., 96 and 101.

Section 10; Application for registration

"(1) Any person who claims to be entitled to a registrable estate in any unregistered land, whether beneficially or as a trustee, may apply to the Registrar in the *prescribed manner* for registration (hereinafter referred to as "first registration") of his estate:

(2) Every application for first registration shall be accompanied by *all the documents of title* to such land in the possession or under the control of the applicant".

Advertisement

"(1) Every application for first registration shall be advertised by the Registrar at the expense of the applicant in the *Gazette* and in such one or more *newspapers*, if any, as the Registrar may decide.

(2) The Registrar may give notice of any application to such persons as he may think fit and shall, whenever practicable, give such notice to the reputed owners of all land adjoining that is comprised in the application, except where such adjoining land is in an area defined in a notice made under Section 9 or is already registered or where the reputed owner or such adjoining land acknowledges in writing that he has no objection to the application."[229]

Section 13; Objections

"Any person who claims to have any estate or interest in the land comprised in an application for first registration may, at any time prior to the determination of the application by the Registrar, give the Registrar *notice in writing* objecting to the first registration of the land in the name of the applicant, and setting out the grounds of his objection."

---

[229] See Section 12.

Section 41; Disposition of land

(1) No disposition shall be registered unless there is furnished to the Registrar, a certificate *in writing* by the Commissioner for Lands signifying his approval to the disposition.

Section 67; Registration of legal personal representatives

"On the death of the owner of any estate or interest, his legal personal representative, on application to the Registrar in *the prescribed form* and on delivering to him an office copy of the probate of the will or letters of administration to the estate of the owner, or of his appointment under Part VIII of the Probate and Administration of Estates Act *(14) or the Fourth Schedule to the Magistrates' Courts Act *(15) shall be entitled to be registered as owner in the place of the deceased."

Registration of survivor of joint owners

"(1) If one or two or more joint owners of an estate or interest dies, his name shall be deleted from the land register on the application of any interested person, accompanied by proof of death.

(2) For the purpose of this section and Section 70, the death of a person *shall be proved by the production of a certified copy* of the relevant entry in a register of deaths, issued under the provisions of the Births and Deaths Registration Act *(16) or, in the case of a person the registration of whose death was not compulsory under that Act, or of a person dying outside Tanzania, buy such evidence as the Registrar may accept as being sufficient."[230]

Section 78; Caveats

"(1) Any person who claims an interest in any registered land or any person who has presented a bankruptcy petition against the owner of any estate or interest, may present a caveat in the *prescribed form.*

(2) Every such caveat shall be supported by a statutory declaration stating the facts upon which the claim is based.

(3) ...

(4) ...

[230] Section 69.

(5) Any person who has presented a caveat may at any time withdraw the same by *a notice in the prescribed form executed and attested in the manner required for deeds by Sections 92 and 93."*

Combination of parcels

"The Registrar may, on *the application in the prescribed form* made with the consent of the Commissioner for Lands, of the owner of Government leases or of rights of occupancy over any contiguous parcels, combine such parcels *by cancelling the folios* of the land register relating thereto and preparing a new folio or new folios in respect of the parcel resulting from such combination."[231]

Section 83; Division of parcels

The Registrar may, on the *application in the prescribed form* made with the consent of the Commissioner for Lands, of the owner of Government leases or of a right of occupancy over any parcel, divide such parcel into two or more parcels by canceling the folio or folios of the land register relating thereto and preparing new folios in respect of the new parcels.

Section 85; Reparcellations

"(1) The Registrar may, on the application in *the prescribed form of* the owners of the Government lease in, or rights of occupancy over, any contiguous parcels, who are desirous of changing the layout of such parcels, and with the consent *in writing* of all other persons in whose names any estate or interest in such parcels is registered or entered and of any caveator and the Commissioner for Lands, cancel the folios of the land register relating to such parcels and prepare new folios in accordance with the revised layout."

The other relevant provisions of the Land Registration Act which have typical physical or offline transactions that are geared towards the use of paper-based methods, the requirement of the presence of physical persons, writing and use of manuscript signatures (not e-signatures) for authentication purposes are highlighted and presented below with some words put in italics for emphasis;

Section 92; Manner of execution of Deeds

"A deed shall be deemed to have been executed–

(a) if *signed* and delivered by a natural person;

(b) if *sealed with the common seal* of a corporation and delivered;

[231] Section 82.

(c) in the case of a corporation not required by law to have *a common seal, if signed* and delivered by such persons as may be authorized on that behalf by any law or by them statute of the corporation or, in the absence of any express provision, by two or more persons appointed for that purpose by the corporation in general meeting".

Attestation

"(1) A deed shall be deemed to be attested if–

(a) when signed by a natural person either as a party thereto or on behalf of a corporation not having a common seal, it is attested by an authorized witness;

(b) when sealed with the common seal of a corporation, it is attested by such persons as may be required by law or by the charter or articles of association of the corporation and also, where such seal is affixed outside Tanzania, by an authorized witness, and the person witnessing the signature of the deed or the affixing of the seal thereto signs an attestation clause in the prescribed form and adds his postal address and qualification to act as a witness.

(2) In this section, the expression "authorized witness" means a person authorized in that behalf by rules made under this Act or expressly so authorized under the hand of the Minister."[232]

Section 96; Filing of powers of attorney

(1) The Registrar shall, on the joint application of the donor and the donee of a power of attorney which contains any power to make applications under this Act to effect dispositions of or otherwise to act in relation to registered land, file such power of attorney. Every such application *shall be in writing* in the prescribed form and shall be executed and attested in the manner required for deeds by Sections 92 and 93.

(2) …

(3) Any interested person may give the Registrar notice in writing that any power of attorney which has been filed under subsection (1) has been revoked by the death, bankruptcy or disability of the grantor or the death or disability of the grantee, accompanied by

[232] See Section 93.

such evidence as the Registrar may require, and thereupon the Registrar shall file the same and endorse notice of such revocation upon the power.

Section 101; Decisions to be in writing

"Where under this Act the Registrar makes any decision or order or does any act he shall, on the application of any person affected thereby, give that decision or order in writing and state his reasons there of or, as the case may be, give his reasons in writing for that act."

Service of notices

"(1) A notice under this Act shall be deemed to have been served on or given to any person–

(a) if served on him personally; or

(b) if left for him at his last known address; or

(c) if sent by registered post addressed to him at his last known address."[233]

2.21.2.3 The Registration of Documents Act, 1924 [R.E 2002], Chapter 117. The most relevant sections of this law that are likely to have an impact in e-commerce include Sections 14, 15, 16, 17, 18-24.

Section 14; Presentation in person or by agent

Every document presented for registration shall be presented by one of the parties executing or claiming an interest under it or by his attorney duly appointed or by an advocate of the High Court, or, if such party is a minor or of unsound mind, by the guardian, next friend, or other person appointed by the court to act on behalf of such a minor or person of unsound mind in the matter, or by the duly appointed attorney of such guardian, next friend, or other person, or by an advocate of the High Court.

Section 15; Presentation by post

A document may be presented for registration through the post or under cover if it is accompanied by the appropriate fee and a letter requesting registration and signed by a person who has power to present the document for registration.

---

[233] Section 110.

Section 16; Identity of person requesting registration

The registrar may, if he thinks fit, take steps to satisfy himself as to the identity of the person presenting a document for registration, and of that person's right to present the document for registration.

Section 17; Power to summon witnesses

If the registrar considers that the testimony of any person is necessary to establish the authenticity of any document presented for registration or the identity of the person presenting a document for registration or his right to present it for registration, the registrar may at his discretion call upon the court of the Resident Magistrate in Dar Es Salaam to issue a summons requiring him to appear at the registry either in person or by duly authorized agent as in the summons may be mentioned and at a time named therein, and may examine the person so summoned on oath which the registrar is hereby authorized to administer.

Method of registration (ss 18-24)

Section 18; Presentation book

(1) The registrar shall keep a book to be called the "presentation book" in which a short description of every document presented for registration with the day and hour shall be entered and, if required by the person presenting the document, the minute of presentation, and for the purpose of priority the time of presentation shall be taken as the time of registration. The registrar in entering memorials upon the documents embodied in the register and endorsing a memorial upon a document to be registered shall take the time from the presentation book as the time of registration.

(2) Documents sent by post or under cover and received during the hours of business shall be deemed to be received simultaneously immediately before the closing of the office for that day and those revolved between the time of closing and the next opening of the office for business shall be deemed to be received simultaneously immediately after such opening.

2.22 *E-commerce and the Company Law*

Company law is another area impacted by the development of technology especially e-commerce. Generally, all companies intending to do business are required under company laws to register their names. The Company laws and Trade Mark laws protect and control companies that abuse the use of names. Due to the development of digital technology most companies are now able to do business online minimising cost and staff. Any company can choose any name for their web or Internet address which is unique and unallocated. However the practise has indicated that some companies are abusing other companies' names or internet domain names. Where an unauthorized individual or company decides to register an Internet address which includes the business name or trade mark of a company it may prevent the genuine company from using its own registered name in an Internet address.[234] This part will not concentrate much on domain name cyber-squatting as the topic is discussed fully in forthcoming chapters dealing with the technology and intellectual property law.

Any company or person intending to do business in Tanzania is required to register its or his name under the Business Names (Registration) Act.[235] This is another example of legislation that is impacted by the evolution of e-commerce.

Section 6 of the very Act provides for the manner and particulars of registration. The section stipulates that:

"(1) Every firm or person required under this Act to be registered shall send by post or deliver to the Registrar at the register office a statement in *writing in the prescribed form* containing the following particulars–

(a) the business name;

(b) the general nature of the business;

(c) the principal place of the business;"

Section 7 further provides for the requirement of signature on the Statement to be signed by persons registering.

The law provides that:

"The statement required for the purpose of registration must in the case of an individual be *signed* by him, and in the case of a corporation by a Director or Secretary thereof, and in the case of a firm either by all the individuals who are partners, and by a Director or the Secretary of all corporations which are partners or by some individual who is a partner, or

---

[234] See Smith & Keenan's, *Company Law* 2005 at page 83. See also *Pitman Training Ltd v. Nominet UK [1997] 8* 538 whereby the Court had to resolve a dispute on domain name cyber-squatting between the two companies.

[235] [R.E.2002] Chapter 213.

a director or the secretary of some corporation which is a partner, and in either of the last two cases must be verified by a statutory declaration made by the signatory."

These provisions do not give room for e-commerce due to the requirement of writing, signatures and use of post as mode of delivery of a statement to the Registrar. All these provisions need to be amended to accommodate the development of ICT specifically the use of e-commerce.

2.23 *The need for reforms on Company law*

In 2002, Tanzania made a great change in her Company Law, which was a colonial replica and came up with the huge new Companies Act of 2002. Despite these changes the new law did not take into account the impact of technology and does not accommodate e-commerce. There are a number of provisions that are a barrier for companies or individuals to transact electronically. For example Section 30 shows typical features of offline laws because according to this provision a company may make a contract in *writing* under its *common seal*. This implies that companies cannot make a contract electronically as under e-commerce there is no requirement of writing and common seal.

Every person or group of people intending to form and incorporate a company that intends to do business is required to prepare a Memorandum and Articles of Association. The law requires Memorandum and Articles of Association to be printed in English, signed in the presence of attesting witness.[236] The UK Companies Act 1985 together with the Electronic Communications Act 2000 take into account the development of technology by giving room for the application of e-commerce. Unlike the UK, the Companies Act and other related laws in Tanzania do not facilitate doing business online.

It is important to look at the features of the UK Company laws with regard to the articles and the development of technology. Under the UK laws it is possible for new articles to be drafted for members' approval which take into account the use of digital technology.

Smith and Keenan's[237] in their book *Company law* argue that under the UK law it is very possible for the notices of meetings of shareholders to be sent electronically. Furthermore, voting on a poll can also be done electronically. More interestingly proxies can be appointed electronically. The Electronic Communications Act[238] provides functional equivalence by recognizing

[236] See Section 4 and 5 of the Companies Act No.12 of 2002.

[237] See Smith & Keenan's, *Company Law*, 2005 at pages 115-116.

[238] See section 8 of the UK Electronic Communications Act 2000.

documents in electronic form or in a data message where the Companies Act requires communication of documents offline. Indeed the Electronic Communications Act seems to modify the Companies Act 1985 to allow electronic communication to take place any time. To this effect, Regulations 60, 61, 62, 63, 111, 112 and 115 allow electronic communications.[239]

2.24 *Absolute Departure from Physical World to Cyberspace Transactions?*

At this juncture it is pertinent to answer the above legal issue using various examples and experience from other jurisdiction. Some might think that the introduction of e-commerce will absolutely change the means and methods of transactions and apply paperless method in lieu of paper based methods. Indeed this is not the case as there are certain exceptions to the use of paperless methods. This means that people might use paperless means of transaction in most transactions but in certain situations they have to rely on apprised methods of transactions. These exceptions have also been recognized at international level by UNCITRAL Model Laws and Common Wealth Model Laws.

These kinds of transactions and legal documents include title deeds and negotiable instruments which need paper based methods by using original documents signed and made by deed or in writing, for example right of occupancy, transfer of deed, bill of lading, assignment of copyright,[240] Contract of Marine Insurance as provided under Section 22 of the UK Marine Insurance Act 1906.

Reference can be made to Section 15 of Common Wealth Model Law on electronic transactions which provides that the Bill or Act does not apply to

(a) The creation or transfer of interests in real property

(b) Negotiable instruments

(c) Documents of title

(d) Wills and trusts created by will

It is important to look at examples and experiences from other jurisdiction at national level. There are examples of laws and regulation from some countries that provide for exception as to the requirements of the use of writing, seal and handwritten signatures in certain transactions and documents as mentioned above. For instance the UK Copyright, Designs, and

239 Visit Table A of the UK Companies Act 1985 and Smith & Keenan's on Company Law 2005 at pages 116-117.

240 See Section 90 (3) of the Copyright, Designs and Patents Act 1988 (UK).

Patents Act provides that some legal documents must be made in deed and in writing. This is reflected in Section 90 (3) which provides that:

"An assignment of copyright is not effective unless it is in *writing signed* by or on behalf of the assignor"(emphasis added). Section 92 further defines exclusive licence to mean "a licence in *writing signed* by or on behalf of the copyright owner authorizing the licensee to the exclusion of all other persons… "(*emphasis added*)." (Copyright, Designs and Patents Act, 1988)

The above provision indicates that certain documents such as probate documents and bill of lading cannot be used electronically in the course of any transactions.

Likewise, the Slovenian's E-Commerce and E-Signature Act (ESA) equally provides some exceptions on the use of paper based method vis-à-vis paperless method. For instance transactions involving the following documents must be in paper form that is in writing and, sealed signed to give them legal enforceability:

(1) real property deeds and contracts;

(2) wills, codicils and testamentary trusts;

(3) division of property between spouses;

(4) disposal of property of persons declared legally incompetent;

(5) inter vivos contracts to divide property;

(6) life-subsystems contracts and weavers of heirship;

(7) donation contracts and donation contracts cause mortis;

(8) contracts of sale with retention of ownership (i.e. contracts for a deed); and

(9) Other legal acts requiring a notarized document.

CHAPTER THREE

IDENTIFICATION UNDER CYBERSPACE

3.1 *Identification of Parties on the Internet*

The growth of Internet-based commerce is likely to depend on, among other things, the quality of the legal rules and enforcement in ensuring that transaction data is protected and secured from electronic misuse worldwide. The problem of identify and verifying the customers/consumers or even the supplier under cyberspace are difficult. This raises some legal issues and concerns. Some scholars have interestingly argued that "in the Internet no body knows you are a dog".[1] Furthermore, the sender of Internet communication cannot be necessarily presumed to be who the receiver thinks it is, nor can the sender always be sure of the recipient's true identity. In cyberspace, companies or individuals might face great difficulty in discerning whether the customer has attained the age of majority or is still a minor as failure to identify a minor might have a great impact on the performance and enforceability and validity of e-contracts.[2] In fact the question of legal capacity under the contract poses a challenge when it comes to the formation of contracts online or the so called cyberspace contracts. This is due to the fact that under cyber or Internet no one knows that he is doing business with a minor or a person with an unsound mind.

It should be remembered that in e-commerce contract, parties for example a supplier and a consumer do not come face to face prior to the conclusion of the contract.[3] The capacity to contract is among the ingredients of a valid contract. One of the essential conditions for the enforceability of an agreement is that the concerned parties must be competent to enter into an agreement. The Law of Contract of Tanzania[4] and the Indian Contract Act specifically require that the parties must be competent to contract. Thus, an agreement is valid and enforceable only if the parties to it are competent to enter into a contract. Capacity to contract means the competence (i.e. capability) of the parties to enter into a valid contract. The term 'capacity to contract' is defined in Section11 of the Indian Contract Act which reads:

> "*Every person is competent to contract who is of the age of the majority according to the law to which he is subject, and who is of sound*

---

[1] Christopher Reed, *Internet Law; Text and Materials* 2000 at page 119.

[2] Ibid.

[3] Instead they use telephone sale, mail order, e-mail, facsimile, etc.

[4] CAP 435.

mind, and he is not disqualified from contracting by any law to which he is subject."[5]

Sellers also need to be careful otherwise they will find themselves selling goods which are not allowed to sell to minors online. Under common law countries like Tanzania, contracts that are made by or with minors other than necessary are voidable.[6] Minors are further not allowed to purchase certain goods and services under certain laws. For instance Section 11 of the Law of Contract Act of Tanzania provides for competency of such persons as follows.

"(1) Every person is competent to contract who is of the *age of majority* according to the law to which he is subject, and who is of sound mind, and is not disqualified from contracting by any law to which he is subject". The age of majority under the laws of Tanzania is 18 years and above.

"(2) An agreement by a person who is not hereby declared to be competent to contract is void".

Distance contracts might lead to the formation of contracts without *consensus ad idem* on the other party as the parties do not have an opportunity to physically meet and make an agreement. Under digital technology it is possible for consent to be rendered unreal by mistake or misrepresentation due to the fact that the parties do not know one another apart from making contracts under cyberspace.[7] Companies wishing to avoid dealing with minors are advised to use Content advisor software, which is found on most web browsers.[8]

3.2 *Legal Regime of Digital Signatures and other E-signatures*

Generally, the purpose of signature requirement under the physical world is to authenticate a document. Furthermore, when a signature is affixed to a document or a contract of sale it symbolizes an intention to be legally bound. Authentication by signature is a big problem in this era of digital technology. In most jurisdictions like Tanzania and other East African Community Member States it seems that the requirement of a signature is only met if a physical signature is affixed to a paper document.

---

[5] See Gogna S., *A Text Book of Mercantile Law*, 2005 at pages 25-30.

[6] See *Mechantile Union Guarantee Co. v. Ball [1937] ALL E.R.1.* See also Contract Laws in Tanzania and compare with English Contract Laws.

[7] For general discussion on the reality of consent, mistake and misrepresentation in contract see Smith & Keenan's on the Law for Bossiness 2006 at pages 15-51.

[8] Turban E., *Electronic Commerce,* Sweet and Maxwell Publishers, London 2002 at page 77.

The so-called electronic signatures do not suffice these legal requirements unless specific provision for electronic authentication has been made. The fact that there are applications available today which make electronic signatures more secure for purposes of authentication than hand-written signatures have not yet found favour with most legislators where formalities are concerned.

The traditional concept of signing a paper document has to be re-evaluated in terms of the electronic bill of lading. In an EDI transaction no "human" signature is required. It has been suggested that such a transaction can be electronically *signed* by means of algorithms contained within their data streams to authenticate the identity of the sender.

The development of ICT has brought new methods of identification electronically whereby electronic documents can be signed by the use of biometric systems, such as finger print or voice recognition, or by rental scanning, etc. The question is how can the parties entering into a cyberspace or distance contract sign while they cannot identify each other. One way of identifying each other on the Internet while communicating and contracting is the use of Digital Signatures. In line with digital signatures which are mainly based on cryptography technology, there exist other means of electronic signatures using various devices that can be used to fulfill the functions offered by manuscript signatures. A good example can be traced from certain techniques that are able to rely on authentication through biometric device based on handwritten signatures whereby a signatory signs manually using a special pen, either on a computer screen or on a digital pad.[9] In this way a handwritten signature can be analyzed by a computer and stored as a set of numerical values, which is then appended to a data message and displayed by the relying party for authentication purposes.

Electronic signature is data in electronic form which is attached to other electronic data and serves as a method of authentication.[10] Digital or e-signatures are created and verified by using cryptography, the branch of Applied Mathematics that concerns itself with transforming messages into seemingly unintelligible form and back into the original form. An electronic signature may take a number of forms; a digital signature, a digitized finger print, a retinal scan, a pin number, a digitized image of a handwritten signature that is attached to an electronic message, or a merely a name typed at the end of an email message.

9 See Article 2 of UNCITRAL Model Law on Electronic Signatures 2001 at page 21. See also Article 2 of EU Directive on E-Signatures.

10 Ibid.

Mathematics of cryptography is used to produce signatures that are functionally equivalent to a handwritten signature. Digital technology has created ways of securing information or data transmitted and stored online through encryption which transforms plain data or text into cipher text that cannot be accessed or read by anyone other than the sender and intended receiver. This process is useful to the e-commerce environment as it can ensure high security through integrity, authenticity, confidentiality, non-repudiation, etc.[11] This is the technology that enables the sender of e-information or electronic documents to create an e-signature. Lloyd Ian[12] in his book *Information Technology Law* argues that electronic signature is very broad which encompasses the use of scanning equipment to create a digital image of a person's signature using encryption among other advanced technology methods.

Generally e-commerce has the ability to reduce the time span between ordering, delivery, invoicing and payment by using the Internet. Electronic commerce has the ability to create a global digital economy. The use of a digital signature shall have the same force and effect as the use of a manual signature if and only if it embodies all the following characteristics:

1) It is unique to the person using it;
2) It is capable of verification;
3) It is under the sole control of the person using it; and
4) It is linked to data in such a method that if the data is changed, the digital signature is invalidated.

3.2.1 Legal meaning of digital signature

According to the Malaysian Electronic Signatures Act, "digital signature" means transformation of a message using an asymmetric cryptosystem such that a person having the initial message and the signer's public key can accurately determine its authenticity.[13] The cryptography technology is the major component of digital technology which uses encryption and decryption to keep the electronic communications and transactions between the parties private and more secure through symmetric and asymmetric cryptography. This unique and new type of signature which is a close parallel to manuscript signature is a "signed" cipher text that can be sent over the Internet and accessed using public

[11] For fuller discussion see Laudon C.K. & Traver G.C., *E-Commerce*, 3rd Edition 2007, at pages 269-273.

[12] Lloyd I., *Information Technology Law*, 3rd Edition, 2000, at page 586.

[13] See Section 2(1).

and private keys supported by digital certificates and PKI.[14] Digital Certificates and PKI help in solving the problem of identity and anonymity by ascertaining:

(a) whether the transformation was created using the private key that corresponds to the signer's public key; and

(b) whether the message has been altered since the transformation was made;

Digital signatures use what is known as "Public-key *cryptography*" which is often based on the use of algorithmic function to generate two different but mathematically related "keys" whereby one such key is used for creating a digital signature and the other one for verifying a digital signature or returning the message to its original form. This technology is believed to solve the problem of exchanging private (secret to the owner) and public keys (widely disseminated) whereby both keys are successfully used for encryption and decryption of messages online. Indeed e-signatures provide effective security on on-line contracts through various means such as biometric method (voice pattern, finger print, imaged handwritten signatures) and digital signatures. While the former involve a unique physical attribute of the parties in contract, the later verifies the authenticity on the origin of communication and the integrity of the content of the message.

Generally, e-signature must fulfill the following requirements:

- Uniquely linked to the signatory. Only one person must possess the private key;
- Capable of identifying the signatory using symmetric key encryption and public key encryption; and
- Linked to the data whose change is detectable.

The advantage of an e-signature is that it cannot be easily tempered with and it can accurately confirm a document is from the intended signatory. Electronic signatures, which identify the person who signed the contract and which fulfil many legal requirements, may be done electronically whereby such a signature authenticates an electronic transmission by identifying the signer and attributing the document to them.

The evolution of digital technology has brought a revolution on paper based or manual signatures (a hand-written form) paving way for electronic or digital signatures, which seem to pose legal uncertainty under offline laws that were created to suit paper based methods. In 1995,

---

[14] Laudon C.K. & Traver G.C., *E-Commerce,* 3rd Edition 2007, at pages 269-273.

the US state of Utah became the first jurisdiction in the world to enact an electronics signature law.[15] In the Utah statute, digital signatures were given legal recognition, but other types of electronic signature were not.

On the other hand, Singapore adopted the so called 'hybrid'[16] modal-a preference for the digital signature in terms of greater legal presumption of reliability and security, but not to the exclusion of other forms of electronic signatures avoiding one-form of technology to the exclusion of others. It has been argued that the hybrid approach is the one also taken by the European Union's E-signatures directives, Japan, Vanuatu, Taiwan, Tunisia, Lithuania, Iran, South Korea, Barbados, Hong Kong, Bermuda, Pakistan, Dubai, Azerbaijan, Finland, Hungary and most recently China.[17] Briefly, one can argue that unlike some commonwealth countries such as the UK, Canada, Australia, Singapore, etc. both the Utah and Slovenia e-signature laws provide more legal recognition on digital signatures than other e-signatures on the simple ground that digital signatures provide a higher degree of security for electronic transactions. Notably, the EU (EU Directive), Singapore, Japan, Hong Kong, Tunisia, China, etc. have adopted the hybrid system that is based on the UNCITRAL Model Laws.

Similarly, the South African law on e-transactions and e-communications provides that,

"Where the signature of a person is required by law and such law does not specify the type of signature, that requirement in relation to a data message is met only if an advanced electronic signature is used".

3.3 *Cryptography Technology (PKI) and Digital Signatures in Tanzania*

The increased use of electronic authentication techniques as substitutes for manuscript or handwritten signatures and other paper based authentication procedures suggest the need for creating a legal framework that will regulate e-signatures. The laws in Tanzania neither cover online transactions nor recognize cyberspace or digital signatures.

Most laws governing business transactions provide that, the contract must be in writing and duly signed or authenticated before a witness. This requirement is no longer applicable in cyberspace world hence off-line laws have to be changed and reformed to accommodate e-commerce principles.

15 See The Icfai Journal of CYBER LAW Vol. VI 2005.

16 Ibid.

17 Ibid.

The current legislation that governs communication, storage of information and transaction in Tanzania and other countries are not in tune with these technological changes. Most legislation still maintain manuscript signatures as a means of authentication of documents and identifying parties creating a discriminatory approach to e-signatures and data messages or alternatives to paper based methods under e-commerce. A good example is the Bills of Exchange Act of Tanzania[18] whereby a signature is an essential to liability. The law further stipulates that "no person is liable as drawer, endorser, or acceptor of a bill who has not signed it as such:

Provided that–

(a) where a person signs a bill in a trade or assumed name, he is liable thereon as if he had signed it in his own name;

(b) the signature of the name of a firm is equivalent to the signature by the person so signing of the names of all persons liable as partners in that firm".

Likewise Section 73 provides that "A cheque is a bill of exchange drawn on a banker payable on demand.

(2) Except as otherwise provided in this Part, the provisions of this Act applicable to a bill of exchange payable on demand apply to a cheque".

It is also important to pay attention to Section 89 of this law which provides that "A promissory note is an unconditional promise in *writing* made by one person to another *signed* by the maker, engaging to pay, on demand or at a fixed or determinable future time, a sum certain in money, to, or to the order of, a specified person or to bearer (emphasis added).

The law goes further by providing more wording that indicates the inapplicability of digital signatures. For instance Section 97 provides that "Where, by this Act, any instrument or writing is required to be signed by any person, it is not necessary that he should sign it with his own hand, but it is sufficient if his signature is written thereon by some other person by or under his authority".

(2) In the case of a corporation, where, by this Act, any instrument or *writing* is required to be *signed*, it is sufficient if the instrument or writing is *sealed* with the corporate seal.

Technology has advanced to the extent of intruding e-cheque which will definitely not be valid under this law.

[18] See CAP 15 RE 2002.

Another outdated law which provides for mandatory requirement of manuscript signatures is the Arbitration Ordinance[19] which provides that:

"When the arbitrators or umpire have made their award, they shall *sign* it and shall give notice to the parties of the making and *signing* thereof and of the amount of the fees and charges payable to the arbitrators or umpire in respect of the arbitration and award.

The law further provides that "the arbitrators or umpire shall, at the request of any party to the submission or any person claiming under him and upon payment of the fees and charges due in respect of the arbitration and award and of the costs and charges of filing the award, cause the award or a signed copy of it, to be filed in the court; and notice of the filing shall be given to the parties by the arbitrators or umpire".

The challenge for Tanzania and other developing countries is how to maintain Public Key Infrastructure (PKI) and verifying or certifying authorities as a way of providing confidence against tempering with keys and e-signatures in general. The government has to decide whether certification authorities are to be operated or under the supervision of government bodies or private sector.

Notably, the Common Law principles that require writing and signatures in the formation of contracts are the main features of laws governing transactions in Tanzania. These requirements based on paper method transactions are not in line with the development of e-commerce. Immediate legal changes are thus required. The requirement of signature of documents or copy of agreements on the parties entering into a contract as considered by the Court in the UK Legislation that the parties must sign their names in their own hand.[20]

The definition of "*writing*" in the current legislation in Tanzania needs to be expanded to include digital documents and electronic transactions in general. In the UK the Civil Evidence Act 1995 has removed previous requirements that documents had to be original in written form to be admissible. The UK has gone further whereby under the CDPA 1988 the word *writing* has been defined to include; "any form of notation or code, whether by hand or otherwise and regardless of the method by which, or medium in or on which, it is recorded."[21]

Likewise, India has given the requirement of writing functional equivalence with electronic records or data message in their law as seen below with added emphasis from the author.

---

[19] See Section 12 and Rule 4 CAP 15 RE 2002.

[20] The Court of Appeal in *Firstpost Homes v. Johnson [1995] 4 ALL ER 355*. The Court considered The Law of Property (Miscellaneous Provisions) Act 1989.

[21] Section 178 CDPA.

1. Where any law provides that information or any other matter shall be in *writing* or in *the typewritten or printed form*, then, notwithstanding anything contained in such law, such requirement shall be deemed to have been satisfied if such information or matter is –
   (a) rendered or made available in *an electronic form*; and
   (b) accessible so as to be usable for subsequent reference.[22]

In Tanzania the Interpretation of Laws Act[23] defines the word "*writing*", and any expression referring to writing to include printing, lithography, typewriting, photography and other modes of representing or reproducing words in visible form. In comparison with other countries legislation like the UK, the Interpretation Laws in Tanzania have not clearly accommodated electronic technologies on data message. The legislators in Tanzania need to borrow this important definition that encompasses both paper-based and paper-less transactions. There is need to prepare an effective legal framework that can regulate and facilitate the use of both digital signatures and other forms of electronic signatures.

When enacting the law that will regulate electronic signatures in Tanzania, digital signatures must be given greater consideration as compared to other forms of e-signatures because this form of e-signature effectively utilizes cryptographic methods that result in a high degree of reliability and security.[24] Tanzania and other East African Community members need to have effective legal framework on e-signatures to enable and facilitate the use of electronic signatures and provide equal treatment to users of paper-based documentation and users of computer-based information. The framework should among other things equally reflect the principle that no discrimination should be made among the various techniques that may be used to communicate or store information electronically, a principle that is often referred to as "technology neutrality".[25]

However there are also some disadvantages of this system to developing countries like Tanzania because the implementation of these forms of e-signatures is very expensive. In addition to that, the proposed law should mandate the accredited Certifying Authorities to issue successful

---

22 See The Information Technology Act, 2000.

23 Section 2 CAP 1 [2002 RE].

24 See The Icfai Journal of CYBER LAW Vol. VI 2005.

25 See the UNCITRAL Model Law on Electronic Signatures with Guide to enactment 2001. In preparing this Guide Model Law the UNCITRAL agreed that the uniform rules to be prepared should deal with such issues as the legal basis supporting certification processes, including emerging digital authentication and certification technology; the applicability of the certification process; the allocation of risk and liabilities of users, providers and third parties in the context of the use of certification techniques; the specific issues of certification through the use of registries; and incorporation by reference (*Fifty-first Session, Supplement No. 17* (A/51/17), paragraphs 223 and 224. See page 12 of the UNCITRAL Document).

applicants and confirm the authenticity and integrity of e-signatures to relying parties. This will simplify the effective implementation and enforceability of the laws. The Certifying Authorities should among other things observe higher security standards and maintain a publicly accessible repository of certificates and public keys.[26] A simple example that can illustrate the rationale behind the use of Certifying Authorities (CAs) for online transactions can be summarized as follows;

If the sender X and receiver Y are in the process of consummating e-transaction, Y needs an independent confirmation that X's message is from X before Y can have faith that X's public key actually belongs to X.

3.4 *Judicial Definition of Writing under Physical World Vis-à-vis Cyberspace Environment*

There are some judicial precedents that can be considered in interpreting some legal provisions that are likely to be impacted by the impact of digital technology. Some cases indicate that the word writing needs to be given equal weight with data and other e-information. Like other countries, Tanzania and other EAC courts also need to deem digital transactions as writing. In *Derby & Co. Ltd v. Weldon*[27] it was held that computer databases (files) were valid documents for discovery. The US is also believed to extend the definition of writing in a broader term to include digital forms,[28] Other laws that indicate the requirement of writing is the Income Tax Act of Tanzania as amended in 2006.[29] While the UK Interpretation Act[30] defines writing to mean "typing, printing, lithography, photography and other modes of representing or reproducing words in a visible form." The CPA 1988 defines writing as including; "any form of notation or code, whether by hand or otherwise and regardless of the method by which, or medium in or on which, it is recorded."[31]

On the other hand the requirement of writing is required for the purposes of evidence under evidence laws and other related laws. In the

---

[26] Ibid at pages 8-9.

[27] [1991] 1.W.L.R 652 at 654. See also Turban E., *Electronic Commerce*, Sweet and Maxwell Publishers, London 2002 at pages 94-95.

[28] Ibid. Code s.1 of The Uniform Commercial Code defines writing as printing, typewriting, or any other international reduction to tangible form. See also *Hawley v. Whipple 48 N.H.487 (1869)* as cited further in Turban E., *Electronic Commerce*, Sweet and Maxwell Publishers, London 2002 at pages 94-95 whereby the court argued that it makes no difference whether that operator writes the offer or the acceptance with a steel pen an inch long attached to an ordinary penholder, or whether his pen be a copper wire a thousand miles long".

[29] See sections 34 and 54 of Cap 332.

[30] Schd 1 of the Act 1978.

[31] Section 178 of the UK Copyright, Designs and Patents Act. See also Turban E., *E-Commerce* at page 95.

UK contracts of guarantees are examples of this kind of contract whereby under Section 4 of the Statute of Frauds 1677 writing is essential as evidence in solving disputes. The said section provides that "no action can be brought unless the guarantee is in writing". In *Action Strength v. International Glass Engineering* the claimant case failed due to lack of evidence in writing.[32]

On the other hand, Australia which has almost the same common law principles with Tanzania has enacted good cyberspace or digital technology legislation thattakes into account the impact of Information and Communication Technologies on trade and business. The most relevant Australian law that regulates e-transactions and e-communication is The Electronic Transaction Act 1999 (cth) that was passed on 30 September 1999.

This cyber law provides an effective legal framework to support and encourage business and consumer confidence in electronic commerce by ensuring that the law treats paper based commerce and electronic commerce equally so that one is not given an advantage over the other. The salient features of this law are mainly based on the principle of functional equivalence - the law should treat paper based commerce and electronic commerce the same; and technology neutrality- the law should not discriminate between forms of technology.

Indeed, the Act aims to facilitate electronic transactions, to promote business and community confidence in the use of electronic transactions and to enable business and the community to use electronic communication with the government.

Furthermore, Section 8 of the said Act provides that "a transaction is not invalid because it took place electronically and in particular that the following requirements imposed by commonwealth law can be met in electronic form":

- A requirement to give information in electronic form (sec 9):
- A requirement to provide a signature (sec 10);
- A requirement to produce a document (sec 11);
- A requirement to record information (sec 12 (1)); and
- A requirement to retain a document.[33]

[32] [2002] 1 WLR 566. See also *Deutsche Bank AG v. Ibrahim* and Others, Financial Times Law Report, 1992. These cases are cited by Smith & Keenan's, *Law For Business*, 2006 at page 140.

[33] See Section 12 (2). For further discussion see Latimer P, *Australian Business Law* 2003 at pages 1283-1285.

3.5 E-signatures in Other Jurisdictions

3.5.1 International and regional level on e-signatures

As highlighted in the foregoing discussion the UN Agency (UNCITRAL) and Common Wealth Secretariat (Common Wealth Model Laws on Technology) have been in front lines in preparing guidelines for countries facing legal challenges brought by e-commerce. In line with UNCITRAL Model Law on E-Commerce, Uniform Rules of Conduct for Interchange of Trade Data (UNCID) by Teletransmission also address EDI agreements.[34] In the process of preparing the Model Law Guide and in defining the scope of uniform rules on electronic signatures, UNCITRAL highly examined various electronic signature techniques currently being used or still under development. The common purpose of those techniques is to provide functional equivalents to (a) handwritten signatures; and (b) other kinds of authentication mechanisms used in a paper based environment (e.g. seals or stamps).[35] The same techniques may perform additional functions in the sphere of electronic commerce, which are derived from the functions of a signature but correspond to no strict equivalent in a paper-based environment. These techniques need to be adopted by developing countries like Tanzania in preparing the laws that will regulate electronic signatures.

As noted earlier that UNCITRAL Model Laws simply provide for functional equivalence between transactions under physical world and cyber transaction, the UNCITRAL has prepared a number of uniform rules on e-commerce and digital signatures. Reference can be made from Article 7 of the UNCITRAL Model Law on E-commerce which provides that:

"Where the law requires a signature of a person, that requirement is met in relation to a data message if;

a) a method is used to identify that person and to indicate that persons approval of the information contained in the data message; and

b) that method is reliable as was appropriate for purposes of which the data message was generated or communicated, in the light of all circumstances, including any relevant requirement."

Briefly Article 7 of the UNCITRAL Model Law on Electronic Commerce mainly focuses on the recognition of the functions of a signature in a paper-based environment. In the preparation of the UNCITRAL Model Law on Electronic Commerce, the Working Group discussed the major functions traditionally performed by handwritten signatures such as to identify a

[34] The US Uniform Electronic Transaction Act 1999 and the Australian Electronic Transaction Act have adopted UNCITRAL MODEL Law on e-commerce 1996 approach.

[35] See UNCITRAL Model Law on E-Signatures 2001 at page 20.

person; to provide certainty as to the personal involvement of that person in the act of signing; and to associate that person with the content of a document. It was noted that, in addition, a signature could perform a variety of functions, depending on the nature of the document that was signed,[36] Likewise, Article 3 embodies the fundamental principle that no method of electronic signature should be discriminated against, that is, that all technologies would be given the same opportunity to satisfy the requirements of Article 6.[37] As a result, there should be no disparity of treatment between electronically signed messages and paper documents bearing handwritten signatures or between various types of electronically signed messages, provided that they meet the basic requirements set forth in Article 6.

On the other hand, the OECD Council has adopted remarkable recommendations that urge member countries to establish compatible, technology-neutral approaches for effective domestic and cross-border e-authentication of persons and entities.[38] This means that the key role of e-authentication can be seen in fostering trust online while enhancing the development of the digital economy. Member States are further urged to review, amend or enact laws that provide effective enforcement approaches and e-authentication guidelines that facilitate identification, security and cross-border authentication.

The UK has implemented the EU Directives on Electronic Signatures[39] and Electronic Commerce[40] via Electronic Communication Act of 2000 which empowers the responsible Minister to modify any statute in order to cope with electronic changes. The powers include reforms on the means of delivery or communication where the law requires such transactions to be made by post, evidenced in writing, handwritten signature or use of original document, deed or seal including mode of payment.

Article 5 of EU Directive on Electronic Signatures provides that:

"1. Member states shall ensure that advanced electronic signatures which are based on qualified certificate and which are created by a secure-signature creation device:

   (a) satisfy the legal requirements of a signature in relation to data in electronic form in the same manner as a hand-written signature satisfies those requirements in relation to paper-based data; and

   (b) are admissible as evidence in legal proceedings.

[36] See The UNICITRAL Model Law on Electronic Signatures, Guide to the Enactment at page 48.
[37] Ibid.
[38] See OECD on Tax and Electronic Commerce at http://www.oecd.org/topic/0,3373,en_2649_33741_1_1_1_1_37427,00.html. Dated 21/7/2007.
[39] OJ 2000 L 13/12.
[40] OJ 2000 L 178/1.

2. member states shall ensure that an electronic signature is not denied legal effectiveness and admissibility as evidence in legal proceedings solely on the grounds that it is:

   – in electronic form; or

   – not based upon a qualified certificate; or

   – not based upon a qualified certificate issued by an accredited certification service – provider; or

   – not created by a secure signature-creation device"

The implementation of e-signatures might be difficult when it comes to proof and identification of the parties. The EU Directive further provides for the remedies to overcome these difficulties by providing mandatory requirements of certification of e-signatures by an independent agency and criteria to be met by the use of "qualified certificate".[41]

3.5.2 Legal consideration of e-signatures from other jurisdiction at national level

Unlike Tanzania, some countries like Australia have used the Utah approach on Digital Signatures.[42] In the US, the Utah Digital Signature Act compliments the UNCITRAL Model Laws by providing satisfaction of signature requirements. For instance Section 46-3-401 of the said Act provides that:

(1) Where a rule of law requires a signature, or provides for certain consequences in the absence of a signature, that rule is satisfied by digital signature if:

(a) that digital signature is verified by reference to the public key listed in a valid certificate issued by a licensed certification authority;

(b) that digital signature was affixed by the signer with the intention of signing the message and

(c) the recipient has no knowledge or notice that the signer either:

(i) breached a duty as a subscriber; or

(ii) does not rightfully hold the private key used to affix the digital signature.

---

[41] See Lloyd I.J., *IT Law* at page 587.

[42] See the Australian Electronic Transaction Act.

Moreover, the Australian government has developed security standards and modules of authentication electronically. For instance The Protective Security Manual (PSM) and the Australian Government Information and Communications Technology Security Manual (also known as ACSI 33) provide the security framework within which the Australian Government operates.[43] The Australian Government e-Authentication Framework (AGAF), with supporting government authentication standards, provide a consistent, whole of government approach to authentication of businesses that conduct electronic transactions with government bodies. Within these and related frameworks, the Australian Taxation Office public key infrastructure (PKI) provides businesses with digital certificates so that they can authenticate themselves to gain access to personalized services within the Business Portal and Electronic Commerce Interface. This infrastructure was developed and implemented prior to July 2000 and is now used by more than 300,000 businesses.[44] As a result of the review of the Gatekeeper Policy, Australian Taxation Office Digital Certificates can now be used by businesses to access other government agency online transactions.

Furthermore, a pilot project extending the use of Australian Taxation Office digital certificates to other agencies commenced on 17 October 2005. Through this pilot project, 200 businesses that deal online with Centrelink will use their Australian Taxation Office digital certificates to authenticate themselves and gain access to secure Centrelink services. Use of Australian Taxation Office digital certificates by businesses to access secure/authenticated services across multiple agencies provide major cost savings for the government. More importantly, it means that a business may need only one security 'credential' to deal online with a range of agencies, making interaction with government both easier and more secure.[45]

Looking at the development of cyber laws in Singapore the country has the Electronic Transaction Act which recognizes digital signature and other related e-signatures. Section 20 of the relevant Act stipulates that:

"When any portion of an electronic record is signed with a digital signature, the digital signature shall be treated as a secure electronic signature with respect to such portion of the record, if:

a) the digital signature was created during the operational period of a valid certificate and is verified by reference to the public key listed in such certificate; and

b) the certificate is considered trustworthy, in that it is an accurate binding of a public key to a person's identity because-

---

43 See the Australian e-government Strategy Document 2006 at page 39.

44 Ibid.

45 Ibid.

i) the certificate was issued by a licence certification authority operating in compliance with the regulations made under section 42;

ii) the certificate was issued by a licence certification authority outside Singapore recognized for this purposes by the controller pursuant to regulations made under Section 46;

iii) the certificate was issued by a department or ministry of the government, an organ of State or a statutory corporation approved by the minister to act as a certification authority on such conditions as he may by regulations impose or specify; or

iv) the parties have expressly agreed between themselves (sender and recipient) to use digital signatures as security procedures, and the digital signature was properly verified by reference to the sender's public key".

The South African Electronic Communications and Transactions Act provides functional equivalence between manuscript signatures and e-signatures. This can be reflected from the following provision:

Signature

12. "(1) Where the signature of a person is required by law and such law does not specify the type of signature, that requirement in relation to a data message is met only if an advanced electronic signature is used."[46]

Malta which uses common laws has a law that provides clear functional equivalence between handwritten and electronic signatures as seen under the following provisions of the law;

"6. If under any law in Malta the signature of a person is required, such requirement is deemed to have been satisfied if such signature is an electronic signature and such signature shall not be denied legal effectiveness on the grounds that it is:

(a) in electronic form; or

(b) not based upon a qualified certificate; or

(c) not based upon a qualified certificate issued by an accredited signature certification service provider; or

(d) not created by a secure signature creation device:

Provided that the electronic signature is in the form of an advanced electronic signature, which is based on a qualified certificate and is created

[46] See Section 13 of the Electronic Communications and Transactions Act.

by a secure creation device, it shall for all intents and purposes of law be presumed to be the signature of the signatory."[47]

In India, electronic signatures and their authenticity have been considered under The Information Technology Act; 2000. This is reflected in the following provisions:

S. 67A. "Except in the case of a secure digital signature, if the digital signature of any subscriber is alleged to have been affixed to an electronic record the fact that such digital signature is the digital signature of the subscriber must be proved."

[S. 85B. "(1) In any proceedings involving a secure electronic record, the Court shall presume unless contrary is proved, that the secure electronic record has not been altered since the specific point of time to which the secure status relates.

(2) In any proceedings, involving secure digital signature, the Court shall presume unless the contrary is proved that:-

(a) the secure digital signature is affixed by the subscriber with the intention of signing or approving the electronic record;

(b) except in the case of a secure electronic record or a secure, digital signature, nothing in this section shall create any presumption relating to authenticity and integrity of the electronic record or any digital signature".

[S. 85B]. Presumption as to electronic records and digital signatures

"In any proceeding involving a secure electronic record, the court has to presume, unless the contrary is shown, that such record has not been altered since the specific point of time to which the secure status relates."[48]

Furthermore Section 5 of The Information Technology Act; 2000 gives the legal certainty electronic signatures as follows:

5. Where any law provides that information or any other matter shall be authenticated by *affixing the signature or any document shall be signed or bear the signature* of any person then, not with standing anything contained in such law, such requirement shall be deemed to have been satisfied, if such information or matter is authenticated by means of digital signature affixed in such manner as may be prescribed by the Central Government.[49]

---

[47] See E-Commerce CAP 426.

[48] See the Information Technology Act; 2000. See also Sarkar S., Law of evidence, 16th Edition, Volume 1, 2007 at page 1382.

[49] Op cit.

Most of these laws that compliment the UNCITRAL and Commonwealth Model Laws on e-commerce and e-signatures attempt to treat e-signatures and data messages as equivalent to manuscript signatures and original physical document in written form.

While the Tanzania Evidence Act does not recognize e-signatures the Evidence Acts in Australia accepts digital signatures as valid identity of the sender, date and identity of the addressee in case of documents sent by e-mail, fax, telegram or telex. Mauritius is also another good example that has gone far in encasing cyber laws such as The Information Technologies (Misc) Act 1998 and The Electronic Transactions Act 2000.

Malaysia is among the countries with various cyber laws that have taken on board all the impacts of digital technology. For instance Malaysia has the Digital Signature Act of 1997 which regulates the use of digital signatures and other related matters. The said law further provides for the certification and licensing authorities.[50]

The most relevant sections in our discussion are 62, 63, 64 and 65. It is pertinent to quote some relevant sections here for the purposes of making comparison with the intended laws that are to be enacted in future in Tanzania. This is useful as far as benchmarking is concerned taking into account that the two countries share the same common law principles. Section 62 provides that "where a rule of law requires a signature or provides for certain consequences in the absence of a signature, that rule shall be satisfied by a digital signature where notwithstanding any written law to the contrary-that digital signature is verified by reference to the public key listed in a valid certificate issued by a licensed certification authority.

(a) that digital signature was affixed by the signer with the intention of signing the message; and

(b) a document signed with a digital signature in accordance with this Act shall be as legally binding as a document signed with a handwritten signature, an affixed thumb-print or any other mark; and a digital signature created in accordance with this Act shall be deemed to be a legally binding signature."

Section 64 further provides that "a message shall be as valid, enforceable and effective as if it has been written on paper if- it bears in its entirety a digital signature; and

(i) that digital signature is verified by the public key listed in a certificate which was issued by a licensed certification authority; and

(ii) was valid at the time the digital signature was created."[51]

[50] The Laws of Malaysia, Digital Signatures Act 1997 (Act 562) and Subsidiary Legislation.

[51] See Malaysian Digital Signature Act of 1997.

Lastly, Section 65 is to the effect that "a copy of a *digitally signed* message shall be as valid, enforceable and effective as the original of the message unless it is evident that the signer designated an instance of the digitally signed message to be a unique original, in which case only that instance constitutes the valid, enforceable and effective message". Other relevant Cyber Laws of Malaysia include The Malaysian Communications and Multimedia Commission Act,[52] The Computer Crimes Act[53] and the Communications and Multimedia Act,[54] e-banking and e-transaction laws. Since Tanzania shares the same legal principles with Malaysia there is a need to adopt relevant cyber law principles under the above mentioned laws.

Slovenia has also not been left behind in enacting cyber laws to enhance economic growth with secure cyber transactions. For instance Slovenia's Electronics Commerce and Electronics Signatures Act (ESA) became effective in 2000 and provides for legal recognition of e-documents and e-signatures. The ESA's e-commerce contract rules cover-attribution, duplication, acknowledgment of receipt and time/place that an e-massage is sent/received.[55] Although all types of electronic signatures are recognized, the digital signature enjoys the most-favored status because it utilizes cryptographic methods resulting in a heightened degree of reliability and security. The ESA provides for the accreditation of certification authorities (CA), but unaccredited CA's are also allowed to operate.[56]

The Law further provides that "if another statute mandates a person to sign a paper document with a hand written signature (or provides legal consequences if a paper document is not signed with a hand written signature), then that statutory mandate will be deemed to have been complied with if the person has affixed his advanced e-signature to an e-document, provided the e- signature is confirmed with a qualified certificate issued by an accredited CA."

It is believed that the rapid development in the use of e-communi cations has dramatically increased the use of cryptography technology such as encryption technologies for e-security, confidentiality and identification making cryptography more advantageous. Other relevant legislation on business transactions that need to be amended to accommodate

---

52 ACT 1998 (Act 588).

53 ACT 1997 (Act 563).

54 Ibid (Act 589).

55 See The Icfai Journal of Cyber Law Vol. VI 2005 at page 8.

56 Ibid.

e-commerce or e-transactions includes the Business Licensing Act,[57] The Capital Markets and Securities Act[58] and the Carriage of Goods by Sea.[59]

Like Mauritius and other countries with modern cyber laws, Tanzania needs to enact e-laws/cyber laws that will address the following objectives:

- Removing uncertainties over writing and signature requirements in e-commerce.
- Enabling electronic filing with public agencies
- Establishing authenticity and integrity of correspondence in electronic medium
- Promoting public confidence in electronic records & electronic commerce
- Enabling citizens to freely access and govern information electronically (e-governance and e-democracy).

3.6 *Exceptions or Exclusion on Certain Documents*

The legal recognition and use of data message and digital signatures under e-commerce as an alternative to paper based method do not mean the absolute departure from tradition methods. There are transactions and some legal documents such as title deeds and negotiable instruments which need paper based method using original documents signed and made by deed or in writing e.g. right of occupancy, transfer deed, bill of lading, assignment of copyright,[60] Contract of Marine Insurance as provided under Section 22 of the UK Marine Insurance Act 1906.

Section 15 of Common Wealth Model Law on electronic transactions provides that the Bill or Act does not apply to

(a) The creation or transfer of interests in real property,

(b) Negotiable instruments

(c) Documents of title

(d) Wills and trusts created by will

(e) Any class of documents, transactions or rules of law excluded by regulation under this Act.

This Law presupposes that probate documents and bills of lading cannot be done effectively electronically. Due to the nature and legal implications

[57] Act No. 25 of 1972) [CAP 273 R.E.2002].

[58] Act No. 5 of 1994) [CAP 79 R.E.2002].

[59] Act (Ordinance No. 6 of 1927 [R.L. Cap. 164]) [CAP 164 R.E.2002].

[60] See section 90 (3) of the Copyright, Designs and Patents Act 1988 (UK).

of these documents, developing countries like Tanzania need to create the legal framework that will allow preparation of e-documents on probate and bill of lading.

On the other hand, the Slovenian's E-Commerce and E-Signature Act (ESA) provides some exceptions and exemptions from using e-documents. Although this law allows the use of electronic documents (E-documents) in lieu of paper documents, there are certain exceptions. For example in the following instances, documents are required to be in paper form to be legally enforceable, and e-documents are not enforceable:

(1) real property deeds and contracts;

(2) wills, codicils and testamentary trusts;

(3) division of property between spouses;

(4) disposal of property of persons declared legally incompetent;

(5) inter vivos contracts to divide property;

(6) life-subsystems contracts and weavers of heirship;

(7) donation contracts and donation contracts cause mortis;

(8) contracts of sell with retention of ownership (i.e. contracts for a deed); and

(9) other legal acts requiring a notarized document.

3.7 *Towards Solutions from International Initiatives*

The United Nations through its Agency known as the United Nations Commission on International Trade Law (UNCITRAL) made great effort in creating guidelines on the enactment of laws on e-commerce and digital signatures. This was done through UNCITRAL Model Laws. These Model Laws have been in place since the 1990s followed by Common Wealth Model Laws with almost the same trend prepared by the Commonwealth Secretariat. Most countries with effective cyber laws have successfully used these model laws as guidelines in reforming and enacting their laws. EU has also created some e-legal instruments such as Directives[61] which oblige member states to reform their laws to reflect these Directives.

The main objective of the UNCITRAL Model Laws was to offer national legislators a set of internationally acceptable rules allowing a

[61] See Article 1 and 2 of Electronic Commerce Directive, OJ 200 L 178/1 and Electronic Signature Directive OJ 2000 L 13/12. The UK has implemented these Directives via Electronic Communication Act 2000.

number of legal obstacles to be removed and creating a more secure legal environment created for e-commerce.

The UNCITRAL Model Law, 1996 has already been adopted or otherwise served as a basis of electronic contracting legislation in a wide range of different jurisdictions, including Australia, Bahrain, Bermuda, Canada, Dominican Republic, Dubai, Ireland, the United States, Jersey, Columbia, France, Hong Kong, Mexico, Philippines, Singapore, Slovenia and the United Kingdom.[62] Singapore was the first country to enact electronic contracting legislation on the basis of the UNCITRAL Model Law.

Indeed the UNCITRAL Model Laws and Commonwealth Model Laws seem to be a better solution for countries that need to reform their laws that were structured to suit paper based environment. These model laws were designed to create and facilitate the enactment of effective cyber laws and an enabling environment for e-commerce development. The Commonwealth Secretariat has developed some Model Law Bills on this subject namely The Model Bill on Electronic Transactions and Electronic Evidence.

While The Commonwealth Model Bill on Electronic Evidence seems to be an overview which mainly addressed the innovations, the model seeks to introduce and accommodate existing evidence laws as well as take into account and adjust to new forms of evidence as a result of the changes in technology. The Model Bill on Electronic Transactions is an overview which focuses on the new forms of transactions ushered in by the technology age and is accompanied by legal interpretations and definitions accorded to such transactions to enable a legislative framework to be sufficiently robust.

In discussing the desirability and feasibility of preparing the new Model Law and in defining the scope of uniform rules on electronic signatures, UNCITRAL has examined various electronic signature techniques currently being used or still under development. The main purpose of these techniques is to provide functional equivalence to (a) handwritten signatures; and (b) other kinds of authentication mechanism used in a paper-based environment (e.g. seals or stamps).

The UNCITRAL intends to develop uniform legislation that can facilitate the use of both digital signatures and other forms of electronic signatures. To that effect, UNCITRAL has attempted to deal with the legal issues of electronic signatures at a level that is intermediate between the high generality of the UNICITRAL Model Law on Electronic Commerce and the specificity that might be required when dealing with a given signature

[62] See UNCTAD on Legal Aspects of E-Commerce for East African Region 2006.

technique.[63] UN introduced a Model Law that can be used and adopted by countries to facilitate the enactment of laws that relate to e-commerce.

The UNCITRAL Model Laws on E-Commerce and Digital signatures might be very useful when enacting our laws. Some relevant Articles are 6 (equivalence of data message to writing), 7 (Signature) and 8 (original documents).

On the other hand, Article 2 of the EU Directive on E-Commerce[64] is also useful in solving requirements under paper based transactions. For instance in dealing and solving the legal consequences posed by the requirement of manuscript signatures under the paper based method when it comes to e-commerce UNCITRAL Model under Article 7 provides that – Where the law requires a signature of a person, that requirement is met in relation to a data message if:

(a) the method is used to identify that person and to indicate that person's approval of the information contained in the data message; and

(b) that method is as reliable as was appropriate for the purpose for which the data message was generated or communicated, in the light of all the circumstances, including any relevant agreement.

In addition, the 1999 OECD Guidelines on E-Commerce might also be relevant and useful in attempting to solve these legal implications brought by the development of IT. International Chamber of Commerce (ICC) Rules for e-trade and dispute settlement are also relevant guidelines for resolving disputes on e-commerce. Other countries like Singapore have enacted their laws in line with UNCITRAL Model Laws. Section 8 of Singapore E-Transactions Act provides for equivalence on digital signatures.[65] The use of the UNCITRAL Model Law can also be useful in solving the problems related to the evidential value of electronic communications, the determination of the place of contract formation and the applicable jurisdiction.

However, the Model Laws and the Guidelines have no legal binding force apart from assisting countries when drafting cyber laws in order to create more uniformity and flexibility. The purpose of Model Laws is to offer national legislators a set of internationally acceptable rules as to how such legal obstacles may be removed and how a more secure legal environment may be created for e-commerce. For instance Article 6 provides that "where the law requires information to be in writing, that requirement is

63 See UNCITRAL Model Law on E-commerce with Guide to Enactment 1996 with additional articles 5 *bis* as adopted in 1998.

64 OJ 2000 L 178/1.

65 See the Singapore E-Transactions Act.

met by a data message if the information contained therein is accessible so as to be usable for subsequent reference".

Developing countries that use a common law legal system can adopt and take on board these Model Laws in creating e-legal framework or cyber laws that will provide functional equivalence and uniform rules that reflect globalization and digital technology.

Airlines are now using Internet sales and e-tickets as a means of reducing distribution costs and saving money in terms of ticketing paperwork and staffing. Customers can now make their bookings and payment online. The said traveling area needs to be regulated to protect customers or consumers and other beneficiaries.

CHAPTER FOUR

Electronic Banking and Other Cyber Payments

4.1 *The Impact of ICT on Banks, Financial Institutions and other Related Transactions*

Financial service providers have been using electronic message transmitted through proprietary software system (intranets) for some time before ICT introduced the Internet.[1] The development of ICT in line with Internet has dramatically replaced the old traditional methods of transaction which has necessitated most banks and other financial institutions in most countries to introduce new technology into commercial activities like Electronic Transfer Fund (EFT) systems such as ATM Cards used for cash withdrawals and electronic funds transfer at point of sale (EFTPOS) systems used for payments for goods and services electronically. As one of the most information-intensive services, finance is at the forefront in the use of modern ICT as a means to achieve efficiency gains in the financial supply chain.[2] In line with this, e-banking or cyber payments are dynamically becoming one of the main delivery channels as they always dramatically decrease the unit cost of financial operations and facilitate e-transactions. Indeed the beginning of this decade has witnessed e-banking and e-payment growing rapidly from developed to the developing countries.

Some countries like Australia have introduced the smart card system to facilitate payment system among other transactions. The term 'smart card' has been used to describe a class of credit card-sized chip devices with varying capabilities such as stored-value cards, contact-less cards and integrated circuit cards (ICC).[3] These differ in functionality, both from each other and from the more familiar magnetic-stripe cards. The ICC (more commonly known as the 'chip card' or 'smart card') provides a toolbox of enhanced capabilities for functions such as access control, payment, information storage, management tools and multiple applications. Smart card technology allows people to access multiple government services more securely, either in-person or online, essentially by providing them with their own miniature computer.

---

1 UNCTAD Information Economy Report 2008 at page xxxi.

2 Ibid.

3 See the Australian e-Government Strategy 2006 at page 26.

There is no doubt that ICT has accommodated the so called exploitation of large international financial transactions among banks and other financial institutions.[4] The use of ICT by financial service providers over the world has greatly increased their communication capacities and speed, decreased transaction costs of financial operations through e-banking and e-payment which have proved to be costless and more business convenient to banks. The development of e-commerce has created modern and new financial demands or needs that cannot be effectively fulfilled by traditional payment system apart from cyber payments system. As a result, most banks in Tanzania and other countries over the world are enjoying the advantages of ATMs which are cost effective; operate 24 hours thus saving in staff costs and premises. Electronic banking or cyber banking is growing very fast over the world including Tanzania. Generally there are five main types of payment systems namely cash, checking transfer, credit cards, stored value and accumulating balance. This payment system has been impacted by the development of ICT under e-commerce environment which has introduced cyber transactions/cyber payments such as digital cash, online stored value system, digital accumulating balance payment system, digital credit card accounts and digital checking. In 2005 the US witnessed credit cards accounting 80% of online transactions.[5]

4.2 *The Magnitude of E-banking in Tanzania*

Cyber banking has been growing very fast in Tanzania. Apart from banks other financial institutions have also embarked on these new methods of electronic financial transactions. There are a number of local examples of organizations and institutions that are involved in e-banking in Tanzania. For instance it has been reported that The Dar Es Salaam SACCOS has entered into a very crucial stage of effecting payment to its members through FBME Banks Fedha Card.[6] This has opened a new chapter on the modernization of SACCOS through application of ICT as part of e-government. The system seems to work very efficiently whereby a holder of a Fedha Card can access their account through ATMs operated by FBNE and Tanzania Postal Bank. Customers can also procure goods and services through TanPay cards. Indeed it has been observed that Fedha Cards "Shirikisho Society" can provide three different types of services which enable members/workers to access salaries, loans and deposits whereby employees and others are able to withdraw their salaries from

4 Ibid.

5 Laudon C.K. & Traver C.G., *E-Commerce,* 3rd Edition 2007.

6 See the *Daily News/Business Standard,* Tuesday September 12 2006 at page 5.

TanPay outlets for cash withdrawals, paying for goods, services, utilities and recharging of their mobile phones.[7] (It's one of the credit cards used in Tanzania)

The term e-banking has been defined as an array of data-processing, electronic and telemetric techniques and infrastructures that make it possible to exchange funds in paperless fashion and consumers where bank services are delivered electronically (Maduegbuo) and (Basle 2001).[8] The creation of suitable mechanisms for enabling different types of payment system to be made through the Internet seems to be a key factor in full realization of its potential as a commercial medium though it can also pose a problem if not well regulated. ICT has facilitated electronic means of payment such as payment cards, ATMs, telephone banking, m-banking, m-payments at a very low cost and more convenient while reducing the role of the use of cash (notes and coins).

An ATM is an electronic banking terminal that accepts deposits and dispenses cash.[9] ATMs are activated by inserting a card like a credit card or Fedha card (Money card) that contains the account number PIN on a magnetic stripe. The ATM operates through calling up the bank's computers to verify the balance, dispenses the cash and then transmits a completed transaction electronically. Under e-commerce technology has been developed to allow merchant server software to create online catalogues and online shopping carts whereby consumers can widely use their credit and debit cards.

The issue is whether the use for example of a credit card system or other related cards electronically is safe, riskless and whether complete anonymity is a desirable feature of a payment mechanism under the lack of effective e-legislation. There is also lack of certainty on e-banking in Tanzania and possibly the region of East African Community whereby electronic banking is growing explosively. E-banking might raise legal issues on the question of privacy as a bank's records of a customer's debit card transaction will always amount to personal data which needs to be confidential given the lack of legal framework that regulate data. A further worry is that a customer's PIN might be obtained by a third party observing the number they key into an ATM. Generally, e-banking and e-payment seem to pose security challenges inviting technology and legal measures for protecting privacy, cyber crimes and other related e-financial crimes.

4.3 *Legal Implication of E-security under E-banking*

The security risk might cause banks and other related financial institutions to lose gain and hope of e-banking if the legal issues and problems are not

[7] Ibid.

[8] See also Bwana J., *E-banking and law in Tanzania* at page 2.

[9] Op cit.

properly addressed through policies and effective legal framework. It is possible for e-payments which involve credit cards, cheques or e-cash to be intercepted by third parties especially where service supplier and the recipient communicate, and the relevant information is misused. For instance if an unauthorised person is able to use an ATM in relation to the customer's account, he will be able to obtain information about the customer, for example, the customer's balance in that account. There are some cases in Tanzania concerning misuse of e-banking through ATM cards that have been reported. For instance on 31 October 2006, one daily newspaper reported that one suspect criminal was arrested by a Police Officer in Mbeya.[10] The accused was alleged to have stolen 6 million Tanzania shillings from various accounts using forged Tembo Cards on CRDB Bank ATMs. The accused admitted to have done illegal e-banking through cash withdrawals from various ATMs in Arusha, Moshi, Dar es Salaam and Mbeya. The issue is how to deal with these culprits while there are no effective laws that regulate cyber crimes such as e-financial crimes, e-fraud and other related offences that are created under cyberspace.

Moreover, other suspects on cyber crimes were reported whereby a CRDB VISA Card brand manager and others appeared before the court charged with TShs 922 theft.[11] While one would expect the accused to face cyber crime or computer crime charges, the accused faced three counts of economic sabotage. This might be due to the lack of cyber laws that address cyber crimes such as illegal access to computer system, e-financial frauds, e-frauds, etc. Another cyber crime incidence on e-banking was also reported in August 2007 whereby two citizens from India and Malaysia appeared before the Court charged with 25 million theft through CRDB ATMs using forged Tembo Cards (debit cards) between 11 and 25 July 2007.[12] E-banking theft has been increasing in Tanzania while the enactment of an effective legal framework for cyber crimes and other related crimes has not been effected. In October 2007 some of the local newspapers reported that one accused employed by the CRDB Bank appeared before the court for charges on theft of more than 62 million Tanzania shillings from CRDB ATM.[13]

In another incident, in February 2009 it was reported that some people were alleged to have stolen $1m from Barclays Bank electronically.[14] The accused persons appeared before the Kisutu Resident Court for allegedly forging swift messages numbers SEQ 000305 and 00041

---

[10] *Mtanzania News Paper*, dated 31 October 2006, at pages 1 and 4.

[11] See the *Citizen News Paper*, Tuesday, 24 July 2007 at front page.

[12] *Mtanzania News Paper* Thursday, 02 August 2007.

[13] See the "UHURU" and "HabariLeo" News Papers dated 16 October 2007 at front page.

[14] See *The Guardian*, Friday March 6, 2009.

respectively.[15] The case which involved almost seven suspects was first reported in October 2008. These cases will attract electronic evidence and cyber crimes whereby the law that has amended the Evidence Act to accommodate electronic evidence in criminal proceedings will be tested.[16]

The major likelihood security risks on e-banking include identity theft such as phishing and spoofing. While phishing involves sending authentic-looking-emails which trick consumers into giving password details by replying to the email, the later involves the use of a fake website that makes customers believe they are using a real site.[17] Other risks include transaction risks, credit risks, funding and investment-related risks, legal and compliance risks.

The Australian government has shown the concern on the whole question of security and privacy under the e-commerce environment. This is evidenced by the Australian e-Government Strategy which highlights among other things that building trust and confidence has been a consistent theme of the government's e-government strategies.[18] Respecting and protecting the privacy and information security of citizens, businesses and community and other organizations will underpin all e-government activities. As part of the government's wider set of initiatives to promote a culture of security in relation to e-commerce, AGIMO, in conjunction with the Privacy Commissioner and relevant security agencies will assist government agencies to understand and implement the government's own legislation and requirements for security and privacy. This will lead to even better protection of people's personal information.

4.4 *Methods and Forms of Cyber-banking Created by the Development of Digital Technology*

It is believed that as technology develops new forms of payment are evolving which do not necessarily require the manipulation of bank accounts or credit facilities, and therefore may be provided by enterprises which do not have authorisation like banks.[19] The said new methods of payment and bank services are generally known as digital cash or electronic money systems, and fall into three types.

Furthermore, the impact of information technology can be observed in four main areas of electronic transfers in banking system namely:

---

15 Ibid.

16 See Act No 15 of 2007.

17 See UNCTAD Information Economic Report, 2008 at page 218.

18 Australian e-government Strategy 2006, at page 14.

19 Reed C., *Internet Law and Text and Materials* 2000 at page 245.

(a) Consumer electronic e.g. Banking, EFTPOS, Internet Banking, Telephone/Screen phone banking, etc. Telephone or screen-phone banking involves a transacting retail business between a bank and its customers. It is done through voice response and recognition. Facilities available are account enquiry, payment of bills, transfer of funds, message service, etc.[20]

(b) Corporate Electronic banking e.g. Financial EDI whereby the process of exchanging information including business data such as invoices, etc. can be done electronically, which is quick and cheap.

(c) Inter-bank Electronic Banking e.g. SWIFT (Society for Worldwide Inter-bank Financial Transfer) and RENTAS (Real-Time Electronic Transfer of Funds). SWIFT has been supplying banks with specific software to enable them to transfer to the new system. Apart from servicing financial service providers, SWIFT Net is also used by major corporations to obtain information for their multiple bank accounts. In 2007 SWIFT made a great step forward by introducing SCORE which enabled for the first time corporations to interact in a standardized way with participating SWIFT financial institutions.[21]

(d) Products (Plastic Cards) e.g. SMART CARDS, Debit Cards, Credit Cards and Charge.

Furthermore, customers are adapting to telephone and Internet banking in Tanzania and other countries which has caused the closing of some bank branches as the use of cash is being steadily replaced with e-payments. There are a number of companies in Tanzania that have introduced mobile banking (m-banking). The Fulusi Africa (Tanzania Limited) has introduced technology process transactions and e-payment through a mobile cellular network (M-Banking). Technology increases and simplifies customers' demands while assuring security in the whole process of payment.[22] According to an interview conducted by a newspaper journalist with Fulusi Africa (Tanzania Limited)'s Managing Director on the definition and the potentials of m-banking, the Managing Director highlighted that m-banking is banking using a mobile handset whereby the users can operate their bank accounts to access balance enquiry, chequebook request, salary alert, money transfer, bill payment and service purchases. This technology allows Mobipawa account holders to easily access their account and make deposits by purchasing e-units that are pegged to the shillings at Mobipawa authorised agents (Pawastation), who can be

---

20 See Chapter on Legal Aspects of E-banking, Institute Bank-Bank Malaysia.

21 See UNCTAD Information Economic Report, 2008 at page 221.

22 See the *CITIZEN Newspaper*, Thursday, 18 October 2007 at page 16.

any financial institutions or business shops.[23] In 2007, some telephone operators like Vodacom in Tanzania started implementing m-commerce by introducing the new technology of money transfer through m-pesa (mobile e-money) system. The system enables the money to be converted into electronic money and the money is sent through SMS. This cheap e-money transfer is sent through an agent and the recipient can get the money anywhere even in rural areas. This is the cheapest money transfer in Tanzania. However all these efforts of m-commerce are done without any legal framework to support the process.

Other banking methods include Internet Banking which uses modern debit cards such as Smart Cards, Home/Office Banking and EDI (exchange of information electronically) which is an electronic bridge between banks and its customers.

The introduction and increasing use of e-banking has been described as the new dynamic change on the current banking scene.[24] It is believed that EFTPOS and debit cards are expected to overtake cheques in the world and in 1998 there were already 1.9 billion ATM transactions worth a total of £98 billion.[25]

Most banks are now using new technology through on-line services whereby customers can open bank account on-line. Customers can use banks to order and purchase services and goods online. Customers can also easily transfer money on-line. It is now becoming common for individuals to order, purchase and download copies of software and make payment by means of a credit card.

4.5 *Concerns and Legal Implications of E-banking*

The issue is whether the use of on-line services guarantees e-security for customers and other beneficiaries. As the exponential advances of technology continue to dramatically facilitate the creation of new advanced methods and approaches to financial service delivery while necessitating the introduction of new electronic financial products these opportunities might be tampered by legal uncertainty.[26] This is a great challenge in countries like Tanzania and other countries that lack regulation in this fast growing area.

There are legal issues which affect the development of electronic financial services in Tanzania. There is no highly assured security against fraud and other related cyber offences given lack of legal framework that regulate this

---

23 Ibid.

24 Bradgate R., *Web linked Commercial Law* 3rd 2000 at page 710.

25 Ibid. See also APCS Payments Market Briefing, July 1999.

26 Job N. Banking and Finance Werks, The Legal Issues affecting the development of electronic financial service provision in South Africa 2002.

area in Tanzania. E-banking through the use of ATM and EFTPOS systems raises a number of legal problems with regard to the effectiveness of the mandate provided by the PIN, privacy, security of the system, liability in the case of fraud or card loss and liability of losses caused by system failure. We need to have an effective legal framework that will not inhibit the development of ICT. Some consumers are reluctant to use credit cards to order merchandise because of the security risks posed by cyber fraud. Online dangers such as fraud, identity, and phishing e-mails designed to trick recipients into revealing personal or financial institution details create threats every day. In the US it is believed that credit card fraud cost Web merchants over $1.4 billion annually.[27] In an effort to try to solve the problem by blocking fraudulent transactions and identify online culprits, the Internet Merchant Risk Council has been helping companies involved in e-commerce by setting up a database to counter credit card fraud on their websites.

It has been suggested that VISA, Master Card and other related financial institutions are in a better position to minimize if not solve online credit card fraud by assuming and accepting to take high risks and liability and installing computer program codes that can assure consumers security. Apart from benefits that have been brought by Internet to consumers and merchants through e-commerce, it is indisputable that this technology has simplified theft online with less risk. Laudon C.K & Traver highlights that the report of Symantec Corporation and the Internet Security Provider indicates that overall attacks against e-business firms averaged 57 attacks per firm per day between July 2004 and June 2005.[28]

In the UK the legal problems in this area were extensively considered by the Review Committee on Banking Services Law and Practice which recommended a two-tier approach to the regulation of such systems, with minimum level of statutory regulation supplemented by a code of best practice.[29]

On the other hand, e-banking will always involve the law of contract and agency whereby banks and their customers will be the parties hence the need for reforms of contract laws to accommodate on-line banking. All these legal issues need to be well addressed in the banking laws and other related financial matters. Unlike Tanzania, the Banking and Financial Institutions Act (BAFIA) 1989 of Malaysia and Bank Negara Malaysia (BNM) Guidelines, address all issues related to e-banking.[30]

---

[27] See Laudon C.K. & Traver C.G., *E-Commerce*, 3rd Edition 2007 at page 246.

[28] Ibid at page 248.

[29] See Para 9.30 as cited by Bradgate R., *Web linked Commercial Law* 3rd Edition 2000 at page 712. See also the case of Chan Man-sin v. AG for Hong Kong [1988] 1 ALL ER on the financial fraud and theft.

[30] See Sections 2, 97, 98, 99 and 119 of BAFIA read together with BNM (Bank Negara Malaysia). The Digital Signature Act 1997, Computer Crimes Act 1997 and Malaysian Payment System Act. See also *Barclays Bank Ltd v. W J Sims Son and Cooke [1980] QB* at 699.

Having realized the development of digital technology and its impact on banking business and other financial transactions, the United Nations through its Commission has introduced UNCITRAL Model Law on International Funds Transfers (1987) and UNCITRAL Model Law on International Funds Transfers (1992) together with UNCITRAL Model Law on Electronic Commerce (1996 and 1998) which seem to solve the challenges brought by digital technology. Any proposed legal framework or cyber laws on e-banking and other related transactions need to reflect these Model Laws and take into account the local environment and society.[31]

4.6 *The Impact of Digital Technology on Other Methods of Payments*

The development of computer technologies has seen people getting paid and purchase electronically under cyber banking. The new methods of payment for goods and services under e-commerce, which can be seen as a logical development of conventional cheques related to Bills of exchange, can affect the Bills of Exchange Law and other related laws on negotiable instruments and financial transactions.[32] There is need to reform the laws regulating payment and transaction methods to take on board the development of digital technology that has brought in alternatives to traditional methods of payment.

4.7 *Legal Barriers on E-banking*

The current legal framework on financial and other related transactions do not suit e-transactions hence it is a barrier to e-commerce development. The laws which regulate negotiable instruments, banking, etc. in Tanzania do not accommodate online transactions or payment in cyberspace rather than off-line transactions. The traditional requirements of writing and manuscript signature which are not tenable under e-commerce are the common features under the laws regulating and governing this area. On the other hand, a new mode of electronic funds transfer (EFT systems-SWIFT) between financial institutions from one country to another is not clearly reflected by the legal frameworks that regulate financial transactions. People can use online payment through the Internet using these cards.

One can observe the features of The Banking and Financial Institutions Act[33] which are not in tune with e-commerce development. Under this law it is not possible to apply for a licence online due to the fact that all

[31] For more reference on e-money transactions see Directive 200/46/EC of 18 September 2000.

[32] See Turban E., *E-Commerce* at page 166.

[33] [CAP 342 R.E.2002].

applications must be in writing and signed manually as opposed to data message and digital signatures.

For instance Section 5 of the said Act provides that:

(1) Every application for a licence under this Act shall be in *writing* and shall include –

- (a) five *authenticated copies* of the law or other statutory instrument by or under which the applicant is established;
- (b) a statement of the address of its head office, and the name and address of every director and of its principal officer;
- (c) ...
- (d) ...
- (e) ...
- (f) ...

(2) The application and every document submitted in accordance with subsection (1) of this section shall be *signed* by the directors of the applicant, or by any principal officer legally authorised to do so. All wording in italics have been made so by the author for the purposes of emphasis to indicate the legal barrier on e-commerce in Tanzania. Section 7, 9, 10, 14, 37 and 47 of Banking and Financial Institutions Act 1991 need to be amended to accommodate e-transactions.

In 2006, Tanzania passed a new law that provides a framework for comprehensive regulation of banks and financial institutions and other related matters. One would expect this law to address all the issues related to ICT.[34] However the salient features of this new law which provide for mandatory writing, handwritten signatures and original documents requirement are almost the same with the former law.

Section 8 provides for the manner and conditions in which applicants are required to fulfil (a) applicant's proposed *memorandum and articles of association* or other charter or instrument of formation required by applicable law:

- (b) ...
- (c) ...
- (d) ...
- (e) ...

[34] Banking and Financial Institution Act No.5 of 2006.

(f) the application and every document submitted with an application shall be *signed* by the directors of the applicant together or by any officer legally authorized to do so.

Section 9 further stipulates for investigation and review of application whereby the provision states that "whenever an application is rejected, the Bank shall provide the applicant with a *written explanation* of the grounds upon which the rejection is based." (*emphasis added*)

Furthermore, Section 30 stipulates that "(1) No bank or financial institution shall, without prior *writte*n authorization of the Bank:-

(a) ...

(b) ...

(c) ....

(d) ...amend the instrument or charter under which it is organized or established".

All these features are not in line with e-commerce or electronic banking which is now growing very fast in Tanzania, Kenya, Uganda, etc.

Looking at the nature of negotiable instruments in Tanzania, it is important to compare the Bills of Exchange of Tanzania and the UK as most of the Laws in Tanzania are derived from British colonial rule which applies common law principles. The combined definition of Bills of Exchange and Cheques under the UK Bills of Exchange Act 1882, which is in parimateria with Tanzania, can be summarized as follows.

> "A Bill of exchange is an unconditional order in *writing*, addressed by one person to another, *signed* by the person giving it, requiring the person to whom it is addressed to pay on demand or at a fixed or determinable future time a certain sum in money to or to the order of a specified person or the bearer."[35] (*emphasis added*)

Section 3(2) of the The Bills of Exchange Act of Tanzania[36] further provides that an instrument which does not comply with these conditions, or which orders any act to be done in addition to the payment of money, is not a bill of exchange. One can further note the provisions that are not in tune with digital technology by stipulating that "the acceptance of a bill is the signification by the drawee of his assent to the order of the drawer.

[35] Refer Section 3 of the UK Bills of Exchange 1882 and compare with The Tanzania Bills of Exchange.

[36] [CAP 215 R.E 2002].

(2) An acceptance is invalid unless it complies with the following conditions, namely–

(a) it must be written on the bill and be signed by the drawee and the mere signature of the drawee without additional words is sufficient;

(b) it must not express that the drawee will perform his promise by any other means than the payment of money."[37]

In the UK all these elements are now contained in an electronic analogy of the cheque through the use of sophisticated cryptography and cyberspace with key features of bill of exchange allowing the creation of digital signatures.[38] However to enable digital money to replace cheques in Tanzania, a new legislation has to be introduced like the UK did.

Section 20 (1) of Tanzania Bills of Exchange provides that,

"Where a simple *signature* on *a blank stamped paper* is delivered by the signer in order that it may be converted into a bill, it operates as a *prima facie* authority to fill it up as a complete bill for any amount the stamp will cover, using the signature for that of the drawer, or the acceptor, or an endorser; and, in like manner".

Section 31, 32 and 84 of the Bills of Exchange Act is also subject to review and amendment to reflect digital technology. The Cheques Act has to be reviewed to accommodate e-transactions.

The impact of Section 23 on the requirement of signature as a conditional precedent for the negotiation and endorsement of the bill can also be observed under Section 32 (1) which provides that:

An endorsement in order to be a negotiation must comply with the following conditions, namely –

(a) *it must be written* on the bill itself and be signed by the endorser ...

Under digital technology (cyberspace) the requirement of writing and signature with regard to negotiation of bills provided under the current law will be different.

In addition to that the new mode of electronic funds transfer (SWIFT) between financial institutions from one country to another can also affect the banking and financial services laws and other related laws in Tanzania such as Banking and Financial Institution Act 1991 and Bank of Tanzania Act 1995. The laws regulating this area have to be amended to accommodate

[37] See Section 17.

[38] Op cit.

the new electronic communication, services, payment and e-transfer of money.

4.8 *Relevance of Model Laws in E-banking*

Article 6, 7, 8 and 9 of the UNCITRAL Model Law and Commonwealth Model Law Bills on E-Transaction, Digital Signatures and E-Evidence are useful in solving the above problems. These Model Laws provide functional equivalence thus where the law requires a signature of a person, that requirement is met in relation to a data message if an electronic signature is used that is as reliable as was appropriate for the purpose for which the data message was generated or communicated, in the light of all the circumstances, including any relevant agreement. It is believed that these Model Laws will assist states in reforming and enhancing their legislation that are based on paper method and come up with uniform laws that allow the use of alternatives to paper based methods of transactions, communication and storage of information at national and international level.

4.9 *Legal Implications of Digital Technology on Competition and Fair Trade Laws*

4.9.1 Consumer protection online

While the development of e-commerce has been generally viewed as being beneficial to consumers as it offers wider choice and more competitive prices, there are also concerns about the vulnerability of consumers to unscrupulous traders operating at a distance, often from a foreign jurisdiction.[39] Consumer transactions on the Internet have become a fact of everyday life for most consumers whereby consumers are not used to this new way of online shopping for goods and services. There are a number of growing illegal activities conducted electronically such as phishing, spoofing, unsolicited e-mails, etc. that put consumers under the risk of losing their money.

The lack of consumer trust and confidence and effective legal framework in the medium and the question of quality of the goods and services are barriers to e-commerce. Consumers' trust in the Internet as a safe medium to conduct successful transactions and consumers' trust in e-commerce suppliers and the quality of the goods and services they provide is crucial for the further development of consumer e-commerce. Online consumers face the same risk like traditional consumers under physical world. No wonder offline offences such as burglary, trespassing, embezzlement,

[39] See UNCTAD on The Legal Aspects of E-Commerce 2006.

malicious destructions, vandalism, etc. committed against offline consumers can also be committed to cyber consumers. The most top nine damaging forms of security and privacy threats to e-commerce include malicious codes, phishing (deception), hacking, cyber-vandalism, credit card fraud, spoofing (pharming/misrepresentation), denial of service attacks, sniffing, insider jobs, etc.[40] These cyber threats which are in most cases in the nature of cyber crimes will be discussed in detail in Chapter 6 of this textbook that will deal with cyber crimes.

In line with consumer protection online, the question of content regulation has been a great debate over the world due to the development of e-commerce, privacy and e-security. Generally, Internet content regulation has been explained as any type of legislation by government or regulatory authorities directed at censoring information and communication on the Internet based on its subject matter, and controlling or attempting to control, access to Internet sites based on subject matter. In most countries the aim of Internet content regulation has mainly focused on protecting children against misuse of the Internet.

The development of e-commerce has created several consumer concerns that must be addressed. For instance the question of anonymity on the Internet makes it difficult to identify people interacting on cyberspace. When transacting locally or through an agent, the physical presence of the supplier or his agent, his local reputation and branding, as well as paper documentation (such as a passport or a lawyer's practising certificate) contribute to establishing a party's identity in an offline transaction. Equivalent mechanisms have to be promoted in the on-line world, such as digital signatures and certificates, to address the problem of identity over the Internet.

In line with these social and legal concerns under e-commerce environment, some literature clearly highlights the vital measures to be taken to secure e-transactions. These include:

- Ensure *integrity* whereby information being displayed transmitted or received on a website or Internet is not altered in any way by an unauthorised party.
- Ensure that e-commerce participants do not deny or repudiate their cyber actions (*non-repudiation*).
- Provide mechanisms that will easily identify a person or entity with whom you are dealing with on the Internet (*authenticity*).

---

[40] See Laudon K. & Traver C., *E-Commerce* 2007, at pages 263-264.

- Ensure that messages and data are accessible to authorized people only (*confidentiality*).
- Establish internal policies and rules that ensure *privacy* online.[41]

There is need to appreciate the role that can be played by effective policy, legal and institutional framework that will regulate the e-commerce environment. This can only be achieved through creating effective legal and policy framework and capacity building in the key law enforcers. The US has passed several legislation to regulate e-commerce such as the Electronic Communications Privacy Act (1986), the National Information Infrastructure Protection Act which criminalises virus distribution, the Computer Fraud and Abuse Act (1986), the Cyberspace Electronic Security Act (2000), The Computer enhancement Act (2000), the Electronic Signature in Global and National Commerce Act (the "E-Sign Law") (2000), the Homeland Security Act (2002), the Patriot Act (2002), the Cyber-squatting Act (1999), etc.

On the other hand, International Chamber of Commerce Commission on e-business, IT and Telecoms (EBITT) has proposed some principles and strategies that can be considered by legislatures, regulatory bodies and law enforcement agencies in making determinations regarding regulation of content on the Internet. The key issues to be considered include:

- Allow self-regulation to demonstrate its efficacy; Filtering, labelling and self-regulation may be addressed by alternative legislation.
- Regulation should be kept to a minimum and deal with specific observed abuses.
- Laws and regulation should be clear, precise and narrowly tailored.
- Legislation should not place additional costs and burdens on business.
- Provision dealing with liability should limit the liability of technical service providers.[42]

4.9.2 Rights of consumers online and the laws in Tanzania in a comparative perspective

Like physical world consumers, cyberspace consumers also need certain inalienable, rights. Under the Internet environment consumers need sufficient information to be able to make an informed decision. Consumers

---

41 Ibid, at page 265.

42 See An Inventory of Policy Positions and Practical Guidance by International Chamber of Commerce Commission on e-business, IT and Telecoms (EBITT), 1st Edition, 2007.

need to be given prior information from their suppliers before any transaction online. This information could include suppliers name and address, the characteristics of goods and services, payment information, clear prices including taxes, delivery or performances of service or contract. The withdrawal and cancel right on the part of the consumer also need to be clearly stated.

EU legal framework on e-commerce has clearly provided necessary rights to consumers that do business online. These rights among others include contact details, e.g. e-mail; geographical addresses of the supplier, registration details of a person or company professional title, the country and VAT Number.[43] Indeed EU Legislation on E-Commerce has gone further by stipulating very crucial provisions on the discretionary right of consumers to cancel their contracts provided they return back goods already supplied to them. However these have certain exceptions in case of gaming, betting, lottery and perishable goods. These rights can also be provided under Tanzania laws and East African Community legislation in general.

The EU legislation on E-Commerce[44] provides a list of information suppliers must disclose on their website and on contracting with a consumer at a distance.

Unsolicited e-mails being sent by suppliers and lack of security to the consumers doing business on-line are also great concerns that need legal protection.

The South African electronic transactions and electronic Communications Act also provides for various consumer rights. This law obliges the suppliers to provide important information to consumers involved in online transactions as follows:

43. (1) A supplier offering goods or services for sale, for hire or for exchange by way of an electronic transaction must make the following information available to consumers on the web site where such goods or services are offered:

(a) Its full name and legal status;

(b) Its physical address and telephone number;

(c) Its website address and e-mail address;

(d) Membership of any self-regulatory or accreditation bodies to which that supplier belongs or subscribes and the contact details of that body;

---

[43] Ibid at page 11.

[44] Distance Selling Directive 97/7/EC and the E-Commerce Directive 2003/31/EC. This Directive prohibits certain types of sales promotions.

(e) Any code of conduct to which that supplier subscribes and how that code of conduct may be accessed electronically by the consumer;

(f) In the case of a legal person, its registration number, the names of its office bearers and its place of registration;

(g) The physical address where that supplier will receive legal service of documents;

(h) A sufficient description of the main characteristics of the goods or services offered by that supplier to enable a consumer to make an informed decision on the proposed electronic transaction;

(i) The full price of the goods or services, including transport costs, tax and any other fees or costs;

(j) The manner of payment;

(k) Any terms of agreement, including any guarantees, that will apply to the transaction and how those terms may be accessed, stored and reproduced electronically by consumers;

(l) The time within which the goods will be dispatched or delivered or within which the services will be rendered;

(m) The manner and period within which consumers can access and maintain a full record of the transaction;

(n) The return, exchange and refund policy of that supplier;

(o) Any alternative dispute resolution code to which that supplier subscribes and how the wording of that code may be accessed electronically by the consumer;

(p) The security procedures and privacy policy of that supplier in respect of payment, payment information and personal information;

(q) Where appropriate, the minimum duration of the agreement in the case of agreements for the supply of products or services to be performed on an ongoing basis or recurrently; and

(r) The rights of consumers in terms of Section 44, where applicable.

(2) The supplier must provide a consumer with an opportunity to:

(a) review the entire electronic transaction;

(b) correct any mistakes; and

(c) withdraw from the transaction, before finally placing any order.

(3) If a supplier fails to comply with the provisions of subsection (1) or (2), the consumer may cancel the transaction within 14 days of receiving the goods or services under the transaction.[45]

Effective regulatory measures and self regulatory codes on supply, advertising and marketing of goods to consumers online should be seen as the way forward for protecting consumers. Countries like Tanzania can learn from other countries like the US, South Africa and UK that already have these laws and regulations in place as part of a benchmarking process.[46] The Tanzania Communications (Consumer Protection) Regulations[47] indirectly provide for rights to information including clear terms and conditions for consumers on electronic communication. For instance Regulation 8 (1) provides that a licensee shall provide a clear and understandable description of available services and the terms, conditions, rates, and charges for services. Furthermore Regulation 8 (2) stipulates that

> *"a basic postal and electronic communication operator shall regularly publish or arrange to be published, directions and guide for the services they offer".*

On the other hand, the primary laws governing consumers in Tanzania such as Fair Competition Act, 2003 primarily protect consumers who are in most cases involved in offline businesses only. The laws hardly apply to the online business such as distance contracts. Arguably, the Trade and Consumer Credit Act lacks e-commerce regulatory framework. This calls for immediate change. The consumers are not confident with regard to the security and identity of the sender or recipient especially when using credit card details on the Internet in the fear that they might be intercepted and fraudulently misused. The laws governing this area will be affected by the development of e-commerce as they have to be changed to overcome the probable legal barriers and implications and risk such as security, transaction costs, limitation of users and privacy over the internet or online contracts.

There is need to create a legal framework that will provide mandatory requirement for the card issuer to reimburse the consumer in case of fraud. Technological protection mechanisms such as cryptography or encryption or digital signatures including Secure Socket Layer (SSL) can also be used

---

45 See Section 43.

46 The US has developed a self regulatory Code known as The Model Code of The International Chamber of Commerce which makes mandatory for any advertising to be legal, decent and truthful. Similarly the UK has The Financial Services and Markets Act 2000 which prohibits persons from communicating an invitation or inducement engages in investment activity online or via website without authorization. See also UNCTAD on Legal Aspects of e-commerce at page 5.

47 Regulations, 2005 made under Section 12 of the Tanzania Communications Regulatory Authority Act 2003.

as a means of security albeit the costs and lack of legal framework that recognize this technology. Consumers are also vulnerable to unsolicited e-mails and spams which call for legislative measures. It is believed that almost 70% of all electronic mail from Asia is spam or unsolicited advertisements.[48] While Philippines seems to have the worst record with spam making 88% percent of all e-mails, China is the largest source of spam by sheer volume.

The laws should further provide for the control of unfair contract terms in consumer contracts and clearly stipulate for substantive control on standard terms. This should be in line with the legal provision that imposes mandatory requirements with regard to the quality and safety of goods or services that are supplied to the consumers. The UK and particularly the EU has gone further in regulating and protecting consumers online.[49]

Competition laws need to be in line with consumer protection online by obliging business people to provide clear and true statements and advertisements while avoiding false trade and price descriptions. Protection of children against certain products is also necessary. This can be done through making laws that provide for verification of age of the consumers.[50]

There is no law that protects consumers against any risks involved in distance selling and buying goods and services online due to the fact that when these laws were passed the online or distance contracts were not in practice in Tanzania. In the UK and other countries most laws were reformed and updated whereby consumers can be protected against numerous risks in distance contracts by way of offline laws, which are equally applicable to the online law.[51] These laws protect consumers against misleading advertisements, unfair or unconscionable term in business to consumer contracts and credit cards transactions on-line. The Sale of Goods Act (UK), The Supply of Goods and Services Act[52] and Consumer Protection Act 1987 offer a remedy to the defective products, etc.

Furthermore, The UK Trade Descriptions Act 1968, The UK Consumer Credit Act 1974 and the EU Directive on Unfair Terms in Consumer[53] contracts all provide a wide range of benefits to consumers doing business online. These laws provide for mandatory terms and conditions to be complied with by the suppliers in all contracts involving consumers before selling and supplying goods and services. These conditions and standards

48 See The Antivirus Firm Report as highlighted in Business Standard (Daily News), Tuesday, March 27, 2007.

49 See The UK Sale of Goods Act (UK) 1979, The Supply of Goods and Services Act and The EU Directive 1994/EC on the Sale of Consumer Goods And Associated Guarantees.

50 Op cit.

51 Ibid at page 30.

52 1982.

53 The Unfair Terms Directive Council Directive 93/13/EEC, OJ L 95, April 21, 1993.

include reasonable skill, care including satisfactory and fitness of the goods and services. The laws further offer remedy for defective products, personal injury, damage to property and certain misleading products, advertisements and statements seeking to restrict consumer rights.[54]

Tanzania and the East African Community in general need to enact consumer protection laws that will specifically regulate distance selling that will equally apply to contracts entered into via the Internet. Self regulatory schemes designed to encourage electronic commerce enterprises to comply with consumer protection are also very important and need to be encouraged worldwide.[55] Furthermore, the UK has an effective regulations that regulate distance transaction which highly protect consumers under cyberspace. For instance the Distance Selling Regulations seems to basically focus on protecting consumers online.

Under the UK Legal System consumers are further protected under The Unfair Terms in Consumer Contracts Regulations[56] which can be used in controlling the possible abuse of clauses which businesses may put into their contracts with consumers especially distance or e-contracts. In addition the Arbitration Act[57] applies the provisions of the regulations to arbitration clauses and an unfair clause cannot be enforced against a consumer who may, therefore, use the civil court system where there is, say, a breach of contract.

It should be remembered that in e-commerce contract parties e.g. supplier and consumer do not come face to face prior to the conclusion of the contract.[58] While Tanzania has not developed a regulatory system that protects consumers involved in e-banking and other related e-business, some countries such as Malaysia have developed guidelines on consumer protection on Electronic Funds Transfers pursuant to Sections 119 and 126 of BAFIA 1989 whereby terms and conditions are well addressed.

The laws in Tanzania neither cover online contracts nor recognize cyberspace or digital signatures. As highlighted in the preceding chapters the laws provide that, the contract must be in writing and duly signed or authenticated before a witness. These requirements are no longer applicable in cyberspace world hence they affect former laws which have to face changes and reforms to accommodate e-commerce principles. There is need

---

[54] See The Consumer Transactions (Restriction) Order 1976, The Business Advertisement Disclosure Order 1977, The Trade Description Act 1968, The Control of Misleading Advertisement Regulations 1988, The UK Sale of Goods Act (UK) 1979 and The Supply of Goods and Services Act. See also Turban E., *E-Commerce* 2002 at page 30-31.

[55] See Reed C., *Internet Law, Text and Materials* 2000 at page 263.

[56] 1999 (SI 1999/2083). See also Smith & Keenan's, *Law for Business*, 2006 at pages 25-26.

[57] 1996, s 89 (as amended by SI 1999/2167).

[58] Instead they use telephone sales, mail order, e-mail, facsimile, etc.

for our country to introduce distance-selling (on-line) laws. These laws should focus on protecting consumers who purchase goods and services over the Internet. This is due to the fact that e-commerce in most cases involves contracting parties and customers do not necessarily come face to face. The current municipal laws are hardly applicable, hard to enforce and difficult to apply unless they are amended. The new law should be consumer informed such that it imposes liability or duty on the suppliers and gives consumers clear and reliable information including clear terms and standards on the websites which can eliminate bad behaviour on the market. Others have suggested the inclusion of the term browse wrap up and click wrap up where consumers can scroll whereby the terms and conditions are available via a hypertext-link.[59]

4.9.3 Consumer protection at international level

At international level the concern of protecting consumers online has been boosted by the creation of International Consumer Protection and Enforcement Network (ICPEN). ICPEN was established in 1992. Unfortunately Tanzania, Kenya and Uganda which form East African Community, are not members of ICPEN. According to the UNCTAD[60] ICPEN has 35 members but none of the members are from Africa.

Some jurisdictions have enacted laws that enable, consumers to benefit a wide range of protection including online and offline contracts. The laws among other things protect consumers against misleading advertising, control specific types of transaction which are thought to pose special risks to consumers, such as credit transactions, and commonly also impose generic controls on unfair or unconscionable terms in business-to-consumer contracts.[61] At regional level a good example is the EU Directive on unfair terms in consumer contracts that is the Unfair Terms Directives Council Directive.[62] Moreover, the EU Directive on the protection of consumers in respect of distance contracts (the Distance Selling Directive)[63] regulates distance selling of goods or services. The Directive protects consumers against any risk involving distance or cyberspace transactions. Indeed this can create confidence on the parties that are involved on on-line transactions. Moreover, the Directive equally provides for vital rights to the consumers such as the right to withdrawal, cancellations, the identity of the suppliers, the price of goods, services, taxes, characteristics of goods or services, clear and comprehensive information including obligations to

59 See UNCTAD on The Legal Aspects of E-Commerce 2006.

60 Ibid.

61 Reed C., *Internet Law and Text and Materials*, 2000 at page 257.

62 93/13/EEC,OJ L 95, 1993.

63 Directive 97/7 [1997] O.J.L144/19. See also Turban E., *E-Commerce* at page 31.

the suppliers.[64] One of the most important provisions in the Directive that highly protects consumers online can be found under Regulation 7 which provides as follows:

Prior to the conclusion of any distance contract or e-contracts the consumer shall be provided with the following important prior information;

- The identity of the supplier and his address,
- Description of the main characteristics of the goods or services,
- The price of the goods or services, and all necessary taxes,
- Delivery costs and right of cancellation,
- The arrangements of payments and delivery or performance,
- The costs of using the means of distance communications,[65]
- The minimum duration of contract and for how long the offer or price remains valid.

More importantly, due to the e-security risk of card fraud, the Directive has gone further in protecting consumers making payments online using their credit or VISA cards by stipulating that a consumer has a right to request payment to be cancelled where it is proved that there has been fraudulent use of the consumer's card in the course of e-transactions. In this situation the consumer is entitled the right to reimbursed with the sum paid.[66] Other legal instruments that protect and provide rights to consumers include the Brussels Convention on Jurisdiction and Enforcement of Judgments.[67]

Jurisdiction problems at EU Level on the applicable law, place of trial and relevant law enforcement agencies in case of dispute between the consumer and supplier (CtoS) are covered by the Rome Convention and Brussels Conventions.

Using self regulation such as Trustmark schemes, Code of Conduct that reflect OECD Guidelines including Alternative Dispute Resolution or On-line Dispute Resolution (ODR) such as arbitration and mediation which are implemented by other countries like the UK and USA can also promote consumer protection and create trust and harmony between consumers and suppliers dealing electronically. Moreover, there are OECD

64 See Articles 4, 5, 6, 7, 8 and 9 of The EU Distance Selling Directive 97/7, [1997] O.J. L144/19. See also David Bainbridge, *Introduction to Computer Law* 2000, at pages 272-274.

65 See also Turban E., *E-Commerce* at page 33.

66 Ibid.

67 The convention solves the jurisdiction problem in case of any dispute whereby the laws and courts of the consumer residence are given jurisdiction.

Guidelines such as the 1999 Guidelines and the 2003 Guidelines which are both very useful for consumer protection and dispute settlements. While the 1999 OECD Guidelines protect consumers in the context of e-commerce, the latter emphasizes on the development and enhancement of dispute resolutions mechanisms and protection of consumers from Fraudulent and Deceptive Commercial Practices Across borders. OECD has further made a milestone history by developing almost nine guidelines for security of information systems and networks. These guidelines include nine principles that are awareness, responsibility, response, democracy, risk assessment, security design, security management and reassessment.

Indeed e-commerce conducted by suppliers and consumers seems to defeat the *caveat emptor* principle under common law statutes as there is no room for the buyer to be aware electronically. There is no doubt that the virtual or 'digital' nature of the agreement theoretically presents no impediment to its recognition under English law as this has already been regulated.

However there are certain regulations in Tanzania that seem to protect consumers in online or electronic communications. These regulations are mainly based on dispute settlement mechanism. For instance The Tanzania Communications (Consumer Protection) Regulations[68] which are administered by the Tanzania Communications Regulatory Authority, provides some relevant provisions as far as consumer protection is concerned.

Regulation 4 obliges *electronic communication* operators or communication licensees to establish a customer care system for their customers to make enquiries and complaints (emphasis added). Furthermore, Section 6 provides for the complaint handling procedures whereby all postal and electronic communication operators are required to notify customers about the availability of consumer complaint procedures and have in place forms to be used for registering complaints. The TCRA is mandated to issue a complaint registration.

4.9.4 Jurisdictional considerations on enforcement of laws that protect consumers electronically

There is no doubt that the question of jurisdiction for the purposes of dispute settlement and enforcement of laws under e-commerce environment and cyberspace in general, might pose some problems and great legal concerns due to the nature of Internet and different legal systems.

[68] Regulations, 2005 made under Section 12 of the Tanzania Communications Regulatory Authority Act 2003.

On the other hand, the United Nations has developed International Laws and Model Laws, with regard to legal recognition of electronic transactions whereby some countries have offered specific legislation affirming their validity. For example, the Model Law on e-commerce of the United Nations Commission on International Trade Law (UNCITRAL) states:

> "In the context of contract formation, unless otherwise agreed by the parties, an offer and the acceptance of an offer may be expressed by means of data messages. Where a data message is used in the formation of a contract, that contract shall not be denied validity or enforceability on the sole ground that a data message was used for that purpose or stored by electronic, optical or similar means, including electronic mail."[69]

Furthermore, Article 15 of UNCITRAL Model Law on E-Commerce results from the recognition that, for the operation of many existing rules of law, it is important to ascertain the time and place of receipt of information. The use of electronic communication techniques makes those difficult to ascertain.

There is also the question of jurisdiction, international enforcement and the applicable laws in case of dispute between consumers and suppliers let alone the high cross-border litigation expenses. It might be difficult to determine the applicable laws, and court and the place of action under cyberspace transaction. There are a number of cases that illustrate jurisdictional problems in this area. The Yahoo case is a good example.

In this case namely *LICRA and UEJF v. Yahoo France; Tribunal de Grande Instance de Paris,* two French human rights organizations brought an action against Yahoo Inco for operating illegal activities on their action website which impacted the consumers and public morality among other things contrary to the French laws. This case involved transaction of Nazi paraphernalia which is illegal in France. Some Nazi items appeared on the Yahoo France auction site whereby the Union Jewish Students in France (UEJF) and the League Against Racism and Anti-Semitism (LICRA) sued Yahoo. The French Court ruled against Yahoo and issued an order prohibiting access to and supply of illegal materials online that affected consumers. The US Court did not honour the French Court decision on the grounds that Yahoo was not bound.[70]

In principle OECD Member countries have agreed common principles which are geared towards providing consumers with effective

[69] See UNCITRAL Model Law 1996/2001.

[70] For detailed discussion see UNCTAD on Legal Aspect for E-Commerce at page 16 2006.

mechanisms to resolve disputes and obtain redress for economic harm resulting from transactions and business conducted under the physical world and cyberspace.[71]

4.10 *Cyberspace Taxation Systems*

E-commerce has been seen as the potential and one of the greatest economic developments of the 21st Century whereby the revenue authorities have a role to play in realising this potential.[72] The impact of digital technology on e-commerce has also posed a great challenge on taxation systems at global level. Most countries like Tanzania apply some principles and guidelines provided under taxation laws for the purposes of determining tax payers who are subject to income and other related taxation. The tradition and general principles of *source, residence and jurisdiction* for the purpose of income tax under the current offline laws might be affected by the global nature of e-commerce due to the fact that Internet has no boundaries, any business or income can be accrued electronically anywhere in the world. There is no doubt that the challenge behind taxation systems is that it is always difficult to tax information products between one country and another. It is extremely difficult to use existing offline laws in Tanzania and other counties to the cyberspace analogues of physical world business.

Unlike indirect taxation such as PAYE, more difficult issues will arise in respect of direct taxation imposed upon businesses and individuals who generate income in respect of operations undertaken in two or more countries. Two issues arise. The first concerns the division between taxes based on the source of income and upon the residence of the taxpayer, and the second concerns the issue where a business may be considered to be established.

4.10.1 Legal analysis on cyber taxation in Tanzania

Under e-transaction it might be difficult to apply the principle of permanent establishment for the purposes of taxing income.

It is important to bring to the attention of our readers some of the relevant sections that are not in tune with electronic taxation. For instance Section 4 (1) which provides for imposition of income tax[73] in Tanzania reads as follows:

"Income tax shall be charged and is payable for each year of income in accordance with the procedure by every person-

---

[71] Ibid.

[72] See OECD on Tax and Electronic Commerce at http://www.oecd.org/topic/0,3373,en_2649_33741_1_1_1_1_37427,00.html. Dated 21/7/2007.

[73] See Income Tax of Tanzania Act No. 4, 2004 as amended by Cap 322 in 2006.

(a) ...

(b) who has a domestic permanent establishment that has repatriated income for the year of income; or

(c) ....

Section 5 of The Amendment of Income Tax Act[74] of Tanzania provides for chargeable income that has a source in Tanzania.

Part VI of the said Act provides for taxation on international matters on the principles of residence and source in determining whether an entity or a person is taxable in Tanzania.

The most relevant sections here are Sections 66, 67, 68, 69, 70 and 71. The sections are provided below for purposes of our discussions as follows:

Section 66 highlights the question of residence as one of the principle determinant of taxation. The section further tries to answer the question as to who qualifies for a residence for the purposes of taxation. The section reads as follows:

"66-(1) An individual is resident in the United Republic for a year of income if the individual–

(a) has *a permanent home* in the United Republic and is present in the United Republic during any part of the year of income;

(b) is present in the United Republic during the year of Income for a period or periods amounting in aggregate to 183 days or more;

(c) is present in the United Republic during the year of income and in each of the two preceding years of income for periods averaging more than 122 days in each such year of income; or

(d) is an employee or an official of the Government of the United Republic posted abroad during the year of income.

(2) A partnership is a resident partnership for a year of income if at any time during the year of income a partner is a resident of the United Republic.

(3) A trust is a resident trust for a year of income if-

(a) it was established in the United Republic;

(b) at any time during the year of income, a trustee of the trust is a resident person; or

[74] See Cap 322 (Income Tax amendments).

(c) at any time during the year of income a resident person directs or may direct senior managerial decisions of the trust, whether the direction is or may be made alone or jointly with other persons or directly or through one of more interposed entities.

(4) A corporation *is a resident corporation* for a year of income if-

(a) it is incorporated or formed under the laws of the United Republic; or

(b) at any time during the year of income *the management and control of the affairs of the corporation are exercised in the United Republic*".

All words in italic are for emphasis purposes to indicate the legal issues that might bring challenges when it comes to the matter of applying these traditional principles of permanent residence under electronic or cyber taxation.

Section 67 further stipulates that "a person shall calculate his income or loss from any employment, business or investment that has a source in the United Republic separately from any income or loss from that employment, business or investment that has a foreign source". On the other hand, Section 68 provides among other things for sources of deductable amounts of income from expenditure or allowances related to movable tangible assets used or embarked by a person in Tanzania. The words "movable and tangible assets" cover intangible goods such as digitized goods that can be bought or supplied electronically under e-commerce. The issue is whether this law covers taxation of income accrued from digitized goods and services which in most cases are neither tangible or movable goods. The said section stipulates as follows:

"68.-(1) Amounts directly included in calculating income have a source in the United Republic where they consist of –

(a) incomings, gains and amounts referred to in Section 8(2)(b), (c) or (d) or Section 9(2)(b), to the extent to which a domestic asset or domestic liability is involved; and

(b) subject to paragraph (a), payments that have a source in the United Republic.

(2) Amounts directly deducted in calculating income have a source in the United Republic where they consist of-

(a) allowances referred to in Sections 13(1) or 17 and expenditure referred to in Section 14(1) to the extent to which-

(i) subject to subparagraph (ii), they relate to domestic assets; or

(ii) where the expenditure or allowances relate *to moveable tangible assets* used by a person who conducts a business of land, sea or air transport operator or chatterer to carry passengers, cargo, mail or other movable tangible assets, the assets are used to carry passengers who embark or cargo, mail or other *moveable tangible assets* that are embarked in the United Republic, other than as a result of transshipment.

The principle of permanent establishment for the purposes of taxation is further enumerated under Section 70 below. The section further stipulates for taxation of intangible assets. However intangible assets are not defined anywhere hence presumably these will not in most cases involve digitized goods and services that are transacted online. In this case people who transact and do business electronically under e-commerce might not be covered by this Act hence they escape e-tax liability.

Section 70.-(1) provides that "the income tax liability under Section 4(1)(a) of a person with a domestic or foreign permanent establishment shall be calculated as if the person and the permanent establishment were independent but associated persons and the permanent establishment were resident in the country in which it is situated.

(2) In addition to taxation in accordance with subsection (1), a person with *a domestic permanent establishment* shall be taxed with respect to the repatriated income of the permanent establishment in accordance with Section 4(1) (b) and 74.

(3) The following assets and liabilities shall be treated as assets or liabilities of the permanent establishment-

(a) *tangible assets* situated in the country of the permanent establishment;

(b) *intangible assets created by or through the permanent establishment;*

(c) *intangible assets,* to the extent that they may be exploited in the market of the country of the permanent establishment.

(4) In addition to the circumstances specified in Sections 39 and 40, the permanent establishment shall be treated as realizing an asset held by it or liability owed by it-

(a) in the case of tangible asset, when the asset is no longer situated in the country of the permanent establishment;

(b) in the case of an intangible asset, to the extent when the asset is available for exploitation in the country in which the owner is resident or a country in which the owner has another permanent establishment."

4.10.2 Legal analysis of cyber taxation from international experience

In any case, the legal question which may have to be determined is whether an organisation which is conducting business over the Internet, for example, a bookshop soliciting orders from UK based customers can be regarded as having an establishment in the UK, which is sufficient to render it liable to UK taxes.

The most relevant legislation governing the administration of taxation especially income tax is the Income Tax Act[75] which in most cases is not designed to facilitate electronic taxation save for off-line taxation.

Article 7 of the OECD is to the effect that "the profits of an enterprise of a Contracting State shall be taxable only in that state unless the enterprise carries business in the other Contracting State through a permanent establishment therein". If the enterprise carries on business as aforesaid, the profits of the enterprise may be taxed in the other state but only so much of them as is attributable to that permanent establishment.

Article 5 cures the problem of determining the notion of permanent establishment which include places where management takes place and the location of branches, offices, factories, workshops, etc. under cyberspace taxation. These include the situation where customers buy and download their digitized goods such as software, data, etc. from a database. Article 5 has defined the permanent establishment to mean "a fixed place of business through which the business of enterprise is wholly or partly carried on". The term permanent establishment includes specifically a place of management, branch, an office, factory, workshop, etc.

While it is a trait principle that in the physical world the laws of a particular country normally have effect within the boundaries of that jurisdiction depending on the geographical location, the Internet world has no such geographical and political boundaries.[76] The principles of establishing applicable laws and jurisdiction in cross-border transactions were developed to suit physical world and paper based transactions before the innovation and use of computer technology.

---

[75] Act No.11 as amended in 2004 and 2006.

[76] See Reed C., *Internet Law and Text and Materials*, 2000 at pages 187-188.

Under digital technology, digitized goods can be ordered, paid and delivered electronically which poses a challenge on taxation systems. Although the laws governing taxation in Tanzania such as income tax has been frequently amended, still the said laws do not reflect e-taxation. There is need to reform these laws to accommodate the impact of digital technology and electronic taxation.

The question is how to conduct and implement electronic taxation at national and international level to avoid tax evasion and double taxation? The cross border nature of Internet transactions poses a challenge. The multiplicity of overlapping applicable laws and jurisdictions can lead to situations where an activity is subject to multiple and contradictory regulation, or to no regulation at all.[77]

While the domicile and jurisdiction problems or uncertainty on all matters related to e-transactions between one country and another country in Europe is well addressed by the Brussels Convention[78] and national laws, this problem lacks legal support in the East Africa region.

It might be difficult to answer the following legal questions given the nature of the current laws that are not tuned to the impact of e-commerce which has resulted from the rapid development of computer technology, Let us assume that two parties are transacting electronically, the questions that might arise are:

- Where is a business regarded to be established for fiscal purposes?
- Where do cyberspace transactions take place?
- Where income is earned in one country by an individual resident or undertaking established in another country where is tax paid?
- How can we avoid double taxation and prevent fiscal tax evasion?
- How can we reform our tax laws to cope with e-developments? How can we assist tax collectors where the transaction is conducted electronically?
- Where and when can taxes be collected?
- Assuming that the goods or services are ordered, paid and delivered online within the country or even between two countries, is tax to be collected?

The concept of establishment seems to be more critical and challenging for income tax purposes. Most tax laws in most countries like Tanzania

[77] Ibid at page 270.

[78] Paragraph 4.14 of the Brussels on Jurisdictions and the Enforcement of Judgment in Civil and Commercial Matter 1968. The UK implemented this Convention via Jurisdictions and the Enforcement of Judgments Act 1992.

apply common law which provides that a business is only liable to income related taxes in a foreign jurisdiction if it is resident or has a permanent establishment there. There is no doubt that every state applies its own system of taxation. However this might not be problem if the existing international harmonisation in using OECD Model Tax convention can be utilized in a uniform way at global level. In this case resolution of this issue is the prime rationale behind the draft of bilateral tax conventions negotiated under the auspices of the OECD Model Tax Convention. The OECD Model Convention which deals with Income and Capital Tax is used by member countries as a model when negotiating bilateral tax regimes to clarify the situation where the tax payer might find himself subject to double taxation in more than one country.[79]

Most tax regimes in some countries including Tanzania do not reflect this convention. These bilateral treaties and convention might be useful in determining where tax due falls and thus avoid unnecessary double taxation.

The most relevant provision is Article 7 of the OECD Model Tax Convention which provides that the profit of an enterprise of a Contracting State shall be taxable only if that state enterprise carries on business in the other Contracting State through a permanent establishment situated therein. With regard to downloaded goods/service or data such as software, audio or visual works the taxation mechanism can be based on Article 5 OECD which provide for the notion of permanent establishment for the purpose of taxation. The article can also solve the question as to whether the database can be considered as stock or merchandise.

Moreover, in the UK concern on e-taxation was raised and three areas where e-commerce and communications offered both opportunities and posed challenges to tax authorities were identified namely taxation administration, compliance and tax evasion issues and taxation rules per se.[80]

---

79 See OECD on Tax and Electronic Commerce at http://www.oecd.org/tdocument/17/0,3373,en_2649_37427_35035793_1_1_1_1_37427,00.html. dated 21/7/2007.

80 See http://www.inlandrevenue.gov.uk/taxagenda/ecom.pdf. See also Lloyd I.J., *Information Technology* at page 594.

CHAPTER FIVE

THE IMPACT OF DIGITAL TECHNOLOGY AND E-COMMERCE ON OTHER AREAS OF THE LAW

5.1 *Brief Overview on Digital Technology*

As observed earlier, the development of Digital Technology in line with e-commerce has a great impact on commercial laws and other related areas of the law. There are also other areas of the law such as Tort Law, Company Law, the Law of Agency and Competition Law, specifically restrictive trade practices that have also been greatly impacted by ICT hence the need for reform. For instance under Tort Law the breach of duty by a person, giving rise to tort liability can happen in both the physical world, by words, or under cyberspace such as defamation by a website, email or negligent advice communicated electronically.[1] Furthermore, a breach of duty of care under cyberspace especially e-commerce that is likely to give rise to action in negligence would definitely be action by data subject against a data controller or user of data storage. This can be more challenging, giving rise and more concern on legal issues and e-security as Internet always allows and encourages free speech which can in most cases lead to e-defamation. It might be difficult to lodge these tort claims in Tanzania and other countries that lack cyber laws that reflect the impact of technology in this area.

The competition laws or anti-trust laws are also being affected by the growth of e-commerce specifically protection of consumers and other small entities. With e-commerce, there is no doubt that consumers doing business on-line are at a higher risk than physical world consumers if there is no clear and effective legal framework to protect their rights against misleading, deceptive conduct, false representation and other related conduct which may be done easily under cyberspace reaching more people. Anti-competitive and restrictive practices such as price fixing, abuse of dominant positions and misuse of market power can occur easily under e-commerce.

On the other hand, the development of technology has also impacted the operation and practice of Company Law in Tanzania. The current company laws and other related business laws in Tanzania do not address all issues related to e-transactions. In Australia there is an agent known as

[1] See Latimer P., *Australian Business Law* 2003 at page 1282.

ASIC which deals and regulates e-commerce and electronic registrations of companies and businesses including electronic lodging of documents and e-licensing. This is done via Corporation Act 2001 which allows e-information, e-filing, e-applications, multimedia disclosure, electronic financial services and on-line banking.[2] This is a challenge to the Business Registration and Licensing Agency of Tanzania (BRELA) which regulates business transactions in Tanzania.

The other areas that are likely to be greatly impacted by the development of e-commerce are insurance laws whereby insurance contracts are in most cases paper based with written and manuscript signature requirements. Most laws that regulate the insurance in Tanzania are typical common laws that apply traditional principles of paper based method which do not take on board the development of technology. In Australia ASIC which is a regulator of financial services facilitates the use of e-application forms and e-disclosure documents by insurance companies through its database.[3]

5.2 *The Legal Implications of Technology on Civil Procedure Laws in Tanzania*

It is pertinent to look at the Civil Procedure Law in Tanzania which is the most consumed law and compare it with the digital technology environment. In short this law shows that all documents that are required in the filing system at the court are supposed to be in writing, signed and original. The law does not allow electronic filing or electronic documents. The most common documents that are used in civil procedures fall under the wording "pleading".

According to the Civil Procedure Act,[4] in civil cases, every suit must be instituted by presenting a plaint to the court or such officer as the court may appoint in that behalf.[5] "A plaint" may be defined as a written statement drawn by a plaintiff or his advocate, which contains in a concise form all the material facts on which the plaintiff relies for the relief which he seeks in a suit.

According to Chipeta B.,[6] a "pleading" has been defined as a plaint or a *written statement* of defence, including a *written statement* of defence filed by a third party, and such other subsequent pleadings as may be presented

[2] Ibid.

[3] Latimer P., *Australian Business Law* 2003 at page 1291. See also www.ica.com.au and www.asic.gov.au where further details of ASIC and e-regulations of insurance are available which include lessons on e-commerce.

[4] CAP 33 R.E 2002.

[5] See s. 22 and O.4, r.1 (1) Civ.P.C.

[6] A Magistrates Manual page 160-162. See also (See O.6, r.1 Civ. P.C.).

in accordance with rule 13 of order 8 of the Civil Procedure Code. In simple terms, a plaintiff's pleading is his plaint, and a defendant's pleading is his *written statement* of defence. All those statements are called pleadings (emphasis added for comparison with data message/e-documents). On the other hand, a "plaint" may be defined as a *written statement drawn* by a plaintiff or his advocate, which contains in a concise form all the material facts on which the plaintiff relies for the relief which he seeks in a suit.

Case laws and some literature (supra) indicate that the rule of pleading is designed to ensure that each party knows what the case of his opponent is.[7]

The other important documents in civil and of course criminal matters are also the summons. There are two main types of summons namely summons to appear and a summons to file a defence. The point of interest on these documents is the ways and methods of serving when compared to electronic procedures under digital technology. According to Order 5 Rule 16 the serving officer shall require the *signature* of the person to whom the copy is delivered or tendered to be an acknowledgement of service endorsed on *the original* (*emphasis added*).

The defendant or agent must be made to *sign* in an appropriate place on the summons as evidence that he has been duly served. It is mandatory that the defendant or agent must sign the summons and a copy of it left with the defendant.[8] The word "sign" here implies hand written or manuscript signatures.

The most interesting means of services of summons is by way of post which appears to be the defeating point when it comes to the application of e-service using ICT in Tanzania.

The Civil Procedure Act of Tanzania provides that "if the court is satisfied that service of summons on a defendant in the ordinary way or by substituted service may cause undue delay and that service could more conveniently be effected by post, the court may order that the summons be served by post.[9]

Order 5 Rule 30 further provides that "Service by post may be deemed to have been effected if:

---

[7] See the arguments by Jessel, M.R., in the case of *Thorp v. Holdsworth, (1876) 3 Ch. D. 637,* on page 639. See also *Gandy v. Caspar Air Charters Limited, 23 E.A.C.A.* 139, Sinclair, V-P., who argued as follows at page 140: "The object of pleadings is, of course, to secure that both parties shall know what are the points in issue between them, so that each may have full information of the case he has to meet and prepare his evidence to support his own case or to meet that of his opponent. As a rule, relief not founded on the pleadings will not be given".

[8] Chipta B.D., *A Magistrates Manual* page 160-5. See also of Mehta C., *Limited v. The Baron Verheyen, 2 T.L.R. (R) 300,* on page 307.

[9] See O.5, r.21 CAP [RE.2002].

1) the summons is returned by the defendant endorsed with an *acknowledgement* of service; or
2) a letter or other document is received from the defendant acknowledging or indicating that he has received the summons; or
3) evidence is produced showing that a *postal packet* was received by the defendant, supported by a certificate of an officer of the court that the postal packet contained the summons (*emphasis added*).

Unlike Tanzania and other East African Community Members legal system, the East African Community rules of court has gone further by putting legal requirements of paper-based methods on equal footing with paper-less method (data message) to some extent as provided under the rules of the procedures of the East African Court of Justice of 2004.[10] This is reflected in Rule 10 which deals with the preparation of documents to be used in court procedures. The rule provides that all documents prepared for use in the court shall be on paper of durable quality, shall be clear and easily legible and may be produced by *computer,* printing, *lithography, stencil duplicating, photography, xerography,* typewriting, or any combination of these *media* (*emphasis added*). However Rule 22 provides for mandatory legal requirement for signature of the registrar and seal of the court, a procedure which cannot be applied under the digital technology unless the words "signature" and "seal" are interpreted equally with e-signatures and other means of e-authentications. The rule reads as follows:

> The notification of a claim or reference shall be signed by the Registrar or an officer authorized by the Court in that behalf and shall be sealed with the seal of the court (emphasis supplied).

The problem of denying an electronic filing system in our legal system can be cured by adopting UNCITRAL Model Laws or using cyber laws from other countries as benchmarks. More importantly Article 10 of UNCITRAL Model Law on E-commerce provides that

"(1) Where the law requires that certain documents, records or information be retained, that requirement is met by retaining data messages, provided that the following conditions are satisfied:

(a) the information contained therein is accessible so as to be usable for subsequent references; and

[10] Made by the East African Court of Justice as mandated under Article 42 of the Treaty Establishing the East African Community.

(b) the data message is retained in the format in which it was generated, sent or received, or in a format which can be demonstrated to present accurately the information generated, sent or received; and

(c) such information, if any, is retained as enables the identification of the original and a destination of a data message and the date and time when it was sent or received."

This article is very important in creating a legal framework that will bless e-government system in Tanzania.

5.3 *Online Dispute Resolution (ODR)*

5.3.1 Disputes settlement in Tanzania under digital technology

While most people in most countries including Tanzania are aware of offline modes of dispute settlement (Alternative Dispute Settlement/ADR), the development of e-commerce has necessitated the formation of new dispute settlement procedures that is Online Dispute Resolution (ODR). Automated dispute resolution processes (ADRP) and automated negation or blind-binding are part and parcel of cyberspace dispute resolution. While ADRP involves dispute process resolution conducted using computer programs without a human intervention practitioner the later process involve computer assisted negotiation whereby a human being is not involved other than software which keeps offers confidential.[11]

Alternative Dispute Settlement (ADR) that is conducted under paper based environment under the physical world in Tanzania includes mediation, conciliation, negotiation and arbitration as provided under the Civil Procedure Code and Arbitration Act. Generally, ADR resolves disputes by using an independent third party. In other words ADR is an umbrella term for processes other than judicial determination in which an impartial party person assists those in a dispute to resolve the issues between them.[12] The object of this mode of alternative dispute resolution is to help the parties reach their own solution since the third party cannot, as a judge can impose a solution upon them. The parties are at liberty to withdraw from the process at any time and they do not have to accept the solution to the problem.[13]

---

[11] See Scott Petterson on ADR. See also automated dispute resolution process or Consumers International (2000) Disputes in cyberspace.

[12] Scott Pettersosn, "Best Practises in organizing and administering an ADR institution", paper presented at ALRAESA Annual Conference, Entebbe Uganda 2005.

[13] See Smith and Keenan's, *Law for Business* at pages 25-27.

On the other hand, mediation conciliation is the process of dispute settlement out of court whereby a third party whom the parties have accepted as mediator will receive written statements from the parties and after that the mediator will discuss the case with the parties.

5.3.2 The legal status of e-ADR in Tanzania

Most laws dealing with dispute settlement procedures such as the Civil Procedure Act,[14] the Arbitration Act[15] especially ADR in Tanzania do not recognize on-line dispute settlements. These laws were designed to facilitate physical world dispute settlement and not cyberspace dispute resolutions. However the judiciary has not been left behind in considering the impact of digital technology under the laws in Tanzania. For instance in 1997 the Court of Appeal of Tanzania made a remarkable decision through the argument raised by learned council before the court. In *Tanzania Cotton Marketing Board v. Cogecot Cotton Company SA*[16] the issue before the court was whether other means of communication including electronic on arbitration procedures can be allowed under the laws in Tanzania.

The Arbitration Ordinance provided mandatory requirement of registering arbitration award to the court *physically* by a person or *registered post only* and any other method of communication applied in forwarding the award would be an improper procedure unknown to the law (emphasis added). This is a remarkable case as far as the physical ADR vis-à-vis cyber ODR and the admissibility of electronic evidence in the court are concerned. The facts of this case are summarized as follows;

The appellant Tanzania Cotton Marketing Board appealed against the decision of the High Court (Miscl. Civil Case No 34 of 1996). The respondent Cogecot Cotton Company SA, had filed an arbitration award in the High Court of Tanzania Dar Es Salaam. Earlier the parties entered into a sale of agreement for the purchase of raw cotton. A dispute arose between the parties whereby the matter was referred to arbitration before the Liverpool Cotton Association Limited. An award was granted in favour of the respondent whereby through Mkono and Company Advocate the said award was filed in the High Court where the appellant raised an objection. The main ground of objection was that in filing the award the proper procedures were not followed as stipulated under the Arbitration Ordinance. The Court was moved to refer to the relevant provision of the Arbitration Ordinance Cap 15. Section 12 (1) and (2) read as follows:

---

14 RE 2002 CAP 33.

15 RE 2002 CAP 15.

16 1997 TLR 165 (CA).

(1) "When the arbitrators or umpire have made their award, they *shall sign* it and shall give notice to the parties of the making and s*igning* thereof and of the amount of the fees and charges payable to the arbitrators or umpire in respect of the arbitration and award."

(2) "The arbitrators or umpire *shall*, at the request of any party payment of the fees and charges due in respect of the arbitration and award and of the costs and charges of filing *the award, cause the award or a signed copy of it, to be filed in the court*; and notice of the filing shall be given to the parties by the arbitrators or umpire." (*emphasis added*)

The court's decision is further reinforced by the learned authors SD Singh in his book, *Law of Arbitration*,[17] in paragraph 18 which stipulates for the filing of award under the India Arbitration Act 1940 as follows:

> "The actual filing by the arbitrator or umpire is not essential as it is sufficient if he causes the award to be filed and even if he forwards the award by post to the court there would be sufficient compliance with the provision of the law…"

Having perused the provisions of the laws and cases[18] in Tanzania and India, the question before the court was whether the law as it stands makes it mandatory for the arbitration award to be filed by the arbitrator himself personally. In reaching its decision the court accepted Dr Kapinga's submission regarding the interpretation of Rule 4. The Court argued that while it is an undisputed fact that under Rule 4 of the Arbitration Rules, 1957, the award is to be forwarded to the Registrar of the High Court by registered post, the words 'registered post' should be interpreted widely enough in order to take into account the current development in communication technology that has taken place since 1957 when the rules were enacted. Earlier in his submission, Dr Kapinga argued that the expression 'registered post' which appears in Rule 4 is not a legal term of art. It should therefore be given a wide interpretation in order to include the modern method of postage which includes other couriers, i.e. DHL, etc.

The court went on further by arguing that the principal legislation does not preclude the award to be filed by other means and the word registered is to be interpreted further to accommodate other current developments in communication technology that have taken place since the law was passed in 1957. Indeed the words by "registered post in a sealed envelope" are

[17] Singh S.D., *Law of Arbitration*, 9th Edition at page 251.

[18] See Indian cases such as *Volkart Brothers v. Achrajiram & others [1933] AIR Sind 160 and Ahmed Musaji Saleji [1912] 40 ILJ 212.*

found under the subsidiary legislation under Rule 4 which seems to be contrary to the principle legislation.

The Arbitration Law in Tanzania further shows that it is not possible to implement ODR which is part of e-commerce and e-government. This is echoed by Section 13 which provides for the procedures for summoning the parties to the dispute and their witnesses as follows:

"1) The court shall issue the same processes to the parties and any witness whom the arbitrator or umpire desires to examine as the court may issue in suits tried before it.

2) Persons not attending in accordance with such process or making any other default or refusing to give their evidence or guilty of any contempt to the arbitrator or umpire during the investigation of the matters referred shall be subject to like disadvantages, penalties and punishments by order of the court on the representation of the arbitrator or umpire as they would incur for the like offences in suits tried before the court." (Arbitration Act CAP 15 [RE. 2002])

As highlighted in the foregoing discussion that the ADR on civil matters such as mediation and arbitration was introduced in Civil Procedure Act under the fourth schedule through Government Notice (GN) No. 422 of 1994, it is also important to peruse the relevant provisions of the G.N and schedule and see whether it is possible to conduct cyber alternative dispute settlement under this law.

The most relevant rules are Rule 1, 17 and 20 of the Second Schedule the Civil Procedure (Arbitration) Rules made under Order 8 and Section 80 of the Civil Procedure Act.

For instance Rule 1 provides as to when and at what parties in dispute can refer their differences to arbitration procedures as follows;

"(1) Where in any suit all the parties interested agree that any matter in difference between them shall be referred to arbitration they may, at any time before judgment is pronounced, apply to the court for an order of reference.

(2) Every such application *shall* be in *writing* and shall state the matter sought to be referred." (*emphasis added*)

Under Rule 10 it is mandatory for an arbitration award to be manually signed award to be signed and filed.

The said rule stipulates that "where an award in a suit has been made, the persons who made it shall *sign it* and cause it to be filed in court, together with any depositions and documents which have been taken and proved before them; and *notice of* the filing shall be given to the parties." (*emphasis added*)

Rule 17 further provides for application to file in court agreement to refer to arbitration

"17 (1) ...

(2) The application *shall* be in *writing* and shall be numbered and *registered* as a suit between one or more of the parties interested or claiming to be interested as plaintiff or plaintiffs, and the others or other of them as defendants or defendant if the application has been presented by all the parties or, if otherwise, between the applicant as plaintiff and the other parties as defendants." (*emphasis added*)

The requirement of the use of paper-based methods such as *writing* and *registered* or signatures can also be observed under Rule 20 which stipulates the manner and procedures of filing an award in a matter that has been referred to arbitration without intervention of court whereby sub-section 2 is to the effect that:

"20 (2) The application *shall* be in *writing* and shall be numbered and *registered* as a suit between the applicant as plaintiff and the other parties as defendants." (*emphasis added*)

5.3.3 e-ADR vis-à-vis ADR under the Labour Laws in Tanzania

There are also other laws that provide for wide range application of ADR mechanisms such as labour laws.[19] These laws which seem to be among current laws provide alternative mechanisms for dispute settlement such as conciliation/mediation, arbitration and adjudication. It is pertinent at this juncture to reproduce some of the relevant provisions and see whether they allow an e-dispute settlement mechanism that is Online Dispute Resolution (ODR).

For instance Section 20 of the Labour Institutions Act indicates the powers of mediators and arbitrators as follows:

"20 (1) Mediators and Arbitrators may summon any person for questioning or to attend a mediation or arbitration...or appear before the court to produce a book or document ...or give evidence in dispute resolution." Under online alternative dispute resolution mediators or arbitrators never come face to face, therefore this provision does not give room for conducting ODR as it is not

[19] See the Labour Institutions Act No.7 of 2004 and the Employment and Labour Relations Act No.6 of 2004.

possible to summon a person online and provide consequences for non-appearance thereof.

Furthermore, there are some rules made under these laws that provide for procedures for alternative dispute settlement mechanisms. These rules include The Labour Institutions (Mediation and Arbitration) Rules 2007.[20] For instance Rule 6 provides for the physical mode of serving documents to the parties in dispute. This rule is to the effect that "a party shall serve *a document* to the other party by *delivering or handing* a copy of the document to the person concerned or representative in *writing*, by leaving a copy of the document at the relevant address or premises, by faxing or by *registered post* to the party intended to receive the document" (emphasis added). As emphasized by the words in italics above , it appears from this rule that electronic filing or sending e-documents electronically is not allowed by the law hence there is no room for ODR.

The matter seems to be more complicated by discriminating the use of data messages or paperless method and the use of technology based dispute settlement mechanisms which are much faster. This is reflected in Rule 7 which provides for the mode of proving whether the documents were properly or genuinely served to the intended party. Under this rule this can only be done by providing proof of mailing the document by *registered post,* a copy of receipt or *statement signed* by the other party. Rule 8 provides for mandatory requirement of physical filing of *original documents* to the Commission of Mediation and Arbitration (CMA) by handing a document to its office or by a registered post (emphasis supplied). In addition to that a dispute can only be referred to the CMA by delivering *signed prescribed forms* or a *written proof referral document* (*emphasis added*).[21] However Rule 32 seems to accommodate the use of data messages or paperless means whereby records of arbitration proceedings can be kept as hand-written notes or as an electronic recording.

5.3.4 The impact of technology on dispute resolution at East African Community Regional level

At the East African Community level, there are also rules that govern Alternative Dispute Resolution (ADR) such as mediation, conciliation and arbitration. These rules very rarely imply the use of cyber mediation or arbitrations (ODR). For instance Rule 3 of the Arbitration Rules of the East African Court of Justice provides for the mandatory requirement of

---

20 G.N. No. 64.

21 See Rule 12. See also Rules 13 and 19 whereby the CMA is mandatorily required to issue a physical written notice for parties to appear.

notification to be made in *writing* when initiating arbitration procedures.[22] This rule does not allow initiation of arbitration online whereby notification could be done electronically using a data message instead of paper-based notification. The rule provides as follows:

"3 (1) A party wishing to have recourse to arbitration of a particular dispute by the tribunal *shall notify* the respondent *in writing* of its request for that dispute to be referred for arbitration and shall therefore submit the request to the registrar." (*emphasis added*)

Furthermore, Rule 5(1), (2) (3) and (4) of the Arbitration Rules of the East African Court of Justice provide modes of submitting pleadings and other communication as follows

"(1) All *pleadings* and other communication... shall be submitted in quadruplicate.

(2) A *pleading* or other *written communication* under these rules shall be validly submitted or serviced only if delivered against a *signed* recipient.

(3) If the parties have so agreed, a party may in order to comply with any time limit, submit or serve a pleading or other communication by electronic communication (emphasis added). Provided that *a signed original* is submitted or served within 7 days from the time of transmission.

(4) A pleading shall be deemed to have been received, in the case of that forwarded by *registered post*, after a reasonable time ... and in the case of electronic transmission on the day when it is sent." (*emphasis added*)

Although sub rules 1 and 2 clearly indicate that it is a mandatory requirement for the submission of pleadings offline to use a paper based method, sub rule 3 and 4 allow electronic filing which implies functional equivalence of paper-based methods and paperless methods or data message. According to these rules there is a likelihood of conducting some mediation or arbitration procedures online.

There is also a question as to whether an arbitration award can be made in a data message and be signed electronically contrary to the requirement of an original document in written form with a manuscript signature. This might not be possible under these rules as the rule provides that "an arbitral award *shall* be made in *writing* and shall be *signed* by

[22] See the Arbitration Rules of the East African Court of Justice made under Article 42 of the Treaty establishing the East African Community.

the arbitrator or arbitrators"[23] (*emphasis added*). To accommodate online alternative dispute resolutions (ODR) under these rules and other related laws, there is need to define the words "writing" and "signature" to include data message and digital signature or e-signature respectively.

Rule 53 of the East African Court of Justice, Rules of Procedure of 2004 provides for the modes of alternative dispute resolutions. For instance Rule 53 (1) stipulates that "mediation or any other settlement shall be conducted by the judge who presides over a scheduling conference and shall be in accordance with guidelines set out in schedule 5". Schedule 5 referred here is to the effect that each party or its representative responsible for making decisions regarding proceedings *shall attend* the mediation session *personally* with its advocate if any (emphasis added). The words in italics indicate that these rules were not intended to give option for parties who would like to use cyber mediation (ODR).

Furthermore, Section 86 of the Employment and Labour Relations Act provides for mandatory requirements for dispute to be solved through mediation by the CMA to be referred in prescribed forms. These prescribed forms which range from F1 (CMAF1) to F7 (CMAF2) are made through GN.N.65 of 2005. These forms provide the mode for serving and submitting them to the CMA as follows:

The form can be serviced by hand, registered post or fax. Furthermore the services of the said forms are supposed to be proved by the following methods:

- By *hand* whereby receipt is supposed to be *signed* by a person who is above 18 years old.
- By the *registered post* through postal authorities.
- By *fax transmission slip* that confirms the fax was usefully transmitted (*emphasis added*).

Section 86 and the rules and referral disputes forms (CMA F1-CMA F2) made thereof indicate that there is no room for the use of alternative dispute settlement online. The law highly prefers the use of paper based methods of dispute settlement mechanisms to paperless dispute resolution mechanisms (ODR).

India, whose laws are *parimateria* with Tanzania has already amended her laws to accommodate the development of digital technology, The government of Tanzania has however not yet amended the Arbitration

[23] Rule 22 (1).

Ordinance to accommodate the development of technology by allowing online dispute resolution (ODR).

The challenge to LDCs like Tanzania is the deployment of connectivity which seems to be a fundamental catalyst for ICT diffusion and digital inclusion. It requires a well developed infrastructure and effective number of Internet hosts per capita, personal computers per capita, fixed telephone and mobile line subscribers per capita, adequate bandwidth, and possible broad band connectivity that supports a high degree of ICT penetration.[24]

It is important to note the position in the UK as compared to Tanzania with regard to ADR and ODR. In the UK, the Civil Procedure Rules 1998, enacted post-Woolf, the courts are said to have been actively encouraging parties to resolve their disputes by some form of ADR and may refuse a party some of his/her costs even when her/she wins his/her case in court if he/she has previously and unreasonably refused to embark upon an ADR procedure because the defendant had refused to engage in alternative dispute resolution.[25]

Smith and Keenan's in their book further argue and highlight important guidelines on the procedures and requirements for fair application of ADR as follows:

- the court has no power to order litigants to mediate. To do so would be a violation of human rights;
- the court does however have a role to encourage ADR;
- all parties to litigation should consider as a matter of routine whether their claims are suitable for ADR;
- where a successful party has acted unreasonably in refusing ADR then the courts can displace the normal costs rule and require the successful party to pay the costs;
- the burden of showing unreasonableness lies with the unsuccessful party;
- while most cases are suitable for ADR there should not be a presumption in favour of mediation.[26]

[24] See Mohamed S. Abdel Wahab, on "online dispute resolution and digital inclusion, challenging the digital divide" MCI Arb., LLM, is an Assistant Lecturer at the Faculty of Law, Cairo University, Egypt and a Researcher and Part-time Lecturer at the School of Law, Manchester University, UK.

[25] See Smith and Keenan's, *Law for Business* at pages 25-27.

[26] Ibid.

5.3.5 *Alternative Dispute Settlements in other Jurisdictions and digital Technology*

Due to the increase in the use of digital technology as a result of the innovation and use of Internet worldwide, the number of disputes arising from the e-commerce is rising. Online mediation and arbitration is now available through certain websites as part of alternative dispute resolution online. Some countries are applying technology online dispute resolution. Laws in some countries like the Philippines have been enacted to recognize these modern modes of dispute settlement resolution. However online arbitration seems to be more expensive compared to online mediation as long as arbitration requires a human arbitrator paid by one party. Numerous websites have been established to help resolve Internet disputes, as well as facilitate the resolution of disputes that occur offline. On the other hand some countries have recognized the use of technology in case management systems whereby the law allows electronic case filing system.

Mohamed A. Wahab in his article titled "Online Disputes resolution challenging the global digital divide" notes that The World Summit on the Information Society; had this to say:

> "*We are also fully aware that the benefits of the information technology revolution are today unevenly distributed between the developed and developing countries and within societies. We are fully committed to turning this digital divide into a digital opportunity for all, particularly for those who risk being left behind and being further marginalized.*"[27]

Although most current disputes that are resolved by means ODR processes are mainly e-commerce related, and the providers are located in high income developed countries, the borderless nature of e-commerce and ODR services makes it possible to extend such services to individuals and businesses in LDCs.[28] In acknowledging the importance of ADR in our information society, the WSIS encouraged the ongoing work for the provision of effective dispute settlement systems, which should certainly include ODR mechanisms.[29] In this case the governments of Tanzania and other East African Community members should support the development and utilization of ODR systems and provide an enabling environment that promotes trust and confidence in new ICT-based applications, especially ODR.

---

27 World Summit on the Information Society; "Declaration of Principles" (2003) at page 2. Available at <http://www.itu.int/dms_pub/itu-s/md/03/wsis/doc/S03-WSIS-DOC-0004!!MSW-E.doc>. ICTs could be defined as a "complex and heterogeneous set of goods, applications and services

28 Op cit.

29 World Summit on the Information Society; "Plan of Action" (2003) op cit. at page 7.

Furthermore, Mohamed S. Abdel Wahab in some of his writings further argues that "the nature and types of disputes prevailing in a society certainly impacts on the prospects of ODR processes".[30] Despite having a bigger role to play in business-to-consumer (B2C) than in business-to-business (B2B) e-commerce,[31] ODR could play a more prominent role in B2B disputes in many LDCs as online connectivity and accessibility for consumers is relatively low in these countries.

Generally, ODR may take place either entirely or partly online and concerns two types of disputes that are those that arise in cyberspace and those that arise offline.[32] Moreover due to the rapid increase in the number of people involved in e-commerce it has become increasingly necessary to design efficient mechanisms for resolving Internet disputes to avoid unnecessary costs as it is time-consuming, expensive under traditional mechanisms, such as litigation, and can raise jurisdictional problems. The cost and effort of resolving a cross-border dispute through the courts means that in practice only the largest claims can be pursued leaving small claims unenforceable.

ODR is possible through websites like Cybersettle and clickNsettle which are fully automated and require little human intervention, while other websites involve a neutral third party as a facilitator. These websites are believed to act as a neutral arena to exchange settlement officers. There is no doubt that undertaking mediation over the Internet ("Cyber-negotiation" and "cyber-mediation") has advantages and disadvantages when compared with traditional, face-to-face mediation.

The dispute settlement or cyber mediation procedure starts with cyber-negotiation whereby the initiating party enters settlement officers ranked for the first, second, and third rounds and expiration dates for those rounds. Computer software send an e-mail or data message to the other party explaining that a settlement offer has been made and requests the other party to put forth counter officers for the first, second and third rounds.[33]

5.3.6 Advantages and Disadvantages of ODR

It is important to look at the advantages and disadvantages of online dispute resolution and see whether it is useful and economical to apply

---

30 Mohamed S. Abdel Wahab, on "online dispute resolution and digital inclusion, challenging the digital divide MCI Arb., LLM, is an Assistant Lecturer at the Faculty of Law, Cairo University, Egypt and a Researcher and Part-time Lecturer at the School of Law, Manchester University, UK at page 12.

31 UNCTAD; "E-Commerce and Development Report" (2003) op. cit. page 179.

32 See Goodman J., on The Pros and Cons of online Dispute Resolution, an assessment of cyber mediation" in *Duke Law and Technology* 2003.

33 Ibid.

the technology based dispute settlement in Tanzania and East Africa Community in general. Indeed cyber mediation has more advantages than disadvantages. The use of ICT in disputes settlement can reduce unnecessary delays of court procedures hence avoid or reduce legal traditional sayings like "justice delayed is justice denied". Conversely, judges, magistrates and arbitrators can conduct court hearings and procedures online using computers with software that allows cyber mediation. The government can amend civil procedure laws and other related laws to integrate various dispute resolution techniques and procedures with the Internet, while at the same time allowing the use of cyber courts and electronic ADR (e-ADR). Like the British, Singapore and other countries, the government agencies and other private entities in Tanzania can establish websites that can create one-way communication between the courts and users or arbitrators and parties to disputes to facilitate dispute settlement online.

In addition to enhancing some of the benefits of traditional mediation, there are also advantages to resolving disputes over the Internet. "The process will allow for greater flexibility, more creative solutions and quicker decision, cost savings, convenience and the avoidance of complicated jurisdictional issues. Unlike traditional mediation, a benefit or mediation over the Internet is that it can provide substantial savings when compared with traditional litigation, which can be extremely costly."[34]

Likewise, legal service fees charged by advocates are more expensive in traditional litigation compared to cyber-mediation. It is believed that the most recognized benefit of on-line mediation is that the disputants do not have to travel lengthy distances to negotiate. If on-line disputes arise between individuals from great distances, and even different countries, at least one of the parties will be required to travel far if they decide to rely on a traditional dispute resolution procedure.[35]

On the other hand, cyber-mediation has some disadvantages over traditional mediation. Whereas traditional mediation does not create a physical record, online mediation creates an electronic record. This could potentially enable a party to print out and distribute e-mail communication easily and without the knowledge of the other party. Goodman J. W. in his article further argues that based on its commercial success thus far, it would appear that the fully automated cyber-mediation mechanisms are proving to be an advantageous forum for a number of disputants. In fact, in the US and other countries cyber settlement claims is said to have

[34] Ibid.

[35] Ibid.

handled more than 60,000 transactions since it went online in 1998, facilitating settlements for more than $350 million.[36]

The challenge in Tanzania is how to implement ODR which is part of e-government under the current offline laws and lack of awareness of ICT and Cyber law among law enforcers. ODR is well developed in developing countries like Philippines which launched the Philippines MultiDoor Courthouse through Cyberspace Policy Centre for Asia-Pacific (CAPCAP) as part of ODR service.[37] Tanzania could borrow the experience from other developing countries like Philippines, Singapore, Malaysia and other countries which have already started implementing ODR by enacting laws and introducing cyber courts.

5.4 *E-government*

5.4.1 Introductory remarks

E-Government (Electronic-government) has been defined as the electronic ways of incorporating all the processes and structures by which the new information and communication technologies can be deployed by government to improve delivery of services.[38] Others have defined e-government as the use of ICT, and particularly the Internet, as a tool to achieve better government.[39] E-government also refers to the use by the general government and public sector of electronic technology to transform the government and citizens by facilitating better service delivery and improving efficiency.[40]

E-government involves "the use of information technologiessuch as Internet, Networks, Mobile Computing by government to enhance and improve the access to and delivery of government services to benefit citizens, business partners and employees. In other words e-government involves utilising Internet based technology to provide seamless access to government goods and services with respect to:

- e-Administration: Govt 2 Govt – Harnessing technology to improve public administration processes for better service delivery;

---

[36] Ibid.

[37] The UNCTAD Information Economy Report, 2008.

[38] Deloitte and Touche, *At the dawn of e-government: the citizen as customer*, at page 1, http://www.deloitte.com/dtt/cda/doc/content/at_the_dawn_of_egovernment%281%29.pdf, (accessed 23/08/04). See also Schiavetta Susan, *Online Dispute Resolution and E-Government: Overcoming the Digital Divide* at page 2. See also Heeks, Richard., e-Government for Development, http://www.egov4dev.org/egovdefn.htm (accessed 23/08/04).

[39] See definition by OECD as highlighted by Dr. Bakari J.K., in his textbook "a holistic Approach for Managing ICT Security in Non-Commercial Organisations, A Case Study in a Developing Country, Universitetssevice US-AB, Stockholm, Sweden 2007 at page 3 of 10.

[40] Ibid.

- e-Society: Govt 2 Citizen – Harnessing technology to integrate public, civil society and private sector interests through processes like e-banking, e-procurement, e-education and e-Health;
- e-Citizens: Govt 2 Business – Harnessing technology to improve the lives of citizens through projects like e-Payment, integrated contact centres, etc;[41]

E-government is also reflected in the following:

- Development of websites in the ministries, departments and government agencies
- Implementation of the Integrated Financial Management Information System (IFMIS)
- Development of the Integrated Payroll and Personnel Database (IPPD)[42]
- Acceptance of e-filing of documents
- E-procurement
- E-taxation, e-returns and e-claims

Briefly e-government involves the process and structures whereby ICT is deployed by various government departments to transform their internal operations and administrations including delivery of services to the public (G2G, G2B, G2C). The users include the citizens, who are users of G2C services, businesses who use G2B services, government entities and employees who are the users of G2G and G2E respectively. Referring to the delivery of government services beyond the traditional brick and mortar by exploiting ICTs, e-government has the potential to revolutionize the way that governments interact with the governed[43] Most governments are now using ICT to facilitate the delivery of service to their citizens. Such integration can take place anywhere such as public sector activities, impacting activities of internal management and administration and the government's interaction with businesses, citizens, and partners, such as ministries and agencies. For instance the Jordanian e-government Strategy highlights four necessary pillars of e-government namely, the institutional framework, the legal framework, ICT infrastructure and the business level.[44]

---

41 Kyama G.E.A.C., E-government consultative workshop, 2005, Nairobi, Kenya.

42 See E-Government Strategy of Kenya 2004.

43 Schiavetta Susan, *Online Dispute Resolution and E-Government: Overcoming the Digital Divide* at page 2. See also Heeks, Richard, e-Government for Development, http://www.egov4dev.org/egovdefn.htm (accessed 23/08/04).

44 See the *E-Government Strategy of the Jordan*, 2006 at page 4.

Most countries that have adopted e-government have structured their e-government into four main areas:

1) Informational portal e-government structure: This is a form of e-government whereby Ministries, Departments etc can host websites which can act as information hubs. Electronic filing of government documents, processing of on online permits, electronic tax payments and the submission of online public employment applications, to mention a few, minimises wasting time in long queues.[45]

2) Legal services portal: The provision of legal services to citizens should be distinguished from judicial functions performed by the courts. The emphasis here is on information, advice or materials that will improve access to justice. This includes; Free-access online laws and regulations to help litigants who represent themselves in court or who may want to acquire a basic and rudimentary understanding of legal processes.

3) Judicial services portal: In this structure, the role of the judiciary in upholding the rule of law, good governance and democracy cannot be over-emphasized be it in developed or developing countries. (a) use of information and communication technology supporting system for recording of court proceedings and e-filing of some documents (b) the development and use of laws and procedures to support the admission of e-evidence in civil and other claims as basis of dispute settlement[46]

4) E-election services portal: This is also a vital aspect of e-government which involves the e-voting system.

Policy and legal framework for e-government is highly needed to make information on government functions, department and institutions activities and services easily accessible. The use of e-government information portal through electronic filing of government documents, processing of on online permits, electronic tax payments and the submission of online public employment applications, to mention a few, will highly minimize wasting time in long queues and reducing unnecessary costs.[47]

While the medium or vehicle through which such e-transactions are conducted is in most cases provided by technology, the rules and regulations for validating and enforcing the transactions are supposed to be stipulated by the law.[48] In this area, it is impossible for the law to exist independently of technology and vice versa. More importantly, the

[45] See Mohammed I. Ahmadu, the legal aspects of electronic government in pacific island countries: a reflection.

[46] See Mohammed I. Ahmadu, the legal aspects of electronic government in pacific island countries: a reflection.

[47] Ibid.

[48] Ibid.

provision of e-legal services by the government such as free access to online laws and case laws as precedents will assist litigants who cannot afford hiring advocates or lawyers to represent themselves before courts. This e-government function of providing wider public access to legal materials will enhance timely access to justice for all.

It is believed that the establishment of appropriate e-government structures in the form of portals for online legal, judicial, corporate, e-voting services, e-tax returns and e-applications of business registration will highly improve the scope of access to government services, create opportunities in rural communities and enhance good governance electronically.[49] The use of electronic signatures in line with Public Key Infrastructure (PKI) using encryption technology will assure e-security, privacy and safeguard the integrity of online transactions and business deals. This will of course be supported by an effective legal framework to effectively support the transition from conventional to electronic signature systems.

E-government promotes efficiency, transparency, accountability and public participation. The Judiciary can deliver justice quickly, timely and efficiently if information and communication technologies (ICT) are effectively applied into the administration of justice. It could be much better to conduct some court procedures such us filing applications including dispute resolution methods such as Alternative Dispute Resolution (ADR) online (ODR) where possible. On the other hand, e-government involves, one-stop Service Delivery, non-stop Delivery and availability of government service anytime and anywhere.

Some scholars have argued that e-Government can be viewed as covering three domains:

- e-Administration – covers improving government processes, by cutting process costs and managing process performance;
- e-Citizens and e-Services – deals with increasing public participation in public sector activities, decisions and actions, and improving public services in relation to quality, cost and convenience; and
- e-Society – relates to the relationship between public agencies and other institutions.[50]

E-Government should be identified as one of the priority areas for bridging digital divide in all government projects and other delivery services. In this way we are talking of e-business, e-governance, and e-democracy.

---

[49] Ibid.

[50] Ibid.

On the other hand e-governance involves, one-stop Service Delivery, non-stop Delivery, government service anytime anywhere[51]:

Some countries such as Malaysia, Singapore, Australia, UK, Canada, South Africa to mention but a few have successfully implemented e-government support by effective legal framework.

Some people are now aware of the concept of E-government in Tanzania. The government of Tanzania established the directory of e-government under the Presidents of Office.

According to D. Sawe, (the former Director of Management Information Systems) the Government of Tanzania has made the following notable e-government progress since November 2004[52]

- Network Management Centre 6 – storey building approved;
- MIS Strategy template successfully piloted in more than three ministries;
- The Tanzania Free & Open Source Software Association (TAFOSSA) all set to be launched before the end of October 2005;
- Preparation of Guidelines on using ICT in public service;
- Initiated monthly gatherings of Govt ICT Contact Persons, as a forum for sharing sectoral progress reports;
- Established a focal point to coalesce and reinforce the many existing, fragmented and isolated e-government initiatives;
- Built a national wide-area network to carry voice and data communications efficiently among all levels of Government.

The government of Tanzania plans to deploy and use fiber optic cable technology in a wider range to facilitate e-government implementation. Fiber-optic technology consists of hundreds of strand glass that use light to transmit data at a fast speed, with less interference and better data security.[53] This technology will later be integrated within East African Community and SADC Member States to facilitate communication and other necessary transactions for the growth of economy within the region. This technology is expected to enhance reliability and the quality of Internet transmission while at the same time creating new business models and opportunities and reducing the costs to consumers dealing online.

---

[51] Devindra R., E-Governance a Technology Perspective, Paper presented at Commonwealth Workshop Cape town SA 2005.

[52] Sawe David J.A., Regional e-Governance Programme: Progress Report from Tanzania 2nd E.A.C., Regional Consultative Workshop.

[53] See Laudon C.K., & Traver G.C., *E-Commerce* 3rd Edition at page 145.

5.4.2 Legal Status of E-government in Tanzania

There is no legal framework in Tanzania that addresses e-government apart from policy. The current laws do not recognize electronic filing and other government services that can be done electronically. The offline laws in Tanzania do not create a trustworthy business and communication environment electronically on issues related to privacy, confidentiality, authentication, integrity, recognition and admissibility of e-records, data message and e-signatures. These legal obstacles need to be further identified and well addressed in order to effectively implement e-government, e-justice and e-commerce in Tanzania. The National Information and Communications Technologies Policy, 2003 addresses the use of e-government. The policy encourages the deployment and use of ICT in e-government and e-commerce. However the policy is not detailed on the implementation and use of e-government and e-commerce.

Some countries like South Africa, Australia, Singapore, Malaysia, Canada etc have legislation and regulations that recognize e-government. The cyber laws in these countries allow electronic filing, recognize digital signatures, e-business and e-evidence. For instance in Canada the Uniform Electronic Commerce Act, seems to be a comprehensive, minimal, and flexible legislation that provides the following opportunities:

- Allows government to deliver programmes and services electronically
- Allows citizens and businesses to provide information to government electronically by reliable means
- Permits parties to enter into electronic contracts
- Technology neutral – does not favour one technology over another
- Allows government to specify what an electronic document has to have or be so that it is equivalent – as reliable – as paper
- Principle of consent – technology not imposed on government, businesses or citizens
- Sets out functional equivalent of "best evidence" rule.

Furthermore, the Electronic Communications and Transaction Act of South Africa clearly addresses e-government services.[54] This is reflected from the following provision:

"27. Any public body that, pursuant to any law:

(a) accepts the filing of documents, or requires that documents be created or retained:

[54] Chapter iv of the Act.

(b) issues any permit, licence or approval, or

(c) provides for a manner of payment, may, notwithstanding anything to the contrary in such law:

(i) accept the filing of such documents, or the creation or retention of such documents in the form of data messages;

(ii) issue such permit, licence or approval in the form of a data message; or

(iii) make or receive payment in electronic form or by electronic means.

On the other hand, India has gone further in recognizing the importance of e-government by giving it legal status under The Information Technology Act.[55] This is reflected from the following provisions with added emphasis by the author, which can be useful in other countries applying common law principles:

S. "6 (1) Where any law provides for—

(a) the filing of any form, application or any other document with any office, authority, body or agency owned or controlled by the appropriate Government in *a particular manner;*

(b) the issue or grant of any licence, permit, sanction or approval by whatever name called in a particular manner;

(c) the receipt or payment of money in a particular manner; then, notwithstanding anything contained in any other law for the time being in force, such requirement shall be deemed to have been satisfied if such filing, issue, grant, receipt or payment, as the case may be, is effected by means of such *electronic form* as may be prescribed by the appropriate Government.

(2) The appropriate Government may, for the purposes of subsection (1), by rules, prescribe—

(a) the manner and format in which such electronic records shall be filed, created or issued;"[56]

(b) the manner or method of payment of any fee or charges for filing, creation or issue of any electronic record under clause (a).

"7. (1) Where any law provides that *documents, records or information shall be retained for any specific period,* then, that requirement shall

[55] An Act passed in 2000 as amended from time to time.

[56] See The Information Technology Act, 2000 as amended. See also the discussion of this Act by Sarkar, *The Law of Evidence*, 2007 Volume 1 and 2.

be deemed to have been satisfied *if such documents, records or information are retained in the electronic form,* if—

(a) the information contained therein remains accessible so as to be usable for a subsequent reference;

(b) the electronic record is retained in the format in which it was originally generated, sent or received or in a format which can be demonstrated to represent accurately the information originally generated, sent or received;

(c) the details which will facilitate the identification of the origin, destination, date and time of despatch or receipt of such electronic record are available in the electronic record:

Provided that this clause does not apply to any information which is automatically generated solely for the purpose of enabling an electronic record to be dispatched or received.

(2) Nothing in this section shall apply to any law that expressly provides for the retention of documents, records or information in the form of electronic records."

8. "Where any law provides that any rule, regulation, order, byelaw, notification or any other matter shall be published in *the Official Gazette,* then, such requirement shall be deemed to have been satisfied if such rule, regulation, order, bye-law, notification or any other matter is published in the Official Gazette or *Electronic Gazette*:

Provided that where any rule, regulation, order, byelaw, notification or any other matter is published in the *Official Gazette or Electronic Gazette,* the date of publication shall be deemed to be the date of the Gazette which was first published in any form."[57]

Furthermore, the US Courts have introduced the so called Electronic Case Filing (ECF) regardless of difficulties and challenges posed by some legal issues such as presumption of delivery, etc.[58] E-filing provides a number of advantages over physical filing as it saves time and costs. There are also a number of cases involving disputes on the challenges and difficulties on the notes and presumption of delivery in electronic case filing system.[59]

---

57 Ibid.

58 See The Icfai Journal of CYBER LAW Vol. 2 at page 19.

59 See *American Boat Co. vs. Unknown Sunken Barge* as cited in The Icfai Journal of CYBER LAW Vol. 2 at page 19.

5.5 *Unanswered Legal Issues under Cyberspace?*

Below are some of the important legal issues that need to be considered under cyberspace:

- Cyberspace is boundary less, so where do things really happen?
- When and where is the contract actually made and enforced under cyberspace?
- When is communication of offer/acceptance deemed to be effective, forming a binding contract in a cyberspace environment?
- Are we able to point out the parties, time and the place where the contract is made electronically?
- Do we still need to apply Postal rule under e-contract?
- Which legal system will apply where two contracting parties are from different countries?
- Which court will have jurisdiction to solve a dispute arising out of two parties from different countries?
- What is the status of electronic documents in Civil or Criminal Trials? "Erosion of Best Evidence Rule?"

CHAPTER SIX

CYBER CRIMES UNDER E-COMMERCE

6.1 *A Brief Overview of Cyber Crimes*

The revolution in information technologies has changed society fundamentally, the way information is processed and stored and is likely to continue to do so in the foreseeable future. Developments in information and communication technologies and the way people use them have outpaced the regulations that govern them.[1] These developments have given rise to unprecedented economic and social changes, but they also have a dark side such as the emergence of new types of crime as well as the commission of traditional crimes by means of new technologies. Notably, developments in technology have introduced new ways of communication and doing business electronically but they have also facilitated the commission of traditional crimes electronically thus introducing new types of cyber offences. It has been argued that the vulnerabilities of digital technologies and inadequate control and security create an insecure environment which allows culprits to take advantage and exploit technologies for illegal purposes.[2] Computer related crime such as cyber crime is an example of the misuse of technologies whereby criminals use computer systems as an object. This calls for effective and appropriate legal framework to be put in place to address all issues including problems and territorial nature of Internet, cyber security, privacy and property rights.

The development of digital technology has exposed more children to obscene materials online such as pornography (particularly depicting adults) and other age-inappropriate and harmful materials, intentionally or not, than was the case before the Internet. In cyberspace, materials depicting extreme violence, degradation and hate are more easily available than was the case previously under the physical world. Currently, violence against children, young people and even women under cyberspace include; grooming, stalking, bullying, production, distribution and use of materials depicting child sexual abuse. Some adults lure children from chat rooms into face-to face meetings where the child is either assaulted or violated. Many unusual challenges confront legislatures, prosecutors and law enforcement agencies in their efforts to combat online grooming and children protection online. This is due to the fact that unusual notions of

1 See ITU Cyber Security Guide for Developing Countries Report at page 5.

2 Ibid.

anonymity and the speed of interactions and relationship forming under cyberspace, as compared with physical settings, require law enforcement agents to act quickly.

Arguably, cyber crimes and other related crimes are just an extension of the ordinary crimes committed under physical world. The difference is that while cybercrimes are committed electronically across cyberspace using non-conventional means, ordinary crimes are committed under physical world using conventional means. Dalal and Sharma argue that computer networks and interconnected information highways have dramatically amplified the opportunities for new kinds of deviant behaviour through a radical metamorphosis of our normative social structures, creation of moral ambiguities and providing a place for criminal countercultures to grow and flourish.[3] Farhan argues that there appears to be a widespread impression that electronic hackers and poor legal rules and enforcement constitute a major threat to the global spread of e-commerce. In particular, many claim that poor legislation and law enforcement create incentives for misuse (hackers) to intensify their fraudulent activities on the Internet. Such fraud is likely to increase the transaction costs of E-commerce and in some cases may create an incentive for hackers.[4] The criminal laws must therefore keep abreast of these technological developments which offer highly sophisticated opportunities for misusing facilities under cyberspace and causing damage to legitimate interests. The evolving cyber-pace offences, in particular those committed through the use of telecommunication networks, e.g. the Internet, such as illegal money transactions, offering illegal services, violation of copyright, as well as those which violate human dignity and the protection of minors are not effectively addressed in most policies and laws.[5]

6.2 *How are E-crimes Defined?*

Electronic crimes or cyber crimes have sometimes been referred to as crimes committed using computer technologies or using information technology such as phishing, hacking, spoofing attacks, defacement attacks, data theft and payment fraud. Briefly the most common cyber crimes include online financial fraud, credit cards fraud, software and data theft, cyber stalking, publication of obscene materials, cyber pornography,[6] software piracy and hacking. As e-commerce differs from traditional commerce in numerous

---

3 See Dalal S. and Sharma R., in "Peeping into a hacker's Mind; Can Criminological Theories Explain Hacking?", in *The Icfai Journal CYBER LAW* Vol. No. 4 , 2007 at page 34.

4 See Farhan AL-Farhan On The Impact of the UNCITRAL Model Law on international legal systems Saudi Arabia information technology development from a legal perspective 2002.

5 See Council of European Explanatory Report on Cyber Crime Convention.

6 Note. Unlike Tanzania, UK etc, in some countries adult pornography is legal.

ways, from the type of communication, supply, delivery and storefront to the methods products or services are delivered to the end consumer, which presents new opportunities for e-commerce crime. The main target of e-commerce crime is information related to financial and intellectual property rights products (e.g. credit or Visa cards, books, CDs, DVDs, and computer programs or software), intelligence (databases containing customers' information), information systems, and services.[7]

The most common e-commerce crimes include computer fraud, obtaining money by deception, theft, dishonestly obtaining money, falsifying documents, hacking, and piracy, cyber money laundering and other related offences. Other cyber crimes include theft of identity, attacks against a person's dignity, crimes against children, attacks on privacy, blackmail, cyber terrorism, distribution of illicit content, etc. Electronic devices such as computers can be used as a target or the tool of criminal activity. Indeed Internet technology facilitates a wide range of illegal activities or infractions such as theft, information sabotage, copyright infractions, breach of professional trust, digital privacy, intellectual property, distribution of illegal content, industrial espionage, denial of services, trademark infringement, domain name cyber squatting, e-frauds, etc.[8]

Identity theft is among the most serious crimes committed electronically. This is a crime whereby someone can obtain key pieces of personal identifying information such as credit card numbers, driver's license numbers and uses them for their own personal gain.[9] This form of e-crime occurs when someone's personal information is accessed, stolen and used without his or her knowledge to commit fraud or other related crimes which can cost time and money. Generally, this crime varies widely depending on the means and mode of commission, and can include check fraud, credit card fraud, financial identity theft, criminal identity theft, governmental identity, a data breach, computer virus, phishing, etc. The offence of identity theft can be done through the following ways which might change as technology develops.

Firstly it can be done through skimming whereby the criminals steal credit/debit card numbers by using a special storage device when processing your card.

Secondly, through phishing whereby the culprits can pretend to be financial institutions or companies and successfully send spam, e-mail or pop-up messages to get you to reveal your personal information. Due to

---

7 Chamard S., Book Review of Superhighway Robbery: Preventing E-commerce Crime University of Alaska Anchorage, Western Criminology Review 5(2), 133-134 (2004).

8 See ITU Cyber Security Guide for Developing Countries Report at page 27-33.

9 See leaflet by the Ministry of Communications and IT of India.

the creativity and brevity of culprits, they can also commit theft of identity by just changing someone's address whereby they divert your billing statements to another location by completing a "change of address" form according to what they want.

6.3 *Cyber Financial Crimes*

The development of digital technology has further simplified money transfer and transactions using tangible products that are information based such as credit cards, Visa cards and cell phones. These information based products can become a crime target or may be used to commit cyber crimes. Fraudulent retailing, financial services fraud, medical services/ product fraud, and other related e-commerce crimes are becoming common. The desire of illegally obtaining bank account and payment card details, which might easily be attempted and accessed using compromised data, means that e-commerce applications, like banking services, are a particularly popular target for fraud and other related e-crimes. Whilst some once-off e-attacks may be the result of disgruntled customers, ongoing and organized e-attacks are more likely to be undertaken internally by staff or externally by organized criminals. Money laundering, which was only common under physical world, is now being committed electronically as cyber money laundering or the use of "cyber money" in money laundering using mobile phones and other computer technologies which pose a great challenge to the current laws that do not address all issues related to cyber crimes. These types of crimes have resulted from the misuse and exploitation of technologies and have made e-commerce in many countries unsafe.

While these technological developments are posing great security challenges, most laws in Tanzania that are related to criminal laws have not been changed to cope with these changes. Laws which were enacted to serve paper based transactions before the development of technology include the Criminal Procedure Act,[10] the Penal Code Act,[11] the Anti-money Laundering Act, the Evidence Act,[12] the Terrorism Act, the Extradition Act, the Copyright Act and other related laws. The adequacy of these offline laws was tested in the landmark case of *Trust Bank Ltd. v. Le-marsh Enterprises Ltd., Joseph Mbui Magari and Lawrence Macharia.*[13] The issue before the Court in this case was whether electronic evidence is admissible under the Tanzania Evidence Act. Though the Law did not recognise e-evidence, the Court accepted such evidence.

---

10 [2002 R.E CAP 20].

11 [2002 R.E CAP 16].

12 [2002 R.E CAP 6].

13 The High Court of Tanzania (Commercial Division) at Dar es Salaam Commercial case no.4 of 2000 (Unreported).

The UK has shown some initiatives on the techniques and means of reducing credit card fraud. Multiple preventive measures have been taken at the following different stages of delivery: card issuance, card acquisition, point of sale, card-not-present sale, and after the sale.[14] Though these initiatives resulted in a significant drop in credit card fraud, experience shows that e-criminals adapt to technological changes and develop new ways of circumventing preventive measures.

There is no doubt that there is need to have effective specific cyber crime and other related crime laws that can appropriately address the complexity and the current unique nature of cyberspace crimes. The current laws and rules of evidence may further need to be modified to accept all digital information with network system integrity together with the use of electronic signatures to authenticate and validate content and e-information. As most people are becoming more and more dependent on commuter networks and other related networks, the importance of assuring e-security supported by effective and appropriate provisions for law enforcement concerns and the whole question of privacy needs to be addressed adequately.

6.4 *The Legal Challenges of Electronic Crimes in Tanzania*

Like any other country Tanzania faces the same e-challenges in combating cyber crimes and other related e-crimes. There are technical and legal challenges that are posed by the development of digital technology and the Internet. For instance there is no doubt that online investment, e-gambling and e-commerce such as sale of imaginary goods and services for real money, make it possible to generate seemingly legitimate revenues that are difficult to monitor, control and impossible to tax and prosecute. ITU argues that e-banking, real estate transactions via the net, the use of virtual front companies and e-cash can all be used to launder the proceeds of crime.[15] Internet can be used as communication mechanism to make criminals escape liability and remain outside jurisdiction where they would be at risk of arrest. A good example is the UK whereby cannabis dealers were able to avoid the application of the UK anti-drugs laws by selling from Dutch websites.[16] Criminal liability on the laws regulating obscenity and indecency is mainly based on possession and distribution of obscene or illegal materials. This means that criminals will only be liable where

---

[14] Ibid.

[15] See ITU Cyber Security Guide for Developing Countries Report at page 33.

[16] See the UK News Report of 1999-2000 as cited by Reed C. in his book tilted *Internet Law, Text and Materials* at page 246.

the culprits commit such offences in a particular country only and not anywhere else. One can observe the problems that are likely to be faced by law enforcement agencies when dealing with offences committed online from another jurisdiction. Let's assume that a person who is not a resident in Tanzania makes and posts obscene material on a certain website which is registered, owned and hosted in another country but the materials are accessed in Tanzania or other countries where such material is an offence. The main legal questions arising from this scenario are:

- *Where is the offence of possession committed?*
- *If under the laws of the hosting website country such acts are not offences, how can such offences be dealt with in a country where it is unlawful?*
- *Can Extradition Treaties and proceedings if available be successful where such acts are offences in another country but not offences in another country?*

Generally, extradition requires an extradition treaty between the countries concerned and can only be available for crimes listed in the Treaty as offences in both countries.

The other legal challenge on cyber crimes is that, electronic evidence can be very difficult to obtain when it is scattered across a system located in different countries whereby success will in most cases depend on the international cooperation between the countries concerned. The following legal questions might arise:

- *How can the relevant information or data be identified?*
- *How can the data be traced or stored?*
- *What are the judicial rules of evidence?*
- *How can the deleted files be recovered?*
- *How can the origin of the e-massage be proved?*
- *How do you establish the identity of a person?*

Most crimes in Tanzania are regulated by laws such as the Criminal Procedure Act, the Penal Code, the Extradition Act and other related laws. However, most of these laws are out of date and do not take into account the development of technology that is always changing very rapidly. These might hinder the development of e-commerce as some of the new offences are not addressed. There is a great likelihood for culprits or criminals to evade their criminal responsibility under the current law provisions. The first concern might be on the whole question of the definition of theft under the current law.

For instance Section 258 of the Penal Code Act defines theft as follows:

(1) A person who fraudulently and without claim of right takes anything capable of being stolen, or fraudulently converts to the use of any person other than the general or special owner thereof anything capable of being stolen, steals that thing.

(2) A person who takes or converts anything capable of being stolen is deemed to do so fraudulently if he does so with any of the following intents, that is to say –

(a) *an intent permanently to deprive* the general or special owner of the thing of it;

(b) …

(c) an intent to part with it on a condition as to its return which the person taking or converting it may be unable to perform;

(d) an intent to deal with it in such a manner that it cannot be returned in the condition in which it was at the time of the taking or conversion; or

(e) in the case of money, an intent to use it at the will of the person who takes or converts it, although he may intend afterwards to repay the amount to the owner, and "special owner" means any person who has lawful possession or custody of, or any proprietary interest in, the thing in question.

(3) When a thing stolen is converted, it is immaterial whether it is taken for the purposes of conversion or whether it is at the time of the conversion in the possession of the person who converts it or whether the person who converts the thing in question is the holder of a power of attorney for the disposition of it, or is otherwise authorized to dispose of it.

(4) When a thing converted *has been lost by* the owner and found by the person who converts it, the conversion is not deemed to be fraudulent if at the time of the conversion the person taking or converting the thing does not know who is the owner and believes on reasonable grounds that the owner cannot be discovered.

(5) A person shall not be deemed to take a thing unless *he moves the thing or causes it to move.* (*emphasis added*) (Penal Code, Cap 16 [R.E. 2000]

This section is paramateria with Section 1 to 6 of the UK theft Act which provides that "A person is guilty of theft if he dishonestly appropriates property belonging to another with the intention of permanently depriving the other of it…"

The main issue here is whether a data message or information which is intangible by nature can be stolen, and if yes, whether the offence can fall under this definition of theft. The words permanently deprived and things that are movable or capable of being stolen do not fit to the current development of technology as theft can take place without necessarily depriving someone of their property. Under the current computer technology some tangible property can be stolen without permanently depriving the owner and the criminals can escape liability or criminal liability as observed in the case of *R v. Lloyd.*[17] The case involved an alleged conspiracy to remove an original copy of film from cinemas overnight so as to produce copies and return the original copy. The issue before the Court was whether the elements of theft under the Law can be fulfilled under the digital technology. The charges were dismissed.

The Australian criminal law had the same provisions with regard to the definition of theft. For instance Section 371 of the Australian Code defines theft as follows:

(1) A person who fraudulently takes anything capable of being stolen, or fraudulently converts to his own use or to the use of any other person any property, is said to steal that thing or that property;

(2) A person who takes anything capable of being stolen or converts any property is deemed to do so fraudulently if he does so with any of the following intents, that is to say;

(a) An intent to permanently deprive the owner of the thing or property of it or any part of it

(b) An intent to permanently deprive any person who has any special property in the thing or property of such special property

(c) ...

(d) ...

(e) An intent to deal with it in such a manner that it cannot be returned in the condition in which it was at the time of the taking or conversion.

However due to the rapid development of computer technology Australia amended the above provisions by updating offences under the Criminal Code Act through the computer offences.[18] The amendments include the inclusion of offences such as unauthorized access, modification and impairment of data, credit cards or other electronic data.

---

[17] [1985] 2 ALL ER 661.

[18] (Cth) 2001.

Likewise, the UK updated her criminal laws and other related laws by enacting some new laws such as the Computer Misuse Act 1990, the Data Protection Act 1998, the Electronic Communication Act 2000, the Criminal Justice and the Public Order Act 1994.

As highlighted by David Bainbridge under the current digital technology it is possible for a person to illegally gain access to someone's bank account and transfer money into his account to gain interest. After a few weeks or months he can return that money, he has gained interest but the account holder has not been permanently deprived of his money.[19]

The other controversial issue under e-commerce is the question of obtaining money by deception as defined under the current criminal law. The word deception has not been defined to fit the current developments of technology as it is now possible for someone like a hacker to obtain money or property by using computers or other related devices.

The criminal laws in Tanzania which are in most cases synonymous with the laws of the United Kingdom provide that a person who by any deception dishonestly obtains property belonging to another, with the intention of permanently depriving the other of it, shall on conviction on indictment be liable to imprisonment. Under normal circumstances there can be no deception if there is no person and it might not be possible to deceive a computer or other related devices.[20] While the UK has amended most of her laws to cope with the current developments in technology to encourage the deployment of ICT especially e-commerce, Tanzania has not yet amended most of her laws save for the Evidence Act.

The topic on cyber crimes will be discussed in detail in the next part of this textbook which will mainly dwell on new types of e-crimes and e-offences.

6.5 *Electronic Documents Vis-à-vis the Best Evidence Rule*

6.5.1 The legal position of e-evidence in Tanzania

The term electronic evidence which has been introduced by digital technology includes data that comprises the output of an analogue device or data in digital format. Unlike physical evidence, electronic evidence cannot be destroyed easily even if the user manages to destroy the data; it is possible to retrieve the data.[21]

---

19 Bainbridge D., *Introduction to Computer Law*, 2000 at pages 301-302. See also R v. Llyod [1985] 2 ALL ER 661.

20 See argument by Lord Moriss in DPP v. Ray [1974] AC 370.

21 See The Icfai Journal of CYBER LAW Vol.6, 2007 at pages 82-83.

Most laws related to business, civil matters and evidence were made to suit the physical world on the use of paper based methods, advocate for the mandatory requirement of original evidence or the so called "best evidence rule" that qualify for admissibility in the court in case of dispute settlements and court procedures.[22] The best evidence rule requires that only original documents can be admissible in the court of laws. Due to the advancement of digital technology, computers, network and other related devices, the use and scope of electronic evidence has been expanding dramatically over the world. While many people in Tanzania are now involved in e-transactions, the absolute reliance of the best evidence rule as a conditional precedent for the admissibility of evidence might hinder the development of e-commerce. Until 2006, electronic documents or data message were not admissible under the legal system in Tanzania.

Under the Evidence Act[23] the best evidence rule excluded the admissibility of secondary evidence unless it is corroborated by primary evidence. However in 2007 the Government of Tanzania passed the Written Laws (Miscellaneous Amendments) Act which amends the Evidence Act, 1967.[24] This law seems to allow the admissibility of electronic evidence. Section 76 of the Evidence Act was amended by this legislation by adding a definition after the phrase "Bankers books". The additional definition reads as follows:

> "Bankers books include ledgers, cash books, account books and any other records used in the ordinary business of the bank or financial institution, whether the records are in a written form or a data message or kept on information system including but not limited to computers and storage devices, magnetic tape, micro-film, video or computer display screen or any other form of mechanical or electronic data retrieval mechanism."[25] (*emphasis added*)

The new amendment law has further brought fundamental changes as far as the legal status and admissibility of electronic records are concerned. This can be observed under the additional section of the new Act to the Evidence Act whereby electronic records or data message are given legal status and can be admissible as evidence before the court. The relevant section provides that:

> "A print out of any entry in the books of a bank on micro-film, Computer, information system, magnetic tape or any other form of mechanical or electronic data retrieval mechanism obtained by

22 See Evidence Act, Civil Procedure Act, Contract Laws etc.

23 CAP 6, [RE. 2002].

24 Ibid.

25 Section 35 of the Written Laws (Miscellaneous Amendments) Act, 2007.

> a mechanical or other process which in itself ensures the accuracy of such print out, and when such print-out is supported by a proof stipulated under subsection (2) of Section 78 that it was made in the usual ordinary course of business, and that the book is in custody of that bank it shall be received as evidence under this Act."[26]

Furthermore subsection (2) provides that "any entry in any banker's book shall be deemed to be a 'document'..."

6.5.2 Has the new law that amended the Evidence Act (1967) cured the problem?

Arguably, one could say that the Written Laws (Miscellaneous Amendments) Act, 2007 has not really cured the problem of legal certainty and admissibility of electronic evidence. This law seems to be mainly based on electronic evidence from banking transactions and admissibility of such evidence under criminal proceedings. It might be difficult to apply such evidence where the only available evidence to be applied in cases related to civil and other related cases or proceedings is e-evidence. All amendment sections provide for admissibility of electronic evidence adduced from the banks whereby the provisions start with the definition of bankers books which include ledgers, cash books, account books and any other records used in the ordinary business of *the bank or financial institution* (emphasis added). This law should recognize the admissibility of electronic evidence adduced from any computer or information system and other related devices be it transaction, communication or cyber crimes rather than basing on financial transactions only.

The question of proof of the integrity of the electronic records or e-evidence has also not been considered. The other important issues that were supposed to be included in the amendment legislation are standard of proof, presumption of computer or information system integrity, proof by affidavit, burden of proof and discretion of the court to consider common law or statutory rule relating to the admissibility of records in other circumstances. Some studies indicate that ccomputer output is no longer confined to computer printouts and scanned documents as highlighted in our law but extends to electronic records generated and stored by an increasing multitude of data processing, storing and transmission devices such as mobile phones, electronic organizers and digital cameras.[27] Technology-centric evidentiary provisions are viewed as somewhat dated. With

---

[26] See Section 36 of the Written Laws (Miscellaneous Amendments) Act, 2007. See also Section 78A of the Evidence Act, CAP 6, [RE. 2002].

[27] See The Technology law development group Singapore academy of law on computer output as evidence consultation paper September 2003.

greater systems and process integrity, not all computer output is considered suspect and computer output provisions designed to check issues of system unreliability seem to better serve the electronic evidence of yesteryears.

Some common law jurisdictions have enacted their laws by taking into account the question of proof of the integrity of the electronic records or e-evidence and computer system generally before giving data messages and electronic communication equal weight with paper based documents. This is reflected from the provisions of Malta Laws as follows;

"7. (1) Unless otherwise provided by or under this Act, if under any law in Malta, a person is required to produce a document that is in the form of a paper, or of any other substance or material, that requirement is deemed to have been satisfied if the person produces, by means of an electronic communication, an electronic form of that document:

(*a*) *having regard to all the relevant circumstances* at the time of the communication, the method of generating the electronic form of the document provided a reliable means of assuring the maintenance of *the integrity* of the information contained in the document;

(*b*) at the time the communication was sent, it was reasonable to expect that the information contained in the electronic form of the document would be readily accessible so as to be useable for subsequent reference (emphasis added);

(*c*) if the document is required to be produced to a person who is neither a public body nor to a person acting on behalf of a public body, then the person to whom the document is required to be produced, consents to the production by means of an electronic communication of an electronic form of the document Provided that:

(*d*) if the document is required to be given to a person, or to another person on his behalf, and the first mentioned person requires that an electronic form of the document be given, in accordance with particular information technology requirements, by means of a particular kind of electronic communication, the person's requirement is satisfied,"[28] and

"8. (1) If under any law in Malta, a person is required to record information in writing, that requirement is deemed to have been satisfied if the person records the information in electronic form:

[28] See Electronic Commerce Cap 426.

Provided that such information in electronic form is readily accessible so as to be useable for subsequent reference and it complies with such regulations as may be prescribed.

(2) If under any law in Malta, a person is required to retain, for a particular period, a document that is in the form of a paper or of any other substance or material, that requirement is deemed to have been satisfied if the person retains an electronic form of the document throughout that period:

Provided that if –

(a) having regard to all the relevant circumstances at the time of the generation of the electronic form of the document, the method of generating the electronic form of the document, provided *a reliable means* of assuring the maintenance of *the integrity* of the information contained in that document; and (emphasis added)

(*b*) at the time of the generation of the electronic form of the document, it was reasonable to expect that the information contained in the electronic form of the document would be readily accessible so as to be useable for subsequent reference; and

(3) For the purpose of sub article (2), *the integrity* of information contained in a document is only maintained if the information has remained complete and unaltered, save for (*a*) the addition of any endorsement; or

(*b*) any change not being a change to the information, which is necessary in the normal course of communication, storage or display."[29]

On the other hand, India enacted an effective law known as The Information Technology Act[30] which provides for the admissibility of electronic evidence among other things. This law has gone further by providing the conditions and rules to be taken into account before electronic records or e-evidence is accepted. More interestingly, the laws further requires the production of a certificate identifying the electronic record containing the statement and describing the manner in which it was produced and giving such particulars of any device involved in the production of that electronic record.

The provisions of this law on electronic evidence prescribe the mode for proof of contents of electronic records with the aim of satisfying proof by secondary evidence. Indeed this facility of proof by secondary evidence

[29] Ibid.

[30] The Information Technology Act 2000.

would apply to any computer output, such output being deemed as a document.[31] This means that a computer output is a deemed document for the purposes of proof.

This is reflected in Section 65B with added emphasis from the author as follows:

[S. 65B. Admissibility of electronic records;

"(1) Notwithstanding anything contained in this Act, any information contained in an electronic record which is printed on a paper, stored, recorded or copied in optical or magnetic media produced by a computer (hereinafter referred to as the computer output) shall be deemed to be also a document, if the conditions mentioned in this section are satisfied in relation to *the information and computer in question and shall be admissible in any proceedings, without further proof or production of the original,* as evidence of any contents of the original or of any fact stated therein of which direct evidence would be admissible.

(2) The conditions referred to in sub-section (1) in respect of a computer output shall be the following, namely:-

(a) the computer output containing the information was produced by the computer during the period over which the computer was used regularly to store or process information for the purpose of any activities regularly carried on over that period by the person having *lawful control over the use of the computer*;

(b) during the said period, information of the kind contained in the electronic record or of the kind from which the information contained is derived was regularly fed into the computer in the ordinary course of the said activities;

(c) throughout the material part of the said period, *the computer was operating properly,* or if not, then in respect of any period in which it was not operating properly or was out of operation during the part of the period, was not such as to affect the electronic record or the accuracy of its contents; and

(d) the information contained in the electronic record reproduces or is derived from such information fed into the computer in the ordinary course of the said activities.

(3) Where over any period, the function of storing or processing information for the purposes of any activities regularly carried on over

[31] See Sarkar S., *Law of evidence,* 16th Edition, Volume 1, 2007 at page 1237.

that period as mentioned in clause (a) of sub-section (2) was regularly performed by computers, whether:-

(a) by a combination of computers operating over that period; or

(b) by different computers operating in succession over that period; or

(c) by different combinations of computers operating in succession over that period; or

(d) in any other manner involving the successive operation over that period, in whatever order, of one or more computers and one or more combinations of computers...

(4) In any proceedings where it is desired to give a statement in evidence by virtue of this section, *a certificate* doing any of the following things, that is to say,-

(a) identifying the electronic record containing the statement and describing the manner in which it was produced;

(b) giving such particulars of any device involved in the production of that electronic record as may be appropriate for the purpose of showing that the electronic record was produced by a computer;

(c) dealing with any of the matters to which the conditions mentioned in sub-section (2) relate, and purporting to be signed by a person occupying a responsible official position in relation to the operation of the relevant device or the management of the relevant activities (whichever is appropriate) shall be evidence of any matter stated in the *certificate;* and for the purposes of Admissibility of electronic records this sub-section it shall be sufficient for a matter to be stated to be best of the knowledge and belief of the person stating it.

(5) For the purposes of this section, -

(a) information shall be taken to be supplied to a computer if it is supplied thereto in any appropriate form and whether it is so supplied directly or (with or without human intervention) by means of *any appropriate equipment;*

(b) whether in the course of activities carried on by any official, information is supplied with a view to its being stored or processed for the purposes of those activities by a computer operated otherwise than in the course of those activities, that information, if duly supplied to that computer, shall be taken to be supplied to it in the course of those activities;

(c) a computer output shall be taken to have been produced by a computer whether it was produced by it directly or (with or without human intervention) by means of *any appropriate equipment.*[32]

According to Sarkar, Section 65B lays down certain conditions which have to be satisfied with regard to the information and the computer or any other related devices in question.[33] In this regard, where those conditions are satisfied, an electronic record shall become admissible in any proceedings without further proof or production of the original as evidence of any contents of the original or of any fact stated in it. When Tanzania enacts laws that relate to electronic evidence we need to consider and if possible borrow some of these key conditions. Our law that amended this Act was supposed to take into account these conditions.

The development of digital technology and the application of ICT are always coming up with new innovations and rapid advancements in hardware and software technologies with widespread usage of the cyberspace. All of these developments and technological changes can and will raise complex issues relating to the reliability, authenticity and weight of electronic evidence if not properly addressed under the relevant laws. It is advised that any court assessing such evidence must not merely direct its mind to the manner of its production in evidence but also to the accuracy and authentication of the evidence.[34] In this regard, Tanzania is required to ensure that the laws of evidence and other related legislation are constantly revised and adapted to the realities of modern business practices and technologies.

It may be more prudent to adopt a technology-neutral non-computer specific approach to admit electronic evidence. It might be useful to borrow the legal position in other countries with effective cyber laws that clearly addresses all issues related to electronic evidence. For instance Singapore amended her Evidence Act and came up with a new law. The Evidence (Amendment) Act 1996 introduced new provisions to "facilitate the use of information technology" and to "provide for the admissibility and weight of computer output produced by any computer or network as evidence in both criminal and civil proceedings". The question of proof of the integrity of the electronic records or e-evidence has also not been considered. The other important issues that were supposed to be included in the amended legislation are standard of proof, presumption of computer or information system integrity. Before a computer output

---

32 See the Information Technology Act, 2000.

33 See Sarkar S., *Law of evidence,* 16th Edition, Volume 1, 2007 at page 1237.

34 See The Technology law development group Singapore academy of law on computer output as evidence consultation paper September 2003.

can be admitted as evidence "for any purpose whatsoever", it must first be relevant or admissible under the Evidence Act or any other written law.[35] This indicates that under Singapore laws, electronic evidence is admissible in both criminal and civil proceedings. The Evidence law in Singapore further provides that "to tender the computer output of an imaged document, the output must be supported by proof that the output is obtained from an approved process and that it accurately reproduces the contents of the original document".

Canada amended her Evidence Act in 1997. The amended at provides that the "best evidence" rule in respect of an electronic record may be satisfied by way of government prescribed "evidentiary presumptions in relation to electronic documents signed with secure electronic signatures" to associate the secure electronic signatures with persons, and the integrity of information contained in electronic documents signed with secure electronic signatures. Furthermore, under the Canadian legal jurisprudence, the law of evidence requires the court to consider the reliability of the record-keeping system and whether such a record-keeping system has adhered to any particular "standard, procedure, usage or practice" in recording and storing the electronic records before the e-evidence is accepted as admissible. The law goes further by providing that in order to prove the authenticity of electronic records, and the integrity of electronic record systems, evidence may be given by way of an affidavit given by a deponent, who only needs to attest to such facts as to the best of his knowledge or belief.[36]

The legal position in the United States is that computer records are routinely admitted pursuant to the Federal Rules of Evidence, which are applicable to both civil and criminal proceedings. In the US, before admitting computer or other related devices evidence, most Federal Courts have based on the application of the hearsay rule to these records, and drawn the distinction between computer-generated records and computer-stored records.[37]

The other important area of information and communication technologies that has been left out by the law that has amended the Evidence Act of Tanzania is the admissibility and proof of electronic signature. Most cyber laws in other countries have considered all these issues in their legislation.[38]

---

[35] Ibid.

[36] See the Canadian Evidence Act 1997.

[37] See The Technology law development group Singapore academy of law on computer output as evidence consultation paper September 2003. See also *Catabran* (*United States v. Catabran* 836 F.2d 453, 457 (9th Cir. 1988) and *United States v. Briscoe.*

[38] Refer Laws of Malaysia, Digital Signatures Act 1997, Computer Crimes Act 1997, UNCITRAL Model Laws and Commonwealth Model Laws.

The word document that appears in the Evidence Act also needs to be redefined to include data message or e-information.

The "document" under the Evidence Act, 1967 as revised in 2002 is defined basing on physical world only and not on cyberspace world as follows:

> "document means any writing, handwriting, typewriting, printing, photostat, photograph and every recording upon any tangible thing, any form of communication or representation by letters, figures, marks or symbols or by more than one of these means, which may be used for the purpose of recording any matter provided that such recording is reasonably permanent and readable by sight."[39] (*emphasis added*)

Section 66 which provides for applicability of best evidence rule whereby documents have to be proved by primary evidence needs to be amended to accommodate electronic evidence.

Earlier before the amendment of the Evidence Act, the Judiciary in Tanzania tested the admissibility of electronic evidence. This was done through the landmark case of *Trust Bank Ltd. v. Le-marsh Enterprises Ltd., Joseph Mbui Magari, Lawrence Macharia*[40] which seem to beneficially erode the best evidence rule admitting computer printout and other related e-evidence under The Evidence Act of Tanzania (CAP 6 R.E 2002).

The court considered the decision of the Court of Appeal in *Tanzania Cotton Marketing Board v. Cogecot Cotton Company SA*[41] which had earlier allowed the electronic communication mode of sending arbitration awards to the High Court contrary to Rule 4 of Arbitration Ordinance.[42] In this case, the issue before the court was whether filing of an arbitration award by DHL courier and not by registered post as required by the law is enforceable.

However, the Government seems to accept the decision of the court by passing the Written Laws (Miscellaneous Amendments) Act which amended the Evidence Act, 1967.

The problem of proof of a fact through a data message under e-commerce has also been a great concern in other jurisdictions. For example, some Latin American countries, have a highly formalised a strict

[39] See Section 3 the Evidence Act, CAP 6 [RE. 2002].

[40] The High Court of Tanzania (Commercial Division) at Dar es Salaam Commercial case no.4 of 2000 (Unreported).

[41] 1997 TLR 165 (CA).

[42] Now [RE 2002 CAP.15].

system of evidentiary admissibility.[43] Some require that evidence presented in a court of law must be in the form of a notarised document. Other countries, such as Singapore, impose a burden upon the party adducing the computer-derived evidence into court to show that the systems from which the evidence was derived were 'operating properly and numerous experts have been used to explain to a court the technical aspects of each component of the system.

6.5.3 *E-Evidence in other jurisdictions*

6.5.3.1 National Level Some countries like UK, Malaysia, Singapore, Mauritius and others have enacted specific effective evidence law that recognizes electronic evidence and all other changes brought by digital technology. The UK amended the Civil Evidence Act 1995 by removing previous a requirement that documents must be original (in a written form) in order to be admissible as "best evidence rule". In 1981 Professor Smith in a learned article on computer evidence developed the ideas put forward in the Statute of Liberty and came up with a rule, which was later accepted by the English Courts.

The rule read as follows:

> "Where information is recorded by mechanical means without the intervention of a human mind, the record made by the machine is admissible evidence, provided of course, it is accepted that the machine is reliable."[44]

The Civil Evidence Act and the Criminal Justice Act 1988 which are the main statutory provisions governing the admissibility and proof of documentary evidence were mainly designed to apply to documents containing computer-stored information. This has been accomplished by providing wide definitions which are widely expanded to include a computer as well as the computer printout from it, in both laws. The laws which allow the admissibility of e-evidence in both civil proceedings and criminal proceedings widely define the term "document" to mean "anything in which information of any description is recorded".

Some judicial cases indicate that the rigid adherence to the original documents or "best evidence rule" is no longer appropriate in this era of digital technology. This historic rule has generated some legal uncertainty

[43] See UNCTAD on Legal Aspects of E-Commerce 2006.

[44] C. Smith, *The admissibility of Statement by Computer* (1981) Crim.L.R.390. This statement was quoted with approval by Court of Appeal in *R v. Spiby (1990) 91 Cr.App.*186. See also Bainbridge D., *Introduction to Computer Law*, 4th Edition at page 291.

in respect of data messages, since the concept of an "original" has little meaning in an e-commerce environment as His Lordship Lode Justice in *R v. Governor*[45] boldly stated that

> "we accept that 'the best evidence rule' saved an important purpose in the days of parchment and quill pens but the invention of carbon papers…and more to come that requirement has gone away".

Furthermore, In *Springsteen v. Flute International* (2001) the Court argued that

> *"The time has now come when it could be said with confidence that the best evidence rule, long on its deathbed, has finally expired."*

Australia has also gone further in enacting and amending laws to accommodate the impact of computer technology on the admissibility of e-evidence. This has been done whereby all provinces or states on their jurisdictions have enacted laws that apply to the admissibility of computer evidence. The provisions of the laws apply to both civil and criminal proceedings.

South Africa, Malaysia and India have also enacted evidence laws that allow the admissibility of computer evidence in both criminal and civil proceedings. Apart from the South African Evidence Act of 1992, there is an Electronic Communications and Transactions Act of 2002 which contains provisions that apply to the admissibility of documents containing electronic representations of information in any form. The Slovenian Electronic Commerce and Signatures Act, 2000 (ESA) provides for legal recognition of e-documents and e-signatures. For instance Article 4 provides that electronic documents or paperless documents shall have equal evidentiary value with paper based documents. The law further stipulates that electronic signatures and e-documents shall have functional equivalence with the paper based statutory requirements for writing, original, and retention.[46]

Furthermore, South Africa enacted the law that provides for admissibility and evidential weight of data messages. This law places physical evidence that is based on the best evidence rule under equal weight with electronic evidence as follows:

Section 14 (1) provides that:

In any legal proceedings, the rules of evidence must not be applied so as to deny the admissibility of a data message, in evidence:

---

[45] [1989] 3 ALL ER 701.

[46] See articles 12, 13 and 14 of ESA.

(a) on the mere grounds that it is constituted by a data message; or

(b) if it is the best evidence that the person adducing it could reasonably be expected to obtain, on the grounds that it is not in its original form.

(2) Information in the form of a data message must be given due evidential weight

(3) In assessing the evidential weight of a data message, regard must be made to:

(a) the reliability of the manner in which the data message was generated, stored or communicated;

(b) the reliability of the manner in which the integrity of the data message was maintained;

(c) the manner in which its originator was identified; and

(d) any other relevant factor.[47]

6.5.3.2 International Level Briefly the UNCITRAL Model Laws have provided guidelines and functional equivalence between e-evidence and best evidence rule and provided both evidence under equal footing under Article 9 which reads as follows:

> In any legal proceedings, nothing in the application of the rules of evidence shall apply so as to deny the admissibility of a data message in evidence: on the sole ground that it is a data message (e-document); or, This topic will be discussed in detail in the forthcoming book on Cyber and Computer related (Part two of Cyber Law). (See the UNCITRAL Model Law on e-commerce, 1999).

On the other hand, The International Standards Organisation (ISO), for example, has adopted a set of standard procedures for the operation of electronic imaging systems. These provisions constitute a basis for the admissibility of computer-derive evidence, while giving such evidence its due evidentiary weight in light of all relevant circumstances.

In contrast to the 1996 Model Law, the Convention does not address record retention and evidential issues; therefore, in the event of a dispute, there may continue to be uncertainties concerning the admissibility and probative value of computer-derived evidence that either party may seek to rely upon.

[47] See The Electronic Communications and Transactions Act 2002.

CHAPTER SEVEN

Technology and Intellectual Property Rights

7.1 *The Impact of Digital Technology and E-commerce on Intellectual Property Rights*

One of the areas in e-commerce that might cause a lot of problems is trading online in goods and services involving Intellectual Property Rights (IPRs).[1] Intellectual Property Rights is a term used specifically for describing certain rights that afford protection to innovative, commercial goodwill and creative endeavour. [2] According to the WIPO Report, the major forms of IPRs for e-commerce can be divided into more than four categories namely, Patents, Trade Secret, Designs, Copyright and Trademarks (Bowyer, 1996). However copyright seems to form a major IPR issue in cyberspace whereby it protects an expression of ideas, and products of human creativity. Copyright is a branch of many forms of IPR that is increasingly important in the Internet era which needs an effective legal framework that takes into account the impact of digital technologies. Digitization of material enables material to be used in different media, to be copied at the same quality as an original, to be manipulated and distorted, and to be distributed throughout the world cheaply, easily and speedily.

IP rights can provide remedies to the rights owners against their misuse, misappropriation and infringement online or offline. The said rights which involve copyright, trademarks, design, patents, etc. are very crucial in the development, commercial exploitation and use of computer technology devices including computer hardware and software and other related applications.

There is no doubt that the rapid growth of the Internet is seen as one of the key technological developments since the introduction of an international legal instrument such as the TRIPS Agreement. The growth of the Internet has had major implications for the treatment and protection of copyright materials and other related intellectual property rights that are published electronically. Technological developments have made copyright material easier to access and reproduce, and more difficult to protect. More recently, with the adoption of the two WIPO Internet Treaties in

---

1 Turban E., *E-Commerce* at page 139.

2 Wilson C., *Nutshells, Intellectual Property Law* 2002 at page 2.

1996, many changes have taken place in the copyright field, as a result of digital technology, opening new horizons for composers, artists, writers and others to use the Internet with confidence to create, distribute and control the use of their works within the digital environment (WIPO Report).[3] Due to the rapid revolution of digital technology, the scope of the subject matter for copyright protection has been expanding. The economic gains from software, multimedia and different technology-based products have reached very significant levels. InThe technology copyright protected material features as one of the main components in electronic commerce and digital transactions.

EAC partner states should, as a first step, commit to implement commonly accepted international Treaties obligations such as the World Trade Organization, TRIPS Agreement and the WIPO Internet Treaties to ensure that IP laws are up-to-date and more effective in dealing with emerging IPRs challenges posed by the development of digital technology.[4] Partner states should also ensure that there are effective civil and criminal remedies available against any IPRs infringement be it in the physical or cyberspace world.

While copyright protects computer software such as computer programmes, databases, etc. as literary works, patent law protects hardware as well as software or computer programmes that show technical effect or contribution. One has to differentiate between Industrial and Intellectual Property rights. While the former include patents, designs, trade or service marks, geographical indications and appellation of origins which involve practical applications, the later in most cases include copyright whose main concern is the protection of rights in aesthetic or artistic works.[5]

There is no doubt that due to the rapid development of digital technology, the World Web has now become the famous Bazaar of Intellectual Property.[6] The Internet does not recognize boundaries as e-commerce allows products to be sold online while protection of intellectual property rights is territorial. Under digital technology IPRs can be infringed anywhere. Intellectual property, which refers to creative rights, now includes intellectual property created electronically. There are some notable difficulties in the application of the 18th Century concept of copyright under digital technology or e-commerce.[7] The argument is based on the fact that a material that appears on a website does not mean that it is in the

---

3 See the relevant Provisions of The WIPO Copyright Treaty 1996 and The WIPO Performances and Phonograms Treaty 1996

4 For instance Article 11 of the WIPO Copyright Treaty requires 'adequate legal protection and effective legal remedies' against circumvention.

5 See Lloyd Ian, *Information Technology* 3rd Edition 2000 at page 304.

6 Opcit.

7 Latimer P. *Australian Business Law* 2003 at page 1277. See also the Australian Evidence Act 1995 Sec.48.

public domain and that it may be copied at will. Furthermore, copyright may be infringed by copying a website or by creating and maintaining hypertext links to other websites. Some authors have argued that copyright law does not recognise a "multimedia" work, and copyright attaches to each of its various elements.

One can clearly observe the difficulty the intellectual property laws in Tanzania and other countries specifically Copyright law faces in keeping pace with changes in technology. Digital technology has transformed the way creators work and how authors and publishers deliver copyright works. It has blurred the lines between copying and reading, sale and reuse, performance and viewing a work. (Hill et al, 1998, p. 1) Due to these rapid changes and growth of the Internet and use of e-commerce, any work may be distributed worldwide, essentially instantaneously and at an insignificant cost. Data transmission is no longer limited to a one-to-one basis, but one-to-many or even one-to-all basis and Internet, is becoming a "broadcasting" system.[8]

Indeed the drafters of the new amendments of copyright laws in Tanzania and EAC in general should make the statutes flexible enough to be applied to future innovations. The Copyright and Neighbouring Act of Tanzania which came into operation in 1999, was passed soon after the enactment of the US Digital Millennium Copyright Act (DMCA) which was passed in 1998. One would expect the Tanzania law to consider some of the provisions in the US DMCA whose main goal was updating United States copyright laws to make them more relevant and flexible given the ever changing digital information climate.

7.2 *Digital Infringement on Copyrighted Works*

Generally, copyright provides for restricted acts on certain rights that belong to the authors and owners. With regard to computer technology and other related technologies, these acts involve copying, issuing copies to the public, adapting, etc. Carrying out these acts without prior permission from the owners, amounts to copyright infringement. Copyright is the most affected area of intellectual property when it comes to the development of digital technology. The most affected areas include the right of adaptation, right of public performance, right of broadcasting, right of distribution and right of rental. An area which has been raising legal concern is the scope of the right of adaptation due to the increased possibilities for adapting and transforming works, which are embodied in

[8] See Fair use in the digital era, Carlos M. Correa Director, Programme on Science and Technology Policy and Management Specialist in Intellectual Property Rights, University of Buenos Aires Argentina.

digital format. Users are now easily able to manipulate text, sounds and images of copyrighted materials electronically. This raises a debate as to the clear and the appropriate balance between the rights of the author to control the integrity of their work electronically by authorizing modifications, on the one hand, and the rights of users to make some changes in digital format, on the other hand.

The ease with which digital information can be reproduced has spawned a market for illegal copies whereby publishers of software, music, video, etc. are losing revenue.[9] Moreover, there has been an unprecedented increase in the number of scholarly and academic works resorting to plagiarism simply by copying existing documents from the web. In other words, one can observe a great variety of possible intellectual property infractions which include forgery of an author's work such as software, design, etc.

Due to the development of digital technology, some countries have reconstructed and redefined some of the restricted acts such adaptation to include the whole process of converting source code into object. It has been further argued that if a person changes a cartoon strip into a narrative this amounts to the infringement of a restricted act, that is adaptation.[10] Unlike in the UK, this is not the case in Tanzania as adaptation includes translation of literary works and musical works only leaving out computer generated works such as cartoons.[11] The works that afford copyright in Tanzania are provided under Sections 5 to 23 of the Copyright and Neighbouring Rights Act.[12] The Act further highlights the restricted and permitted acts on the use of copyrighted works. While literal and non-literal copying of computer programs might amount to copyright infringement in other jurisdictions, the Copyright and Neighbouring Act of Tanzania seems to be silent on electronic infringement. The UK Law that regulates copyright reflects this under Section 17 (2) which effectively states that copying in relation to Literary (which include software); dramatic, musical and artistic work includes reproducing the work in any material form which include storage in any medium by electronic means.[13] This means under the UK Law, non-exclusive licence is required for one to be permitted to copy someone's computer programmes and other related software.

---

9 See ITU Cyber Security Guide for Developing Countries Report at page 41.

10 See Bainbridge D., *Introduction to Computer Law* 4th Edition, 2000 at page 41.

11 Ibid at page 29.

12 [Cap 218 R.E. 2002]. See also the argument in *IBSCOS Computer Ltd v. Barclays Mercantile Highland Finance Ltd [1994] FSR 275* as cited by Bainbridge D at page 29-30.

13 Compare the UK CDPA Act (Section 17 (2) and (6), 1988 and the Copyright and Neighbouring Act of Tanzania 1999. See also Section 21 (4) of the UK CDPA Act 1988 which has defined the word translation in relation to computer programmes in relation to source and object code. See also Section 50B of the UK CDPA Act, 1988 as to whether de-compilation of computer programmes amount adaptation hence infringement under the Copyright law in Tanzania.

This legal requirement needs to be provided under the copyright laws in Tanzania to encourage innovators and creators of software.

The development of digital technology brought by the innovation and use of computers has brought a great impact on copyright. This is the most affected area of intellectual property because of the development and use of information and communication technologies. Technology has greatly facilitated more and more computer users to access legally and illegally copyrighted materials electronically. This has lead to more disputes on intellectual property rights arising out of misuse of these rights.

Electronic shopping and pirating of IP materials have been growing very fast as online shopping grows, so do the dangers. This has been experienced in many countries, in the UK; James Bond has been the victim of online pirates.[14] The Business Standard reported that the latest film in the British spy series was circulating on the Internet and on illegal DVDs available in the streets of London. The movie was reported to have been illegally downloaded off the Internet by more than 200,000 people by November 24, 2006 according to a piracy surveillance specialist.

According to Federation of the Phonographic Industry (IFPI) it is believed that by 2006 the global revenue from music downloaded onto computers and mobile phones doubled to about 2 billion dollars and by 2010 it is expected that at least one quarter of all music sales worldwide will be digital.[15] There is great likelihood of physical world musical sales to be overtaken by digital sales as indicated in Korea, China and other countries.

To cope with these rapid changes, some countries like the US enacted an effective legal framework to regulate these areas for the purpose of protecting copyright owners and other consumers. Likewise, the Chinese Government signed MOU for enforcement with four US and British industry associations namely Motion Picture Association of America, The Business Software Alliance, The Association of American Publishers and the Publishers of the UK for better protection of online copyright.[16]

Generally, infringement may take two forms namely primary and secondary depending on the infringers. For instance primary infringement occurs where restricted acts are carried without the permission of the copyright owner while secondary infringement (done by someone other than a primary infringer) is concerned with large scale infringement taking place with actual or constructive knowledge. In other words, while primary infringement normally is done by people who are directly involved with misusing copyrighted works, secondary infringement involves people in a

[14] See the *Business Standard* dated 28 November 2006.
[15] Ibid, Tuesday January 23, 2007.
[16] Op cit, Tuesday December 2006.

commercial context dealing with infringing copyright or helping primary infringers. Copyright in a work is infringed by a person who does not hold a licence to the work uses the work or authorizes another to do any of the acts restricted by the copyright.

Sections 23, 24, 25 and 26 of the UK CDPA are very exhaustive in covering both offline and online infringement of copyrighted works. The act stipulates that secondary infringement of copyrighted works include:

- possessing or dealing with infringing copy[17]
- providing means for making infringing copies[18]
- permitting use of premises for infringing performance[19]
- provision of apparatus for infringing performance,[20] &
- importing copyrighted works.

Generally, a person infringes the copyright in a work if he does one of the restricted acts or authorizes another to do one of the acts in relation to a substantial part of the work without the permission of the copyright owner and such a person may be sued by the copyright owner (or an exclusive licensee of the owner) for infringement.

On the other hand, some judicial decisions have developed some theories on copyright infringement. This is reflected in the famous US case (NAPSTER) which is a typical and landmark case on cyberspace infringement of copyrighted works.

The US Digital Millennium Copyright Act (DMCA) was the relevant legislation enacted in reaction to past technological developments that were seen as threatening the traditional commercial interests of copyright owners. On the other hand, Section 24 of the UK CDPA provides for limited liability of ISPs such as vicarious liability where they have knowledge of illegal activities taking place online.

This development has not been able to take into account the prospective developments in computer technologies and changes in how cultures use those technologies that may threaten or enhance (or both, simultaneously) copyright owners' interests.

A material contribution occurs on the part of the contributory infringer towards facilitating or inducing primarily infringing conduct.

---

17 Section 23.

18 Section 24.

19 Section 25.

20 Section 26.

The example most often given of a material contribution one that extends back to the first case of secondary liability for copyright infringement is that of making available a site or facility through which the primary infringement is carried out. Contributory liability requires that the secondary infringer must have knowledge or have reason to know of direct infringement as highlighted by the court in *Cable/Home Communication Corp. Network Produs Inc.*[21] It was believed that Napster had both actual and constrictive knowledge that its users exchanged copyrighted music online.

Vicarious liability occurs where the secondary infringer is in some position of authority over the primary infringer. A person is vicariously liable for the copyright infringements committed by another when he is in a supervisory relationship with the primary infringer and receives some financial benefit from the infringement.[22]

Infringement elements can be summarised as follows:

What both of these theories of secondary liability share is the element of control on the part of the secondary infringer over the conduct of the primary infringer. In the case of contributory infringement, the control is exercised through the knowledgeable giving or withholding of the material contribution necessary to carry out an infringing activity.

The first applications of theories of secondary liability to new technologies that make mass copying possible were not conceptually different from the earliest, low-technology cases. In *M. Witmark & Sons v. Pastime Amusement Co*[23] the secondary infringer operated as a nexus for the primary infringing activity and enjoyed some reward from being in that position.

7.3 *The Role and Liability of Intermediaries in the Infringement of Intellectual Property Rights*

The use and commercial exploitation of Internet technologies for the purposes of making transactions possible and effective online requires the full participation of intermediaries such as Internet Service Providers (ISPs/OSPs) who are often unconscious actors.[24] ISPs and OSPs are the main

[21] 902 F.2D 829, 845 & 846 N.29 (11th Cir.1990). See also *Religious Tech.Crte. v. Netcom On-line Communication Servs., Inc.*, 907 F.Supp.1361, 1373-74 (N,D.Cal 1995).

[22] *Shapiro, Berntein & Co v. H.L.Green Co. 316 (2d Cir 1964).* See also Dr T. Hays (Lecturer at the University of Aberdeen 2003), The Evolution and Decentralization of Secondary Liability for Digital infringement of Copyright-Protected Works in the US.

[23] 298 F. 470 (E.D.SC. 1924), aff'd Pastime Amusement *Co. v. M.Witmark & Sons, 2 F.2d 1020* (4th Cir. 1924). See also Dr T. Hays (Lecturer at the University of Aberdeen 2003), The Evolution and Decentralization of Secondary Liability for Digital infringement of Copyright-Protected Works in the US.

[24] Reed C. *Internet Law and Text and Materials* 2000 at page 29.

firms that provide the lowest level of service in the multi-tiered Internet architecture by leasing Internet access to home owners, small businesses, large institutions or organizations.[25] They further facilitate transactions and communications between the end users and identification of parties. Consequently, the interjection of Internet technology into the relationships between infringers, their facilitators, their superiors and their customers adds an additional complex layer of potential responsibility.[26] Central to these relationships, at their nexus, are Internet service providers. ISPs, for the most part, do not provide their own content, meaning that they do not interject material of their choosing into the Internet rather, they act strictly as facilitators providing access to the Internet to their customers. ISP in most cases acts as a host connected full-time to others hosts, and provides access and other services to its subscribers.[27]

The interconnection of multiple ISPs (peer 2 peer) makes up the Internet, the customers of some ISPs acting as consumers for the content provided by the customers of others. During the relevant period, approximately 1992 through 2000, ISPs were seen as the primary facility providers for the nearly autonomous digital transactions of an unlimited number of Internet users.[28] While there were relatively few ISPs they could be seen as having most, if not all, of the attributes of a secondary actor capable of being either contributory or vicariously liable for infringing transactions passing through their computer networks. The liability on ISPs might arise through copying, possession[29] or transmission of copyrighted materials.

ISPs provided so much of a nexus for infringing activity and their control over the medium of exchange, particularly in the case of the provision of bulletin-board services (BBS) that primary, as opposed to secondary liability, was attributable to them. In *Playboy Enterprises, Inc. v. Frena*,[30] a small BBS was held primarily liable for the copyright violations committed by its customers in regard to the unauthorized dissemination of protected photographs and the District Court, noting that intent and knowledge are not elements of primary infringement, did not hesitate to hold the operator liable. Later on in another case known as *the Scientology case*[31], a different District Court applied contributory liability to an ISP that provided access to the use of the Internet to a customer who posted copyright-protected religious material to a bulletin board.

---

[25] See Laudon C.K & Traver C.G, *E-commerce*, 3rd Edition, 2007 at page 136.

[26] Dr T. Hays (Lecturer at the University of Aberdeen 2003), The Evolution and Decentralization of secondary Liability for Digital infringement of Copyright-Protected Works in the US.

[27] See Reed C., *Internet Law and Text and Materials* 2000 at page 29.

[28] Ibid.

[29] See Section 23 of the UK Copyright, Designs and Patents Act.

[30] 839 F. Supp 1552 (1993).

[31] *Religious Technology Centre v. Netcom On-Line Communications Service 907* F.Supp.1361 (N.D. Cal. 1995).

The legal formulation of this secondary liability was based on the knowledge on the part of the ISP of the infringing nature of the material passing through its computer network. The court held:

> "*If plaintiffs can prove the knowledge element, [the ISP] will be liable for contributory infringement since its failure to simply cancel [the primary infringer's] infringing message and thereby stops an infringing copy from being distributed worldwide constitutes substantial participation in [the primary infringer's] public distribution of the message.*"[32]

Contributory liability which originated from the USA Copyright law was established on the basis of the ISP's general knowledge of the primarily infringing activity combined with the ISP's contribution and its users. Title II of the DMCA retains the classifications of primary and secondary liability for infringement of copyright in digitised works, and it incorporates that public policy of promoting the development and expansion of the Internet through the creation of various exceptions to liability. These exceptions only apply to ISPs that engage in one or more of four categories of protected activity.

7.3.1 The Implications of Digital technology of MP3—Peer 2 Peer File Sharing

The impacts of digital technology and the development of e-commerce can be observed from intellectual property rights point of view whereby copyright specifically musical works are now more vulnerable to infringement. The invention and the use of software using Mp3 files for downloading and storing compressed music files under the so called peer-to-peer technology poses a great challenge to copyright owners and the music industry in general. The software allows very large audio files to be compressed and stored on a PC's hard drive. This compressed file can be burned onto a blank CD and can be e-mailed to friends, posted on a website, loaded on a personal player, etc.[33] MP3 music files under e-commerce have a great impact on copyrighted works. This is affecting the traditional methods of music distribution and unfairly infringing the copyright of music distributors and musicians. Some people in developing countries like Tanzania have been using this technology to infringe other people's copyrighted works irrespective of the exiting copyright laws which do not seem to clearly address digital infringement of copyrighted work.[34]

---

[32] Ibid page. 1374.

[33] See Michael Chissick, "Intellectual Property Rights" in Turban E., *E-commerce* 2002 at pages 152-153.

[34] Adam Mambi, "Copyright Infringement on Music Industry and the impact of technology on IP in Tanzania", Dissertation submitted at the University of Aberdeen for LLM Requirements in 2003.

In 1998, the US passed the Digital Millennium Copyright Act (DMCA) for the purposes of implementing the 1996 WIPO Treaties and address controversial issues brought by digital technology, specifically digital infringement of copyrighted work. The said law provides for the provisions which criminalise circumvention of anti-piracy measures in software among other things. The first application of the DMCA to Online Service Providers (OSPs) transactions was in the *A & M Recordings, Inc. v. Napster.*[35] In this case, the plaintiffs were engaged in commercial recording, distribution and sale of copyrighted musical composition and sound recordings. The complainant alleged that Napster was a contributory and vicarious copyright infringer. Napster, Inc. operated as a central registry for MP3-format music files stored in the computers of its customers. Through its website, Napster provided its customers with its own "Music Share" software that enabled customers to share MP3 music files with other customers. Through the use of the software, Napster was able to provide all of its customers with a database giving information about which music files were available and from who.

The software combined with Napster's database allowed customers to copy any of the millions of music files directly available from Napster customers' computers, giving Napster a financial benefit in the form of advertising revenue in relation to third-party advertisements exhibited in the Music Share software, and depriving the recording industry of an estimated $100 million due to the resultant copyright infringements.[36] The US Court of Appeal the 9th Circuit in Napster February 2001 ruled that Napster was liable for contributory, vicarious and secondary infringement based on direct infringement by its users. Napster was originally a company that made software that allowed users to use MP3 files share in their MP3 libraries with each other by P2P. The Recording Industrial Association of American (RIAA) took Napster to Court. Napster claimed that it was not liable but just a service provider. The Court held Napster liable. It was further argued that without safe-harbour protection, Napster could be held liable for secondary infringement of the copyright in the recorded music copied by its customers. At the trial court level, Napster was held liable under a contributory and vicarious infringement theory. That liability was endorsed on appeal, as was vicarious liability.[37] This represents a fusion of the two theories on copyrighted works infringement that can be observed under e-commerce transactions.

Key to the application of this liability is the ability of an ISP/OSP in question to control the activities of its customers. Because of Napster's

---

35 No.00-16401, No.00-16403, US Court of Appeals for the Ninth Circuit. 239 F.3d 1004; 2001 U.S.

36 See Turban E., *E-Commerce* at pages 140-142.

37 Ibid.

position as the nexus of the MP3 file exchange, it was in a technical position to control the activities of its customers. Because that relationship existed as long as the customers used the "Music Share" software, the relationship was ongoing and concurrent with the primary infringing activity.

In the US, the situation has always been alarming despite the DMCA and the decision of the Court in the Napster case. For instance in 2001-2005 the case of *Metro Goldwny Mayer Studio v. Grokster* knocked at the US Supreme Court Door whereby the court unanimously decided that all Internet file sharing services such as Grokster, StreanCast, Kazaa could be held liable for digital copyright infringement if it could be proved that their software was intended to be used for such illegal activities. This was due to the fact that the music industry legal filings claimed that more than 90% of the music/songs downloaded by almost 36 million Americans via P2P file sharing networks was being done illegally. Furthermore, in *A & A Records Inc. and Ors v. Internet Site known as Fresh Kutz and Anor*, the Court ordered, amongst other things, that the owner of the website or its agents stop from continuing to infringe the record companies' copyright, from destroying any records and computer files connected to the website, and to block access to all infringing copies of musical recordings on the website.[38]

Looking at the nature of copyright law in Tanzania one might argue that the role and liability of intermediaries is not well addressed by these laws. Likewise, downloading and uploading of copyrighted materials which in most cases leads to digital infringement are not addressed by IP Laws. The solution is to borrow the experience from other countries like the UK, MALTA, USA, etc. and come up with an effective legal framework that addresses the impact of digital technology on IPRs.

7.3.2 Software and Computer Programs Piracy

Computer software seems to be a relatively recent and very unique intellectual property that serves both as an expression of an idea and the idea itself. Software has been defined to include computer programs or series of instructions copied into temporary or permanent memory on a computer which may subsequently execute those instructions.[39] Software is produced in a variety of human- readable and other very unreadable languages.

Generally, software and other related computer programmes are protected by copyright law from infringement.[40] However the protection

---

[38] See White SW Computer Law Report at www.computerlaw.com.au on 8/9/20008.

[39] See The Icfai Journal on CYBER LAW, 2007 Vol. 2.

[40] See the discussion in the *Sega Enterprises v. Richards [1983] FSR 73* and *Apple Computer Inc. v. Computer Edge Pty Ltd [1984] FSR 481.*

of software from illegal copying is also available under patent, and trade secret laws or the law of confidence. Consequently, computer programs, databases and other related works created using computers or stored in computers including computer generated works afford copyright protection as literary works provided that they are fixed/recorded or in a form of expressed ideas but not ideas themselves.

The UK CDPA defines literary works that afford copyright as follows:

(1) In this part – "literary work" means any work, other than a dramatic or musical work, which is written, spoken or sung, and others accordingly include -

(a) *a table or compilation other than a database,*

(b) *a computer program,*

(c) preparatory design material for a computer program, and

(d) *a database*[41]

On the other hand, The Copyright and Neighbouring Rights Act[42] of Tanzania provides that literary and artistic works shall include:

(a) books, pamphlets and other writings, including computer programs;

(b) lectures, addresses, sermons and other works of the same nature;

(c) dramatic and dramatico-musical works;

(d) musical works (vocal and instrumental), whether or not they include accompanying words;

(e) choreographic works and pantomimes;

(f) cinematographic works, and other audio-visual works;

(g) works of drawing, painting, architecture, sculpture, engraving, lithography and tapestry;

(h) photographic works including works expressed by processes analogous to photography;

(i) works of applied art, whether handicraft or produced on an industrial scale;

(j) illustrations, maps, plans, sketches and three dimensional works relative to geography, topography, architecture or science.

---

41 See Section 3.

42 See the Copyright and Neighbouring Right Act [CAP 218 R.E 2002].

Unlike other laws in other jurisdictions, the definition of literary works in the copyright law of Tanzania does not include computer programs and other related software. In addition the Act provides a limited definition of computer programs. The Act defines "computer program" to mean a set of instructions expressed in words, codes, schemes or in any other form, which is capable when incorporated in a medium that the computer can read, of causing a computer to perform or achieve a particular task or result.

This Act needs to be amended to expand the definition of literary works to include computer programs and other related software. The words "computer programs" also need to be redefined so as to provide effective protection against infringement. A new definition may confer protection upon the set of instructions itself which is adapted to the nature of copyright which includes the stored set of instructions in a non-sensate form such as electrical impulses based on the notion of expression or description made in language, code or notation.[43]

The drafters of the law can study the amendments that were made by Australia when they amended their Copyright Act, 1968 and enacted new effective law that has further taken into account the current development of digital technology. This was done via the Copyright Act, 1984 which further redefined computer programs to provide more protection under copyright. The definition of "computer program" which was introduced by the 1984 amendments to the Copyright Act 1968 (Cth) focuses upon "an expression, in any language, code or notation" (1) s.10(1) of a set of instructions of the designated kind rather than upon the set of instructions itself.[44]

The Copyright Amendment Act 1984 (Cth) amended the definitions in s.10(1) of "literary work", "adaptation" and "infringing copy" and added new definitions of "computer program" and "material form". The definition of "literary work" was amended to include:

(a) a table, or compilation, expressed, in any words, figures or symbols (whether or not in a visible form) and

(b) computer program or compilation of computer program This Australian Act further re-defined a computer program as

"an expression, in any language, code or notation" of a set of instructions (whether with or without related information) intended directly or after either or both of the following:

(a) conversion to another language, code or notation, of a set of instructions

---

[43] See the discussion by lawyers on White SW Computer Law, IP & IT Lawyers, AUSTRALIA.

[44] Ibid.

(b) reproduction in a different material form; to cause a device having digital information processing capabilities to reform a particular function"

Moreover the Act further defined material form as; "in relation to a work or adaptation of a work, (it) includes any form (whether visible or not) of storage from which the work or adaptation or a substantial part of the work or adaptation, can be reproduced."

Most copyright laws provide some restricted acts for software or computer programmes namely copying, issuing copies to the public, making an adaptation, etc. with an exception of fair dealing. As technology develops, many authors are under risk from digital infringements of their copyrighted and other IP related works. It is believed that through the considerable pressure from the computer industry especially the lobby group FAST (The Federation Against Software Theft), Australia amended the Copyright Act and passed an amendment law in 1985 which made it clear that a computer programme is protected as literary work."[45] This approach was followed by the UK under its legislation on Copyright, Designs and Patents Act (CDPA).[46] This law was further modified and amended to take on board the EU Directive[47] provision of legal protection of databases.

Digital technology has also impacted on software copyrighted works. Some countries such as China have been blamed by some reports for software piracy. For instance it has been reported that by 2006 four in five software programs installed in China were illegally obtained.[48] The survey of 102 countries by the Bossiness Software Alliance, an industry group which has been lobbying for copyright protection, calculated that software piracy cost the legitimate sector nearly $40 billion in 2006.

The software and other related computer programs industry is suffering from unprecedented piracy. Piracy can occur in the following ways:

- Multiple Installations – This involves installing more copies than you have licensed.
- End-User Piracy – This is copying a program illegally or using unlicensed software in the work place.
- Client/Server Piracy – This is whereby a program is accessed by more end-users than the company has licensed.

---

45 Bainbridge D., *Introduction to Computer Law*, 4th Edition 2000 at page 4.

46 See Section 3 of the CDPA 1988.

47 EU Directive on the legal protection of databases (OJ[1996] L 77/20. The UK implemented and simplified enforcement of this Directive by enacting the Copyright in Databases Regulations 1997 and the amendments of CDPA.

48 See Daily News (Business Standard) on Technology, Tuesday, May 2007 at page 8. It was further reported that around 35% of Software installed in the same year were illegally obtained.

- Online Piracy – This is when software is downloaded from the web and installed but not paid for.

In *IBCOS Computers Ltd v. Barclays Mercantile Highland Finance Ltd,*[49] which involved writing of computer programs the Court had little difficulty in finding that there had been copying, showing the usefulness of including deliberate mistakes or redundant elements in copyright works. He also held that copyright subsisted not only in the *individual programs* but in the whole suite of programs as a compilation because the selection and arrangement of the programmes required *skill and judgement.* However in *Total Information Processing Systems Ltd v. Daman Ltd*[50] the court departed from this position by arguing that linking several programs together does not constitute an original compilation.

Furthermore, in *Autodesk Inc. v. Dyason*[51] , Autodesk Inc., a Californian company, owned the copyright in a computer program known as "AutoCAD". The program enabled a user to produce drawings which assisted in the drafting of architectural and engineering plans and designs. Autodesk Australia Pty. Ltd., a Victorian company, was the exclusive licensee of Autodesk Inc. In this case it was noted that the first appellant, Autodesk Inc., is a Californian company which owns the copyright in a computer program known as "AutoCAD". The AutoCAD program enables a user to produce drawings which assist in the drafting of architectural and engineering plans and designs. The letters "CAD" in AutoCAD stand for "computer assisted drafting". The second appellant, Autodesk Australia Pty. Ltd., is a Victorian company which is a wholly-owned subsidiary of the first appellant. Autodesk Australia Pty. Ltd. is the exclusive licensee of Autodesk Inc. throughout Australia with respect to its copyright in AutoCAD.

To avoid piracy of this kind, the appellants developed a hardware device, called an "AutoCAD lock", without which the AutoCAD program cannot run. Autodesk Inc. and Autodesk Australia Pty. Ltd. succeeded in their action in the Federal Court (Northrop J.) against Kelly and the Dyasons for infringement of copyright. In another similar case that is *Computer Edge Pty. Ltd. v. Apple Computer Inc*[52], the Court held by a majority that, whilst two Apple programs written in source code (i.e. programs devised by programmers in high level computer language) were literary works within the meaning of the Copyright Act and so were protected by copyright.

[49] [1994] FSR 275.

[50] [1992] FSR 171.

[51] [1992] HCA 2; (1992) 173 CLR 330 (12 February 1992). See also the discussion by lawyers on White SW Computer Law, IP & IT Lawyers, AUSTRALIA.

[52] *[1986] HCA 19; (1986) 161 CLR* 171 as discussed by lawyers on White SW Computer Law, IP & IT Lawyers, AUSTRALIA.

The question of intellectual property rights protection for computer software was raised during the 1970s, when the world realized that software products and other related computer programs are valuable commercial goods in their own right and not only as application technologies linked to the market for computer systems.[53] Some of the first countries that adopted IP legal framework to protect software from piracy were the US followed by Europe and Japan which introduced various frameworks of copyright laws which differed according to national legal context as well as differing cultural attitudes towards intellectual property.

The current legal framework in Tanzania might not be useful in the fight against online piracy on IP rights. Due to lack of effective legal framework that provide IPRs protection electronically, most authors, innovators or creators of those rights are vulnerable of online infringements and economic loss as pirates can just access and download free of cost electronically. For instance it has been learnt that the Indian Film Industry has been losing a lot of money to online piracy as unknown and unidentifiable people can just illegally access relevant sites watch and download movie clips and other copyrighted materials and store them electronically/online.[54]. While there is no doubt that the Copyright and Neighbouring Act in Tanzania does not have clear and specific provisions on management and control of online piracy and other related illegal activities, it is advised to use digital management and limited term licence on software with one package instalment for each computer.

7.3.3 International Initiatives on Digital Infringement of Intellectual Property Rights

At international level most international legal instruments provide for reciprocal protection on illegal copying and infringement between members through legal instruments. The most relevant legal instruments include the Berne Convention and the Universal Copyright Convention administered by WIPO and the 1961 Rome Convention. The Conventions are very relevant as far as copyright protection on software such as computer programs is concerned. The Berne Convention specifically obliges member states to provide effective standards of protection and rights to the authors and owners of copyright such as right to reproduce the work,[55] to perform the work publicly[56], to translate the work[57] and adapt the works among other restricted rights. In line with these conventions there is an umbrella

[53] See The Icfai Journal of CYBER LAW, 2007 Vol. 4.

[54] Ibid at pages 5-6.

[55] See Article 9.

[56] Article 11.

[57] Article 8.

agreement known as TRIPS Agreement which obliges members to provide national protection and comply with international conventions on intellectual property. While the Berne Convention 1886 seems to be based more on the protection of authors' rights (*droit de'auteur*) or literary and artistic works, the 1961 Rome Convention goes further to protect neighbouring rights or entrepreneur works[58] (*droit voisins*) including phonogram producers, performers and broadcasters. However both conventions share the same national treatment principle.

Initially the Berne Convention did not seem to reflect the impact of digital technology until it was modernized via other Conventions. The impact of digital technology on copyrighted works has been considered via Article 20 of the Berne convention, the WIPO Copyright Treaty 1996 and the WIPO Performances and Phonograms. These Conventions which appear to cope with digital technology grant exclusive rights to others, performers and producers in making their copies available to the public by wire or wireless means.

The relevant Article reads as follows:

> "*Performers shall enjoy the exclusive right of authorizing the making available to the public of their performances fixed in phonograms by wire or wireless means...*"[59]

The phrase "by wireless" suggests the protection of IP rights in line with computer technology. Furthermore, these Treaties address issues related to electronic rights management systems, computer programs and databases.[60] Article 4 of the WIPO Copyright Treaty 1996 is to the effect that the protection applies to computer programs in whatever mode or form of expression.

The phrase "anonymous and unpublished works" provided under Article 15 also suggests protection of IP rights related to computer technology. The WTO TRIPS Agreement also provides protection on intellectual property resulted or related to digital technology such as software and biotechnology products. Arguably The World Intellectual Property Organization (WIPO) took a further step as far as digital technology is concerned by adopting the WIPO Treaty and the WIPO Performances and Phonograms Treaty in 1996.

---

[58] Examples of these types of works include sound recordings, cable programs, broadcasts and the typographical format of published editions. *Droit d'auter* include works created by authors such as literary works that is to say books, music, art, and films.

[59] See Article 10 of the WIPO Performances and Phonograms Treaty 1996.

[60] See Articles 4, 5, 7, 11 and 12 of The WIPO Copyright Treaty 1996.

More importantly, the WIPO Copyright Treaty, 1996 has gone further in addressing the possible challenges and impact that has been brought by the development of digital technology. The Treaty seems to extend the protection of authors' right to copy to the right of dissemination of their copyrighted works online. The relevant Article is Article 8 which reads as follows:

> "*Without prejudice to the provisions of Articles 11(1) (ii), 11bis(1)(i) and (iiO, 11ter(1)(ii), 14(1)(ii) and 14bis(1) of the Berne Convention, authors of literary and artistic works shall enjoy the exclusive right of authorizing any communication to the public of their works, "by wireless means" including the making available to the public of their works in such a way that members of the public may access these works from a place and at a time individually chosen by them.*"

Furthermore, the WIPO Copyright Treaty further obliges the contracting parties to provide adequate legal protection and effective legal remedies against the circumvention of effective technology measures that are used by authors in connection with exercising their rights under the Treaty or the Berne Convention, that restrict acts, in respect of their works, which are not authorized by the authors concerned or permitted by the law.

The Treaties update the international protection of copyright and related rights significantly, not least with regard to the so called digital agenda which improves the means to fight and curb for physical and digital piracy worldwide.

Tanzania is among the members who have acceded these international conventions on IP.

However most laws related to IP in Tanzania and other EAC Member States do not fully reflect these Conventions and do not take into account computer technology. In addition Tanzania has not signed and ratified all these important Conventions which provide protection on intellectual property rights that are technology based. Furthermore, the country has not signed and ratified the Convention relating to the Distribution of Program-Carrying Signals Transmitted by Satellite of 1974 due to the fact that at that time broadcasting technology was still at infancy stage. It is hereby recommended that the country should sign these Conventions and other related conventions to ensure more copyright protection under this era of information society as we have already moved from analog to digital technology.

To promote strong protection of intellectual property available over digital networks the International Chamber of Commerce (ICC) has recommended the following points in some of their reports:

- Effective and timely implementation and enforcement of the WTO Agreement on Trade Related Aspects of Intellectual Property Rights (TRIPS)
- Timely ratification of the WIPO Copyright Treaty and the WIPO Performances and Phonograms Treaty[61]

On the other hand, the EU has responded to the technological developments by introducing the Cable and Satellite Directive. The Directive which seems to be more elaborative on the impact of digital technology, obliges members to create an effective legal framework that legally recognizes that copyright and related rights should include the right to authorize communication to the public by satellite.[62] Indeed the Directive has gone further in trying to solve jurisdictional problems on cyberspace by clearly defining the place where such communication can take place. The Copyright Law in Tanzania does not clearly give such right which is very important as far as Information and Communication Technology is concerned.

Furthermore, at the EU level the European Patent Convection (EPC) explicitly restricted the scope of software patents. For instance Article 52 of that Act provides that:

> "inventions not 'susceptible of industrial application,' which do not provide a concrete 'technical result', are not considered patentable under European Patent Office (EPO) rules.".

The Convention further provides for unpatentable subject matter which includes "schemes, rules and methods for performing mental acts, playing games or doing business and computer programs. Although the language sounds fairly resolute and still holds true for most software "as such", however the amendments to the Convention made in 1985 recognized that a program in combination with a machine may be patentable if the program causes the machine to operate in a new "technical" way or produces a "technical effect".

7.4 *Software Contracts and Copyright Licensing*

License is the most common method of acquiring computer software including computer programs. A licence is normally granted by the copyright owner to the applicant and the latter is normally given permission to use such copyrighted work in return for a fee while the owner still retains his copyright. Once a copyright owner grants a licence to a person, he may

---

[61] See An Inventory of Policy Positions and Practical Guidance by International Chamber of Commerce Commission on e-business, IT and Telecoms (EBITT), 1st Edition, 2007.

[62] See Articles 2 and 4 of the Directive, 1993. See also Lionel B. and Sherman B., *Intellectual Property Law* at pages 45-47.

permit that person to do an act within the scope of the owner's exclusive rights. The licence for most intellectual property rights may be expressed, implied or contractual depending on the agreement between the parties.[63]

License agreement and assignment of copyright on software presupposes contracts that in most cases impose duties on both parties associated with the intellectual property rights. To avoid copyright infringement it is necessary to obtain a licence in order to legally use software. This can be either exclusive licence or transfer of right to use through copyright assignment.

Assignment and licenses of copyrighted works and database rights are extensively provided for under the UK Copyright, Designs and Patents Act as follows:

(1) Copyright is transmissible by assignment, by testamentary disposition or by operation of law, as personal or moveable property.

(2) An assignment or other transmission of copyright may be partial, that is, limited so as to apply –

 (a) to one or more, but not all, of the things the copyright owner has that exclusive right to do;

 (b) to part, but not the whole, of the period for which the copyright is to subsist.

(3) An assignment of copyright is not effective unless it is in writing signed by or on behalf of the assignor.[64]

All contract issues related to terms of contracts warrants, indemnities liability and arbitrations are also common features under computer software and even hardware contraction be it assignment, granting licence or contract for writing software. Reference to the above discussion can be made from C*ircuit systems Ltd & Basten v. Zuken Redec UK Ltd*[65] *Orino Finance Ltd v. Crown Financial management (1994*) and *The Salvage Associate v. CAP Financial services Ltd.*[66]

On the other hand, the licence agreements for off -the-shelf software which also involve *sui generis* contracts the copyright owner normally

[63] See *Trumpet Software Pty Ltd v. Ozemail Pty* (Federal Court of Australia, Tasmania District Registry General Division, Unreported No. TG 21 of [1995]) whereby the Court discussed the position of non-contractual licences. In this case Trumpet produced software and distributed it as shareware. This arrangement constituted a licence binding the recipients of the software.

[64] See Section 90 of CDPA 1988.

[65] [1995] Const. LJ, 201. See also Section 16 and 17 of CDPA 1988. See also Bainbridge D., *Introduction to Computer Law*, 4th Edition 2000 at page 240

[66] [1995] FSR 654.

prefers to set out conditions of use of software and confirm copyright subsistence before granting licence to a purchaser.[67]

In most cases the contracts between software authorities and publishers, the terms of the licence is exclusive implying that the author will grant the publisher the sole right to deal with the software in return of agreed royalty payments. It appears that all these transactions involve the contract and sale of goods laws which unfortunately are not in tune with computer technology development in Tanzania. While it has been argued by different scholars that a contract for the acquisition of software alone cannot be a sale of goods contract as the title to the software is normally not transferred and computer programs or databases are not goods.[68] This can cause difficulties for Judges, magistrates and other lawyers to clearly interpret these contracts given the nature of the laws governing transactions in Tanzania.

The Copyright law in Tanzania provides for general rules of contracts on authors' work. This is reflected in the Copyright and Neighbouring Rights Act[69] as follows:

> *S.22 The general rules of the law of contracts shall apply to other questions relating to contracts for use of authors' works other than uses provided for under this section.*

Furthermore Section 23 provides for the contracts for commissioned works as follows:

"(1) Where a contract has been concluded for the use of a work to be created (commissioned work), the user shall be under the obligation to make a declaration concerning acceptance of the work within two months from the date on which the work was handed over, unless the law otherwise provides; if the user fails to make such a declaration within the time fixed by law, the work shall be deemed to have been accepted.

(2) Within the time open for acceptance of the work the user shall be entitled to return the same to the author for correction or amendments, such request shall be initiated by him in writing, taking into consideration the purpose for which the creation of the work was agreed upon. Justified requests for correction or amendments can be repeatedly made to the author, by fixing suitable dates therefore; if the author refuses to comply with such a request or the amended

[67] See in Bainbridge D., *Introduction to Computer Law*, 4th Edition 2000 at page 240.

[68] See in Bainbridge D., *Introduction to Computer Law*, 4th Edition 2000 at pages 70-75.

[69] See [CAP 218 R.E. 2002].

work does not qualify for the stipulated purpose either, the user may terminate the contract and shall be obliged to pay in consideration of the work done by the author an appropriate amount less than the remuneration agreed upon for the use of the work."

7.5 *Intellectual Property Rights and Electronic Publishing*

It is believed that the innovation and development of computer technology and other related technologies under the so called digital era has changed most traditional norms that are linked with copyright and other related rights.[70] Musical works, sound, data, broadcasting and communication can now be digitized and transmitted electronically to the public in real time in a cheap way. The world of digital technology has made possible for all manner of works such as information or data, literature, music, industrial design, etc. to be stored and made available electronically in a digital form using databases.[71] The Berne Convention in which Tanzania is among the signatories provides for the right of communication to the public whereby authors can enjoy such exclusive rights.

The Article stipulates as follows:

> "Without prejudice to the provisions of Articles 11(1), 11 bis (1)(i) and (ii),11 ter (1) (ii),14(1) (ii) and 14bis (1) of the Berne Convention, authors of literary and artistic works shall enjoy the exclusive right of authorizing any communication to the public of their works, by wire or wireless means, including the making available to the public of their works in such a way that members of the public may access these works from a place and at a time individually chosen by them."[72]. (*emphasis added*)

The advantage of publishing copyrighted work on the Internet which makes a work available to a wider audience might also attract misuse and infringement of copyrighted materials. This might be done through publication by means of multimedia and the Internet which in some cases has made ISPs liable for copyright infringement. There is no clear definition of the term "electronic publishing" in most states. Some scholars have argued that e-publishing includes publication by one of the following methods:

---

[70] Edgar T., "Multimedia Convergence and the future of copyright in Broadcasting", *The Uganda Law Journal 2003* at page 179.

[71] See Lloyd J.I., *Information Technology Law*, 2000.

[72] Article 8.

sale, rental or lending of a physical carrier containing a copy of the work or works in question- for example, CD-ROM, magnetic disk or magnetic tapes.[73]

It is very possible for three-dimensional works and moving images to be expressed digitally and, using appropriate software, displayed on screens, copied, manipulated or transmitted anywhere in the world "at the touch of a button".[74]

In line with these developments, the technology of multimedia (CD-ROM) can offer large storage for various copyrighted works such as literary works, film, music; photographs, etc. on a single disk or displayed on screen and made available to a wide audience at minimal expense.[75] A number of academic journals/articles, papers and books are now appearing on the Internet making authors vulnerable to IP infringement.

On the other hand, it is possible for some publishers of newspapers, magazines and other publications to publish or even reproduce articles from their publications in electronic form such as onto CD-ROMS or on a website. The rights to electronic reproduction for publishers need to be clarified through obtaining the written permission from authors before the original publication to avoid unnecessary legal concerns and disputes. The dispute and claim over the copyright infringement thorough e-publishing is sometimes common. This is reflected from the US case of *Tasini and Ors v. The New York Times Co and Ors.*[76] In this case a group of six freelance writers sued a number of publishers for copyright infringement arising either from reproducing their articles on a CD-ROM or an online text retrieval system. The Court found that the selling of the articles for inclusion in a data base of all articles featured in the original publications and the publication of these databases did not constitute a copyright infringement as the CD and the online service were a revision of the original published edition which was within the rights of the Publisher.

While it has been argued that some people view the Internet as equivalent to the public domain that can be freely copied and used, others argue that this view is misguided as some people depend on copyrighted works to earn their income.[77] Publications of some materials such as cable programs, broadcasting, and literary works which in most cases are copyrighted works can be made extensively by multimedia or the Internet and

---

[73] See Bainbridge D., *Introduction to Computer Law* 4th Edition 200 at pages 73-75.

[74] Ibid.

[75] Ibid.

[76] US Court of Appeal case, August 1997. See also Australian WHITE SW Computer Law. IP and IT Telecommunications Lawyers.

[77] Ibid.

accessed by a lot of people all over the world. While in Tanzania there is no specific provision under the Copyright and Neighbouring Act that could protect e-publishing of these copyrighted works, some countries like the UK provide for the effective protection of such works. For instance the CDPA, 1988 as amended clearly defines copying to include storage in any medium by electronic means and the protection goes on further by recognizing broadcasts, cable programs and other online publishing.[78]

The development of digital technology has made it possible for copyrighted work to be published and accessed electronically thus giving more benefits to computer users. On the other hand, technology has put authors at risk of losing their rights and earnings when their works are placed electronically via electronic databases given inadequate intellectual property cyber laws. This is reflected from the US case of *New York Times Company, inc al., petitioners v. Jonathan Tasini et al.*[79] This case concerned the rights of freelance authors and their publishers who published their works electronically in a database that was easily accessible to computer users. The authors complained about copyright infringement because of the inclusion of their articles in the databases. The computer program enabled computer users to search indexes and abstracts and be able to view each article, print or download it onto a disc. The joint authors filed a civil action alleging infringement of their copyrighted works facilitated by electronic publishers namely LEXIS/NEXIS and University Micro Films International (UMI) through placement and sale of their works including CD-ROMs in the NEXIS, NYTO and GPO databases. The authors sought declaratory and injunctive relief and damages. Under the US Copyright Act, as amended in 1976 copyright subsists in original works of authorship fixed in any tangible medium of expression. There was no doubt in this case that copyright subsisted in the collective work which vests in the collective author.

This case indicates the way freelance authors who experience significant copyright infringement are threatened by economic loss due to the digital revolution that has given publishers new opportunities to exploit authors' works. Similar incidences are being observed in Tanzania as many people are now able to view, print and download electronically published works for business while authors are not benefiting due to the lack of legal framework that reflects the new media or digital technology. These cases are not even reported in the courts or any institutions administering intellectual property rights. The best way for authors to benefit is to enter into a licence agreement with electronic publishers or any other publisher allowing them continued electronic reproduction of the author's work in return for fees or royalties.

[78] See Section 17 (2) of CDPA 1988. See also section 7 (1) of the CDPA 1988.

[79] Supreme Court of the United States, 121 S.Ct.2381 2001.

More legal problems might result from the widespread use of electronic storage and publishing of works. It is believed that the first case on the copyright nature of the Internet was heard in Scotland. It involved Web pages of Shetland Times on which extracts of news items appearing in printed editions of its newspapers were placed. In this landmark case it was claimed that the copyright in the headlines had been infringed[80] by including headlines in a cable program service.

There are also concerns on the advantages, disadvantages and dangers of using and e-publishing intellectual property rights in various websites over the world. For instance in The *Shetland Times Ltd v. Wills and Zetnews Ltd,* Shetland Times (ST) published a newspaper – The Shetland Times and the defendants published another newspaper – The Shetland News (SN). It was later reported that ST established a website on which they featured various articles from their paper. SN was also operating a website which had links to headlines on ST's site.[81] By using these links, readers bypassed the need to visit ST's home page and did not see the advertisements placed there. ST claimed infringement of copyright as SN reproduced the headlines from ST by providing the links and the text of the articles when it was displayed on the user's screen. An interim injunction preventing SN from using such links was granted by the Scottish Court on the basis that incorporation of links to headlines provided at another site constituted an infringement of copyright which subsisted in the headlines and articles as cable programs and the headlines alone as literary works.

Another relevant case to be considered at this juncture is *Ticketmaster Corporation v. Microsoft Corporation* (US Case) which highlights the legal consequences of using contents from another party's website without prior permission from the owner. The facts of this case as reported in a document on Intellectual Property, Information Technology & Telecommunications Lawyers from Australia are as follows;[82]

Microsoft linked one of its websites (http://seattle.sidewalk.com) to the Ticketmaster website (http://www.ticketmaster.com). Later on, Ticketmaster claimed that this linking enhanced the value of Microsoft's website while diminishing the value of Ticketmaster's website by, amongst other things: depriving Ticketmaster of advertising opportunities; publishing erroneous information; and diluting the value of Ticketmaster's relationship

---

[80] *Shetland Times ltd. V. Dr Jonathan Wills [1997] FSR 604.*

[81] See White SW, Computer Law, Intellectual Property, Information Technology & Telecommunications Lawyers on The Legal implications of E-commerce accessed at www.computerlaw.com on 8/9/2008.

[82] The Legal implications of E-commerce by White SW Computer Law, Intellectual Property, Information Technology & Telecommunications Lawyers accessed at www.computerlaw.com on 8/9/2008.

with MasterCard, a major advertiser. Ticketmaster raised several intellectual property misuse claims such as trade mark infringement and misleading and deceptive conduct. It has been argued that permission should be sought before establishing a link to a site to avoid possible legal ramifications even if there is good and reasonable intention of bringing more business to the linked site.[83]

Indeed under the current technological development it is possible for one to access and acquire Intellectual Property Rights materials to one's website from another website attracting legal battles on the possible misuse of IPRs. This is reflected by the US Judiciary on the complaint lodged by The Washington Post, Time Inc, Cable News Network, Times Mirror, Dow Jones and Reuters New Media as follows;

In February 1997, a complaint was lodged by The Washington Post, Time Inc, Cable News Network, Times Mirror, Dow Jones and Reuters New Media against Totalnews in the New York District Court. The plaintiffs claimed that Totalnews had, by "framing" and "linking" their content to the Totalnews site, amongst other things, misappropriated valuable commercial property, engaged in false representation and advertising, committed Federal Trademark dilution, infringed their registered trade and service marks and copyright (including domain names).[84]

7.6 *The Role of Internet Service Providers (ISPs) on e-publishing*

It is indisputable that ISPs play a big role for computer users to easily access materials published or stored electronically. In some cases ISPs have been held liable for copyright infringement due to the fact that they facilitate access to materials on the internet and gain financially. Moreover, through their agreements with persons to whom they provide access, ISPs have some measure of control, and they can tell their clients or users to adhere to copyright law and not to make infringing material available to others, whether on a web page or by transmitting by e-mail.

Internet Service Providers may be vulnerable for copyright infringement in a number of ways. Copyright in a work is infringed by a person who without the licence of the copyright owner does, or authorizes another to do, any of the acts restricted by the copyright.[85] It is possible that an ISP could be accused of being a joint infringer along with the client responsible for making infringing material available through its service. Joint infringement occurs

[83] Ibid.

[84] Ibid.

[85] See Section 16, UK-CDPA 1988.

where two or more persons act in concert pursuant to common design to infringe. ISPs do have some control as they can monitor and check what is being made available through their service. They can erase or block infringing material. The problem they have is that the sheer volume of material involved makes effective control and policing almost impossible. The best they can do is to warn their clients about the dangers of copyright infringement. Liability to ISPs applies to others who facilitate access to material over the Internet. Thus, libraries with online facilities or employers who allow or encourage employees to make use of the Internet should be careful as regards copyright infringement by their clients or employees. Education and vigilance seem to be the key words in respect of Internet.

In the US in the case of *Marobie-FL Inc v. National Association of Fire Equipment Distributors ("NAFED") and Anor,*[86] Marobie sued NAFED for, amongst other things, copyright infringement. NAFED's website contained clip art which was available to download. The Court found that NAFED's actions clearly constituted copyright infringement. Marobie also sued the internet service provider that hosted NAFED's website, but the Court found that there was no liability on the part of the service provider for providing the means to copy, distribute or display the copied clip art.

The EU has recognized some rights related to copyright that are subject to infringement electronically by introducing the Council Directive.[87] Article 8 of the Directive provides among other things "that member states shall provide for performers the right to authorize or prohibit the broadcasting by wireless means and the communication to the public..."

The East African Community can also adopt the same regional framework like the EU.

While some countries and regions like EU have introduced legal instruments that regulate e-commerce that aim at promoting business or transactions to be conducted electronically whereby goods and services are supplied electronically using distance selling contracts, there is no such legal framework within the EAC region.

7.7 *Commercial Exploitation of Intellectual Property Works Published Electronically*

In any case where someone needs to commercially exploit works published electronically (whether by cable, broadcast or in multimedia products) he can provide for access by means of a licence agreement.[88] This can be

[86] See SW Computer Law on IP and IT Telecommunications at www.computerlaw.com.au

[87] Council Directive 93/83/EEC of 1993 read together with Council Directive 93/98/EEC.

[88] Bainbridge D., *Introduction to Computer Law* 2000 at page 81.

done through granting of a licence to the publisher who will pay licence fees or royalties in return of permission to use the work. For instance a computer program-copyright owner can decide to grant exclusive right to a software publisher. A licence is always necessary because accessing the works will involve acts that are restricted by copyright. For example, retrieving a document from a database will require a copy to be made in the computer's memory and permission to do this must be obtained from the copyright owner. Any use of a work involving computer technology will usually require copies to be made even if they are only transient. It is an infringement of copyright to make a transient copy. Briefly copyright can be assigned through giving, selling, leasing or licensing. In Tanzania exclusive rights of authors of copyright works can enjoy and commercially exploit their economic rights through assignment and licensing under the Copyright and Neighbouring Act, 1999.[89] The relevant sections of the law provide that;

S. 16. Assignment of author's rights

"(1) The rights referred to in section 9 shall be assignable in the whole or in part.

(2) Any assignment of a right referred to in section 9 shall be in writing signed by the assignee.

(3) An assignment, in whole or in part, of any right referred to in section 9 shall not include or be deemed to include the assignment of any other rights referred to therein.

(4) Notwithstanding the provisions of section 21 the assignment of right in future work shall be void.

(5) The transfer of ownership of the original or of one or several copies of a work shall not imply the assignment of right in the work." (Ibid)

S. 17. Licences

"(1) The author or other owner of copyright may grant non-exclusive or exclusive licences to others to carry out, or to authorize the carrying out of certain specified acts covered by his or its economic rights.

(2) A non-exclusive licence shall entitle the licensee to carry out the act concerned concurrently with the author or other owner of copyright and concurrently with any other possible non-exclusive licensees.

[89] See the Copyright and Neighbouring Act [CAP 218 R.E 2002].

(3) An exclusive licence shall entitle the licensee to carry out the act concerned to exclusion of all others, including the author or other owner of copyright.

(4) A licence shall be considered to be exclusive only if the licensing contract contains words to that effect, or if the obvious intention of the contracting parties to that effect clearly result from the circumstances. The licensee shall have "*locus standi*" to sue in his own name for an infringement of any exclusive right conferred on him.

(5) Failure to mention the scope or ways and means of carrying out the acts for which a licence is granted shall be deemed to limit the licensee to such ways and means that are necessary for the purpose that may be reasonable presumed to be envisaged by the contracting parties when concluding the licensing contract.

(6) Only the economic right explicitly mentioned in the contract shall be considered part of the licence.

(7) Unless the licensing contract provides for a shorter period, the validity of the licence expires fifteen years after conclusion of the contract or, if this period is shorter, on the expiring of the contract an assignment on the basis of which the assignee has granted the licence.

(8) Any grant of exclusive licence, shall be valid only if it is the subject of written contract signed by the contracting parties." (Ibid)

The law further provides rights to transfer to the authors whereby the user shall be entitled to transfer the rights conferred on him under the contract for the use of the work only with the consent of the owner of copyright unless otherwise provided for by legislation.

Digital technology poses considerable challenges to copyright law specifically computer programs, databases and other multimedia products. All these forms of electronic publishing are capable of copyright subsistence and other IP Rights. In all cases, the individual works so made available may be subject to copyright. Copyright may also subsist, in the broadcast or cable program, database and other compilation. It is also important to look at the potential role and liability of Internet Service Providers (ISP) for copyright infringement.

7.8 *Relevance of Intellectual Property Law under the Information Society Era*

Intellectual property law is a very important area of law because it is the key protecting tool in the era of digital technology which is made up of various things related to innovation in computer hardware and software and other intangible things such as ideas, signs, inventions and data or information. There is no doubt that in an information society era, intellectual property rights have become the essential legal framework protecting the information assets of rights-holders, in the form of trademarks, copyright and database rights or patents.[90]

The basic principle of intellectual property protection is to reach an acceptable compromise between granting incentives to the inventor through temporary monopoly rights on the commercial exploitation of his invention and favouring the diffusion of knowledge by compelling him to disclose the principles of his invention. In the option of software protection through copyright, the problem is that copyright protects expression of ideas and not the ideas themselves.[91] This approach is in line with fair competition rules for the purposes of protecting consumers and others against restrictive trade practices and other unfair terms. However ideas that are not in the form of an expression but lead to innovations might be protected under patent rights.

Furthermore, intellectual property law can be used to regulate the creation, use and exploitation of mental or creative labour including works related to Information Technology.[92] IPRs are promptly protected through laws that create private property rights in creative endeavors and innovations for the purposes of assuring control over their commercial exploitation while at the same time providing rewards and incentives for the creators/innovators. Examples of IP rights that afford protection to innovative and creative endeavors include copyright, patent, trademarks or service marks and designs. These rights provide a basic framework of protection from piracy and plagiarism of computer programs and works created using a computer.[93]

7.8.1 Usefulness of Intellectual Property Rights to the creators/inventors and commercial exploitation of technology

The rights associated with intellectual property are of immense importance to those involved in the development, exploitation and use of computer hardware, software and other applications. Intellectual Property Rights

[90] See UNCTAD on Legal Aspect of E-Commerce 2006.

[91] See The Icfai Journal of CYBER LAW, 2007 Vol II.

[92] See Sherman B. and Leonen B., *Intellectual Property Law 2002* at page 2. See also Article 2 of WIPO Convention of 1967 which provides that Intellectual Property includes the rights relating to literary, artists and scientific works, performances and performing artists, photographs and broadcasts, invention in all fields of human endeavour, industrial designs, trademarks and commercial names and designation.

[93] Bainbridge D., *Introduction to Computer Law,* 4th Edition 2000 at page 7.

protection gives an incentive to creators and innovators to develop knowledge-based businesses. IPRs/ICT/Computer Law provides the manner in which Computer Technology affects the relationship between individuals in terms of rights and duties. On the other hand, IP endows rights on the owners of the works of copyright or proprietors of patents to exploit their works or inventions while imposing a correlative duty on others not to do certain acts in relation to the subject matter of the rights. Consequently, both patent and copyright seek to protect creative or intellectual effort by conferring an exclusive right on the owner in respect of the exploitation of such protected works.[94] Initially copyright was seen as the most relevant shield on computer technology products. However as technology develops with more inventions, other IPRs are also becoming very useful tools on computer technology products.

On the other hand, data protection law imposes obligations on data users and grants rights to individuals who have their personal data stored on computer by others. IP gives rights that protect creative works, inventions and commercial goodwill under computer technology. Indeed, copyright is the most important subject as far as computer technology is concerned as most things seen on computer screens and other related devices are copyrighted works. Patent which in most cases is termed as a statutory right that gives monopoly and exclusive right to the owner to use inventions is the second important area of IP that can be useful in the deployment of IT and protection of technology products. Generally the patent system is mainly concerned with the practical application of innovative concepts that require some physical end product consisting of the subject matter of protection.[95] In this case it is important to note that ICT products mostly depend on computer software for their operation. Computer software consists of instructions recorded in intangible form on a storage device. Computer software and other related applications can be effectively protected through intellectual property rights such as copyright and patents.

The question of patentability that is novelty,[96] inventive step and industrial applicability are the main pillars and prerequisites for obtaining patent rights. Patents like trademarks are granted nationally whereby the owner deserves a statutory monopoly over a defined area of technology for a period of time e.g. 20 years.

Unlike copyright, patent protects ideas themselves. Although in the eyes of the law it appears that patent seems to be the least relevant IPR to

[94] Lloyd I.J., *Information Technology Law*, 3rd Edition 2000 at page 305.

[95] Ibid at page 308.

[96] See *Quante Ltd v. Spaceward Microsystems* [1990] RPC 83 and www.patent.gov.uk/dpatents/canipub.html. See also Lloyd I.J., *Information Technology Law*, 3rd Edition 2000 at page 308.

an e-commerce/e-business, however the growth of e-commerce and e-patent in other developed jurisdictions like Europe and US have made patent to be one of the hottest topics in e-commerce.[97] Patent protection is important to ensure e-commerce businesses benefit from the invention they make.

7.8.2 Copyright and Information Technology

Copyright is the property right subsisting in original literary, dramatic, musical and artistic works including secondary, entrepreneurial or derivative works. Some authors have argued that copyright is the term used to describe the area of intellectual property law that mainly regulates the creation and use of cultural goods such as literary works including computer programs.[98] Copyright protects expressions of ideas put into some permanent form (*fixed, written or recorded*). In line with this, there are moral rights which grant the author the right to be identified as the author of the work and the right to object to derogatory treatment of the work. Section 3 of the UK Copyright, Designs and Patent Act 1988 provides that for copyright to subsist in a computer program it must be original and it must be recorded. This implies that the work of the author must be the result of his skill, labour and judgment as highlighted by Petrson J. in *University Press of London v. University Tutorial Press Ltd.*[99] Section 3 (2) of the UK Copyright, Designs and Patents Act (CDPA) provides that "copyright does not subsist in a literary work, until it is recorded, in writing or otherwise". The UK CDP seems to compliment the EU Council Directive on Copyright (Computer Programs), which provides that "only the expression of a computer program is protected and that ideas and principles which underlie any element of a program, including those which underlie its interfaces, are not protected by copyright under this Directive".

The said Directive clearly states that the author of a computer program shall be the natural person or group of natural persons who has created the program with exception that where a computer program is created by an employee in the execution of his duties or following the instructions given by his employer, the employer exclusively shall be entitled to exercise all economic rights in the program so created, unless otherwise provided by contract.[100] The unauthorised reproduction, translation, adaptation or transformation of the form of the code in which a copy of a computer

---

[97] Lloyd I.J., *Information Technology Law*, 3rd Edition 2000 at pages 308-375.

[98] Sherman B.B.L., *Intellectual Property Law* 2002 at page 27. See also P. Goldstein, "copyright" (1990-1) 38 Journal of The Copyright Society of the USA 109.

[99] [1916] 2 CH 601. Compare this position of UK with Tanzania under Copyright and Neighbouring Act and the US on the doctrine of "Sweat of brow" as highlighted in *Feist Publications Inc. v. Rural Telephone Service Co Inc (1991) 111 S Ct 1228).*

[100] See Articles 1 and 2 of Copyright (Computer Programs), Council Directive, 14/05/1991, No. 91/250.

program has been made available constitutes an infringement of the exclusive rights of the author. Remedies for copyright and database infringement on cyberspace are not different to infringement on any other medium. The likelihood problem might be the place to sue where infringement has occurred electronically given the fact that copyright is limited to national boundaries, while cyberspace has unlimited boundaries.

It is quite common to see some people commissioning and engaging some experts in Information and Communication Technologies to create Internet sites. The legal issues that are likely to arise include ownership of IPRs that are associated with creativeness and innovations in designing those valuable sites such as websites. Generally, the developer of the site will in most cases be the owner of intellectual property rights such as copyright unless parties entered and signed terms of copyright assignment.[101] Otherwise there might be legal consequences for one party to copy and use creative copyrighted materials and designs found in the designed website without prior permission from the author.

7.8.3 The development of digital technology on Intellectual property status

During the 20th Century, the development of the information technology era highly impacted on intellectual property rights. Intellectual property was regarded as a major tool for protecting creations and innovations which emerged due to the development of technology. Copyright is the most important area of intellectual property that protects software such as computer programs, databases and other related programs. Most things seen in the computer face (software) are protected by copyright. Computer software or programs are regarded as literary works hence copyrighted works except where they lead to technical contribution. One can examine the relevance of copyright to computer software in two main areas. Copyright is very vital in the protection of material on a website on e-commerce such as written material e.g. advertisement – literary work, images – original images such as drawings, graphic charts, maps, diagrams, and photographs are protected as artistic works.[102] Copyright can further protect the layout of a webpage, music and audio visuals and databases where investment, skill and labour is applied. It has been observed that the underlying difficulty with protecting software under copyright law is that the expression readily transforms into an embodiment that is a concrete, tangible, and useful process which typically falls within the exclusive province of patent

[101] See White SW Computer Law, Intellectual Property, and Information Technology & Telecommunications Lawyers at www.computerlaw.com.au.

[102] See Turban E., *E-Commerce* 2002 at pages 144-145.

law. However, certain works of software may not be sufficiently "concrete" and "tangible" to be protected under patent.[103]

The first concern is the protection of computer software and, in particular, computer programs and databases from unauthorized copying while the second area is related to the works of various types which have been created by or with the aid of a computer or are stored and accessed or made available electronically.[104] Whilst Copyright law protects computer software, whether it includes programs, databases, computer files or printed documentation, patent law protects new and inventive forms often incorporated software.[105] Computer software includes computer programs, databases and other related programs. Certain acts restricted by copyright under computer programs include copying, issuing copies to the public and making an adaptation of course with an exception of "fair dealing". The case of *IBCOS Computers Ltd v. Barclays Mercantile Highland Finance Ltd*[106] illustrates more on the relevance of copyright law on computer programs and copyright infringement with regard to computer software.

The innovation of computer technology has raised some legal questions as to the authors and owners of works generated or produced by computers and other related devices. For instance in works produced by or with the aid of a computer, human skill can reside in the person who enters information into the computer to produce the output or in the programmer who writes the program being used or a combination of programs. Section 178 of the CDPA defines a work as 'computer-generated' when it is generated by a computer in circumstances such that there is no human author of the work. Works created with the aid of computer, human skill can reside in the person who enters information into the commuter to produce the program. In *Express Newspapers plc v. Liverpool Daily Post & Echo plc*[107] grids of random selected by computers were held to be protected by copyright.

While the UK CDPA[108] clearly recognizes and protects works produced by or with the aid of a computer, the Copyright and Neighbouring Act in Tanzania is unclear and silent on these types of works. In such a situation it is difficult to determine the author or owner of the computer generated works and the works produced with the aid of computers. In most cases works involving computers can be divided into 2 or 3 categories; namely;

---

[103] See The Icfai Journal of CYBER LAW, 2007, Vol. II.

[104] See Bainbridge D., *Introduction to Computer Law*, 4th Edition 2000 at page 23.

[105] See Sec.1 of the UK CDPA 1988. Read also Article 5 TRIPS and other International Instruments on Copyright e.g. WIPO Treaty, Berne Convention 1886, Rome Convention 1961, Universal Copyright Convention 1952.

[106] [1994] FSR 275.

[107] [1985] 1 WLR 1089.

[108] See Section 9(3) and 178.

works created using computers, works created by computer and intermediate works.[109]

Furthermore, it is pertinent to consider the question of employee-employer relationship and freelance computer programmers in determining the authors and owners of copyright. The question of control, contract of service and contract for service are relevant determining factors as to the ownership of copyrighted works. Section 61 of the Labour Institutions Act of Tanzania provides for the presumption of employment. The law tries to answer the question as to who is an employee as follows:

"61. For the purposes of a labour law, a person who works for, or renders services to, any other person is presumed, until the contrary is proved, to be an employee, regardless the form of the contract, if any one or more of the following factors is present";

(a) the manner in which the person works is subject to the control or direction of another person

(b) the person's hours of work are subject to control or direction of another person

(c) in case the person is working for an organisation, the person is part of that organisation

(d) ...

(e) ...

(f) the person is provided with the tools of trade or work equipment by the other person; or

(g) the person only works for or renders services to one person. (Footnote material: The Labour Institution Act, 2004)

Generally, where the work is created by an employee in the course of his employment the author and owner of that work will be an employer unless otherwise stated.

Having realised that computer programs are not well protected by the current legislation the EU made important initiatives in protecting copyrighted works such as computer programs through enactment of Computer Directive Program which protects computer programs via *sui generis right*, copyright and patent.[110] The term of duration compliments with the Berne Convention that is life of the author and fifty years. Furthermore, EU made another great step forward in the field of Information Technology

---

[109] Bainbridge D., *Introduction to Computer Law*, 4th Edition 2000 at page 68.

[110] Copyright (Computer Programs) Council Directive, 14/05/1991, No.91/250 which came into force in January 1993.

by passing another important Directive that protects electronic databases, copyright and provides *sui generis right* in the database.[111] On the other hand, Article 10 of The TRIPS agreement provides for the protection of computer programs and data. The article stipulates that computer programs whether they are in source code shall be protected as literary works under the Berne Convention.

The 1996 WIPO Copyright Treaty which brings the application of traditional exclusive right within cyberspace environment also equally protects computer software or computer programs as copyrighted works.[112] For instance Article 4 provides that

"Computer programs are protected as literary works within the meaning of Article 2 of the Berne Convention. Such protection applies to computer programs, whatever may be the mode or form of their expression." Article 8 of The 1996 WIPO Copyright Treaty came into place to secure the Berne Convention. Article 8 of the Berne Convention provides that:

> "... authors of literary and autistics shall enjoy the exclusive right of authorizing any communication to the public of their works, by wire or wireless means..."(*emphasis added*)

The 1996 WIPO Copyright Treaty came into place at the right time to secure the Berne Convention which was being affected by digital technology.

Unlike East African Community countries (Tanzania, Kenya and Uganda), the European Union has recognized the importance of harmonized protection of intellectual property rights such as copyright in the fast growing information society given the rapid impact of technology. This has been done via the Directive on the harmonisation of certain aspects of copyright and related rights in the information society.[113]

An effective harmonized legal framework on copyright and related rights, through increased legal certainty with technology neutrality and while providing for a high level of protection of intellectual property, will foster substantial investment in creativity and innovation, including network infrastructure. This will in turn lead to growth and increased competitiveness of the industries in our region, both in the area of content provision and information technology as highlighted under the EU Directive (supra). The Directive develops and updates principles in the preceding Directives and places them in the context of digital technology.

111 Database Directive (1996).

112 Adopted by the Diplomatic Conference on 20 December 1996.

113 Directive 2001/29/ec of the European Parliament and the Council of 22 May 2001 on the harmonization of certain aspects of copyright and related rights in the information society.

Technology is always changing dramatically while legal instruments to cope with these changes are not coping with technological changes. Even the adoption of the two WIPO Treaties in 1996 that has taken into account some concerns on digital technology, fall short of keeping up with technology. WIPO needs to do more to keep pace with these rapid changes in technology. Since the enactment of Copyright and Neighbouring Act of Tanzania in 1999, which has little to do with the legal implication of digital technology on copyright, many changes have taken place in the copyright field, as a result of digital technology. Composers, artists, writers, authors and other copyright owners are not very confident to create, distribute and control the use of their works within the digital environment. As the revolution of digital technology takes place rapidly, the scope of the subject matter for copyright protection is also expected to expand rapidly.[114] While the economic importance of computer technology products such as software, multimedia has been growing very fast, copyright protected material seem to be seen as one of the main protection tools in e-commerce and other related digital transactions.

There is no doubt that technological development is multiplying and diversifying the vectors for creation, production and exploitation in our country which necessitates the creation of new legal concepts for the protection of intellectual property to respond adequately to digital technological challenges and economic realities such as new forms of exploitation. Adequate legal protection of IP under the information society is necessary to safeguard and guarantee the creators reward and encourage more innovations, creativeness and investment.

The EU also aimed to promote and develop e-commerce by enacting Electronic Commerce Directive 2000 which encourages business online and protection of copyrighted works online by providing liability for ISPs.

7.8.4 Relevance of Patent on computer technology and e-commerce

A patent is a limited monopoly on innovations or inventions that is granted for 20 years in return for the disclosure of technical information for scientific and industrial reasons.[115] Unlike copyright which does not protect ideas which are not expressed except fixed works whose right arises automatically, patents protect ideas and can only be granted where the applicant satisfies registration procedures. The patent must contain almost

[114] See the WIPO Report on the Copyright in Digital Era.

[115] See Sherman B.B.L., *Intellectual Property Law* 2002 at page 315.

four key parts namely an abstract, description of the invention, claims and drawings. These are the key components and essential parts of the patent that need to be submitted by the applicant of patent right to any patent office. Patents cannot be granted on excluded subject matters unless they meet the legal requirement related to patentability subject matters.

Generally, most products such as software and other related computer programs are protected under the copyright regime due to the fact that these are literary works. Earlier the only relevant area for protecting information related products such as software and technology activities was copyright. At that time software was seen as an art or craft rather than an industrial process or product.[116] Since the 1970s the world has witnessed the legal implications of technology on IP and the role of patent law with regard to computer related inventions. However the development of technology has greatly influenced patent to be granted on software and other related applications on certain conditions. Patent law generally provides protection for a "process" or "machine" assuming it meets the arduous standards of patentability, including novelty and utility. It has been argued that the major problem with applying patent law to software is that software often can be reduced to mathematical calculations or manipulations of data, bringing it dangerously close to "abstraction".[117] The question is how to grant patent to computer programs "as such".

Some have also argued that trade secret law may be the only body of intellectual property law that does not pose substantial new hurdles with respect to software.[118] Indeed, trade secret law is one of software's most useful forms of protection as it generally provides protection for almost any form of knowledge so long as it is not "general knowledge". Trade secret law is particularly useful in aiding the protection of high level source code (e.g., Java, C++, and BASIC) which has the benefit of almost built-in secrecy such that it can remain substantially independent of the machine code into which it is ultimately compiled and distributed.[119]

At this juncture one might refer to some precedents on this matter by examining the two decisions namely *IBM*/Computer Programs (T935/97) and *IBM* (T1173/97) as cited by Lloyd J. in his book *Information Technology Law*[120] While the first case concerned a method of allowing information in a data-processing system that involved software, the latter related

---

[116] Lloyd J.I., *Information Technology Law*, 2000 at pages 3006-3007.

[117] See The Icfai Journal of CYBER LAW, 2007 Vol. 2.

[118] Ibid.

[119] Ibid.

[120] Ibid.

to resource recovery in a computer system.[121] The Technical Appeal Board observed the scope of the exclusion of computer programs as such under the law. It was decided that computer programs as such were not patentable due to the lack of technical character but software or computer programs that show technical contribution to the solution of technical problems are patentable.

However the question is how to determine that a computer program has a technical character. Some scholars have suggested that this legal question can be solved by working at the technical effects or the solutions to a technical problem.[122]

In the foregoing two cases it was noted that the patentability of a computer program will depend on the fact that the product resulted in additional technical effect that went beyond the normal physical interaction between the program or software and the computer hardware where the program operated.[123] However the determination of the technical contribution as a pre-requisite for accepting or refusing patent application might be difficult in developing countries like Tanzania due to the low level of the development of technology. This has also sometimes been the case even in well developed countries like the UK, US, etc. as observed by the British Comptroller in Fujitsu's application for patent.[124]

Indeed the IBM case seems to be the landmark case as far as the protection of information technology products is concerned. Our courts in Tanzania and EAC generally, might benchmark and follow this approach. This could well be supported by the amendment of legal regime governing patents in Tanzania to accommodate the development of technology. The current patent law and regulations in Tanzania and other EAC countries were enacted before the current development of technology. The Patent Act 1987 needs to be reformed to take on board all technological developments by considering the patentability of software and other related applications where technical effect are proved.

Technical subjects that have recently attracted a lot of patent interest include methods of ensuring transmission and, in particular, payment methods as well as technology for managing the load amongst the connected computers that form the basis of the Internet. There had been a great deal of legal debate as to whether software and other related computer programs should be patented or copyrighted. Judicial interventions have tried their level best to cure this problem. It is worth mentioning the

---

[121] See Bentley L. and Sherman B., *Intellectual Property Law* 2002 at pages 390-391.

[122] Ibid at pages 390-392.

[123] Ibid. See also IBM 1935/97 and Article 52 (2) and (3), EPC.

[124] [1996]. See also Bentley L. and Sherman B., *Intellectual Property Law* 2002 at page 375.

land mark case from US namely *Computer Associates v. Altai*[125] as cited by Lloyd Ian in *Information Technology Law* at page 306 whereby the Court of Appeal had this to argue:

> "*General we think that copyright registration, with its indiscriminating availability – is not ideally suited to deal with highly dynamic technology of computer science...patent registration with its exacting up-front novelty and non obviousness requirements, might be the more appropriate rubric of protection of intellectual property of this kind.*"[126]

On the other hand, The TRIPS Agreement seems to provide room for the patentability of computer programs or software related inventions. This can be echoed from Article 27 which stipulates that:

> "*patents shall be available for any inventions whether products or processes in all fields ... enjoyable without discriminating as to ... field of technology*".

The pivot role of patent on software or computer program based on technical contribution can also be seen under e-commerce whereby patents might be granted to software or computer program products that are distributed online over the Internet.

Following the IBM decision, the UK has made changes on its legal framework and guidelines to accommodate the patentability of computer program invention related on the basis of technical effect as required by EPO.[127]

There is now an exception to industrial applicability on patentability. This is in relation to software and other computer programs where there is a substantive technical effect/contribution.[128] While initially computer programs and other software were not patentable on the grounds of excluded subject matter, software developers are now comfortable of patenting their software or computer programs provided they are able to prove technical

---

[125] 982 F 2d 694.The first case in which software was involved concerned Slee and Application *[1966] RPC 194.* as cited *by* Lloyd J.I., *Information Technology Law.* See also Burroughs Application [1974], IBM Application [1980].

[126] 982 F 2d 694 at 712.

[127] See Lloyd J.I., *Information Technology Law* 2000.

[128] Refer to European Patent Convention and CDPA UK. See also *Fujitsu Application, The Times March 14, 199.* Lloyd J.I. in his book *Information Technology Law* argues that the report of the Parliamentary Office of Science and Technology on Patents, Research and Technology indicates that between 1990 and 2000 the European Patent Office granted around 10,000 patents for software related patents while refusing 100 applications.

contribution.[129] However there is no doubt that patent application and registration is so demanding with and costly as compared to copyright which arises automatically and can be protected equally anywhere in the world under the Berne Conventions and other related international conventions. In *Interactive Gift Express v. Computer service, 2001* the court ruled that patent would not cover web-based businesses although the court of appeal reversed the decision allowing patent in such inventions. Furthermore, in *the British Telecommunications v. Prodigy Communications, 2001* web-based hypertext linking was held to qualify for patent protection.

The European Patent Office (EPO) came up with guidelines on the mode of determining whether software or computer programs show substantive technical contribution. These approaches require courts or patent registry offices to consider whether technical means are used to produce a result or solve a problem and whether the invention produces a technical result.[130] Some European countries courts like the UK have followed the EPO approach irrespective of great criticism.

Indeed the adoption of Trade Related Aspects of Intellectual Property Rights (TRIPS Agreement) Protocol related to the General Agreement on Tariffs and Trade (GATT) has cemented and simplified the effective protection of Intellectual property rights including technology products such as computer programs and semi conductor products or integrated circuits. This is reflected from the relevant Article of this international legal instrument:

...available for any inventions whether products or processes, in all fields of technology ... *(provided they meet patentability requirements)* ... patent shall be available and patent rights shall be enjoyable without discrimination as to the place of invention, *the field of technology...*[131] (*emphasis added*)

This provision of the Article has opened reasonable "Pandora's box" for patent rights on software-related inventions.

Although Tanzania has signed and ratified the TRIPS Agreement its implementation has not yet started effectively in some areas of patents whereby the effective implementation will start from 2016.

---

[129] In *Merril Lynch's Application [1989] EPOR 561-606* The Court dismissed the application for Patent for Computer program on the ground that the contribution made by the invention was limited to the field of business hence excluded subject matter which is unpatentable. See also Bently & Sherman, *Intellectual Property Law* at pages 373-375.

[130] See Wilson C.A. Nutshell on Intellectual Property Law at page 10. See also EPO Decision from Viacom's Application 1987.

[131] Articles 27 and 5. See also Lloyd JI, *Information Technology Law* at page 314.

Some Judicial decisions have indicated that even encryption methodologies are patentable because they have a technical effect and make contributions involving certain technical problems.[132]

On the other hand, while the US patent system seems to take a liberal attitude towards patentability of business methods and technology, the Swedish Patent and Registration Office and the EU or European Patent Office do not indicate such generous attitude when it comes to affording software and methods patent protection.[133]

Software and other related computer program inventions might be under vulnerable challenge in Tanzania due to lack of legal framework that recognize these products as part of patent system. The patent system in Tanzania is governed by Patent (Registration) Act[134] which does not reflect the development of computer technology on software products. Sections 8, 9, 10 and 11 provide for patentability of an invention that is a novelty, inventive step and industrial application. For instance computer programs and other related applications might not meet these requirements.

Practically the Business Registration and Licensing Agency of Tanzania (BRELA) the institution that is mandated to regulate and licence industrial property rights has never received any application of patent on software given the nature of the current laws. To complicate matters more, the term technical contribution does not appear in the law. Software and other related computer programs might get a little shield from the Copyright and Neighbouring Act. However there is room for protecting software-related inventions under patent or copyright at international level under the above mentioned International Conventions and Protocols if signed ratified and domesticated by Tanzania.

The legal system on patent in the UK has now recognized the importance of patenting software related inventions on the ground of technical contribution. This has been ignited by the judicial decisions such as VICOM, IBM, etc. and the EU Patent Convention. As argued by Lloyd in his book *Information Technology Law* one of the main issues in these cases especially IBM was to determine when a computer program constituted more than one abstract creation and exhibited a technical character in its own right, independent of linkage with a tangible object.[135]

Consequently the court argued that

> "*...a patent may be granted ... in every case where a program for a computer is the only means, or one of the necessary means, of obtaining*

[132] See *Badger Co.v. Application, [1970] RPC 36 and IBM Corp application [1980] FSR 564.*

[133] Law and Information Technology Swedish Views, Swedish ICT Commission Report at page 117.

[134] Cap 217 [R.E.2002].

[135] Lloyd J.I., *Information Technology Law*, 2000 at page 364.

technical effect achieved by the intentional function of a computer itself under the influence of the program at hand"[136]

This means that where computer programs or software-related inventions are able to produce technical effect or contribution within the meaning of Article 52 (1) of European Patent Convention there is no reason for refusing the patent application.

Computer technology patents may affect competition laws whereby consumers are charged more for patented products. Compulsory licensing for inventions related to health care or pharmaceutical products is one way of controlling abuse of patent monopoly.

7.8.5 Relevance of trademarks and service marks to computer technology

A trademark or service mark can be defined as a sign, symbol or distinguishing feature that distinguishes the goods or services of one undertaking from those of another undertaking.[137] The EU Council Regulation[138] defines Community Trade Mark to include "signs that are capable of being represented graphically, particularly words, including personal names, designs, letters, numerals, the shape of goods or of their packing, provided that such signs are capable of distinguishing the goods or services of one undertaking from those of other undertakings." Trade and service marks might also be an important area in the development and commercial exploitation of ICT. There are some examples of trademarks that can be observed in the computer industry namely *Acer,* Motorola, IBM, TOSHIBA, SONY, Microsoft, *HP, Dell,* etc. Historically trademarks have been legally protected due to the fact that they operate in public interest as they provide crucial information related to the goods required by the consumers as well as increasing the efficiency of the market.[139]

As part of Intellectual Property Rights (IPRs), trademarks constitute property rights conferring the proprietor the exclusive right to certain forms of use of the mark.[140] Before the development of digital technology and the rise of www or .com trademarks had a very limited role in ICT. With the emergence of Internet domain names trademarks are very

---

[136] See pages 871-877.

[137] Reed C., *Internet Law, Text and Materials* 2000 at page 41.

[138] Article 4 Council Regulations (EC) No. 40/94. See also Section 2 of Article 15 of TRIPS Agreement.

[139] See Benly L. and Sherman B., *Intellectual Property Law*, 2002 at pages 662-663.

[140] Lloyd I.J., *Information Technology Law,* 3rd Edition 2000 at pages 456-460. See also section 2 of the UK Trademark Act 1994 compare with Trade and Service Mark Act of Tanzania CAP 326 [R.E.2002].

relevant as many other forms of products and services under IT will benefit from this area of industrial property law. The development of e-commerce which has facilitated the sale and supply of goods or services online has relatively created a relationship between trademarks and internet domain names. Trade and service marks are becoming more significant in the ICT industry, particularly in their use on the Internet as domain names.

With the advent of Internet many, companies are opening their business online using trademarks or domain names. Like any other form of product, it is also possible for IT related products to seek protection under trademark law and the law of passing off. Conversely companies using ITV, IPP TVT, Coca-Cola, and Airlines, etc. will opt to register their domain names as a trademark under cyberspace. There are many Internet related trade or service mark and domain name disputes.

Where someone registered a domain name incorporating someone's trademark then he might be liable for trademark infringement. One of the key barriers in e-commerce is the protection of trademarks. Many times the domain name also includes the trademark of the company (e.g. Microsoft) by taking the TM and adding a Top Level Domain (TLD) designator (such as .com, .net. However, there is no requirement for a domain name to be a trademark. Trademarks are not only relevant to domain names but also online advertisements through various websites. Due to the massive proliferation of websites, there is a great deal of competition to attract potential visitors to a site in preference to numerous other sites which may have similar information. One method used is to include "meta tags" on the pages, which constitute your site. Meta tags are a form of computer code, which is analyzed by the search engines, but not visible in the normal viewing layout of a web site page.[141] Commonly, meta tags include subject headings which you anticipate people will use to find the information contained on your website. Suffices to say few things on trademark and domain names will discussed at this stage as this will be discussed in depth on the topic on domain names in the forthcoming pages.

At international level there are legal instruments on trademarks such as The Paris Convention, TRIPS Agreement, Madrid Agreement on International Registration of Marks 1891 and the Madrid Protocol 1989. For instance Section 2 (1) Article 15 of TRIPS provides that:

Any sign, or any combination of signs, capable of distinguishing the goods or services of one undertaking from those of other undertakings, shall be capable of constituting a trade mark. Article 16 confers exclusive

[141] See White SW Computer law presentation in www.computerlaw.com as accessed on 9/8/2008.

rights to the owner of registered trade mark. See also Articles 6, 7, 8 9 and 10 of the Paris Convention for the Protection of Industrial Property.[142]

7.9 *The Development of the Law of Confidence and its Relevance to Intellectual Property Rights*

7.9.1 A conceptual analysis of the law of confidence

The law of confidence is mainly concerned with the protection of qualifying information secrets whether they are trade secrets, secrets of a personal nature or concerning the government.[143] It is a form of protection which can also be used widely for the protection of certain intellectual property rights such as copyright in software or computer programs. This branch of intellectual property law can also be found on implied or express obligation of confidence, contract law with a duty of confidentiality and employee confidentiality. The relationship between employers and employees are in most cases governed by express terms incorporated under the contract which bind both parties to keep certain information confidential. Some of the relevant authorities to substantiate this argument include *Denco Ltd v. Joinson*[144] which was also cited by Bainbridge D. in his book *Introduction to Computer Law* whereby an employee who had a right to access to certain information in his employer's computer system allowed another employee to illegally access parts of the restricted computer system. The employee was summarily dismissed. When he went to the court to challenge his dismissal the court blessed the dismissal.

In *Redrock Holdings Pty Ltd & Hotline Communications Ltd v. Hinkley*[145] which involved computer software for class library the key legal issue discussed was whether class library and Internet software written by an employee in the course of his employment belongs to him. The other issues to be determined were whether there was a contract of employment or a contract for employment and how to control a highly skilled and professional employee. Furthermore, the court analysed some landmark legal issues as to whether or not a software developer is free to develop a software program for a client that is similar to a program which was previously developed by them for another client.

In addition, the court argued on the criteria to be used in determining the owner of the copyright under the employer-employee relationship. In

[142] March, 1883, The revised BRUSSELS on December, 14, 1900 and Lisbon on October 31, 1958 and STOCKHOLM on 1967 and 1979.

[143] Bainbridge D., *Introduction to Computer Law*, 2000 at page 91.

[144] [1991] IRLR 63 cited by Bainbridge D., *Introduction to Computer Law* at page 94.

[145] [2001] VSC 91 (4 April 2001). See also White SW Computer Law, IP and Information Technology & Telecommunications lawyers at http://www.computerlaw.com.au

this situation, the court identified and raised some legal issues such as (a) the contractual obligations owed to the original client, (b) who is the copyright owner of the source code (including library code) and (c) whether the original program was written using confidential information supplied by the original client.

According to the White SW Computer Law, IP and Information Technology & Telecommunications lawyers, the Court argued that there was no dispute that Mr Adam Hinkley was the author of the programs in question. Rather, the issues in contention concern the identity of the owner of the copyright in the programs. In addition to claiming copyright in the programs, Redrock alleged against Mr Adam Hinkley that there was; (a) breach of certain contractual obligations which it asserts are to be implied into his contract of employment; (b) breach of obligations under the Australian Copyright Act and the *Corporations Law*; and (c) breach of certain fiduciary obligations.

The Court further argued that "it thus appears, and rightly in my respectful view, that, the greater the skill required for an employee's work, the less significant is control in determining whether the employee is under a contract of service. Control is just one of many factors whose influence varies according to circumstances."[146] The court concluded that the evidence about control does not in the circumstances of this case establish that Mr Hinkley was employed under a contract for services. It is almost impossible to give a precise and clear definition of the distinction between a contract of service and a contract for services.

In the matter of Telephonic Communicators International Pty Ltd v. Motor Solutions Australia Pty Ltd & Others,[147] some of the key illegal issues discussed by the Court included whether or not a software developer is free to develop a software program for a client that is similar to a program which was previously developed by them for another client. The court also discussed sub issues as follows:

(a) Whether there are contractual obligations owed to the original client, (b) who is the copyright owner of the source code (including library code) and (c) whether the original program was written using confidential information supplied by the original client.

The above case involved software that was developed for training systems used for staff in car dealerships. Mr Phillis had begun to develop these training tools and systems in about 1990. The intellectual property rights in the training products were transferred to Telephonic Communicators

[146] Ibid.

[147] See Steve White, Principle White SW Computer law, DEVELOPING SIMILAR PROGRAMS FOR COMPETITORS.

International Pty Ltd (TCI), a company owned by Mr Phillis's family. The claims of the similarities of programs and the breach of confidence did not succeed as there had been no written contract dealing with a duty of confidentiality owed to TCI by Logea or Mr Murray. The information supplied by Mr Phillis to Mr Murray involved the disclosure of the various training programs written by Mr Phillis. As these programs were provided to various clients of TCI, and in the absence of contrary evidence, the Court held such information was not secret.[148]

There is no clear definition of this area from any statute in most countries in the world save for case laws and equity which have expanded the scope and limitation of the applicability of this branch of law and protection of property rights such as trade secrets and business know-how.

In the UK this area of law has been indirectly legislated through CDPA 1988 whereby Section 117(e) provides that

> "*nothing in this part effects the operation of any rule of equity relating to breaches of trust or confidence...*" (*emphasis added*).

The TRIPS Agreement is the most useful international instrument that recognizes and protects undisclosed information. For instance Article 39 under Section 7 provides among other things that;

> "...Members shall protect undisclosed information and data submitted to government or government agencies." The Article goes further by stipulating that "Natural and legal persons shall have the possibility of preventing information lawfully within their control from being disclosed to, acquired by, or used by others without their consent so long as such information is secret, has commercial value..."[149]

In Tanzania there are some laws that indirectly provide for the importance of confidentiality and non-disclosure of certain information. For instance Section 59 of the Labour Institutions Act provides for as to when breach of confidentiality becomes an offence as follows:

> "59 (1) ...it shall be an offence for any person to disclose any information relating to the financial or business affairs of another person if that information was acquired in the performance of any function or the exercise of any power under this Act".[150]

---

[148] See Steve White, Principle White SW Computer law, DEVELOPING SIMILAR PROGRAMS FOR COMPETITORS.

[149] See Article 39(2) of the Agreement on Trade Related Aspects of Intellectual Property Rights (TRIPS AGREEMENT) 1994.

[150] Act No.7 of 2004.

However, under the same provision there is an exception to certain information which can be disclosed and such disclosure does not amount to breach of confidence or an offence.

Likewise, Section 101 of the Employment and Labour Relations Act[151] similarly provides for confidentiality with the same words including exceptions as follows:

> "101 (1) ...it shall be an offence for any person to disclose any information relating to the financial or business affairs of another person if that information was acquired in the performance of any function or the exercise of any power under this Act."

In Tanzania, the question of confidentiality is further stipulated under the Employment and Labour Relations (Code of Good Practice). The relevant provision provides as follows;

"56 (2) An employer shall not be required to disclose employee information that is;

(a) is legally privileged

(b) is confidential and if disclosed may cause substantial harm to the employee...

(c) is an employee's private personal information, unless the employee consents to the disclosure of that information."[152]

There are various authorities from the UK that explain the principles and guidelines on the rights and breach of confidence and their consequences as developed by the court. For instance in *Faccenda Chicken Ltd v. Fowler*[153] the Court of Appeal developed the following principles:

Where there is a contract of employment the employee's obligations will normally be determined form the nature of the contract.

(a) In the absence of express term, the employee's obligations would be implied.

(b) While still in employment, there is an implied term imposing a duty of good faith.

(c) Protection of information which under implied terms against disclosure by an ex-employee all attention should paid on the nature of

[151] See Act No. 6 of 2004.

[152] See G.N. No. 42 of 2007.

[153] [1986] 1 ALL ER. See also Bainbridge D., *Introduction to Computer Law*, 2000 at page 96.

employment, information and the employees stress on the confidential nature of relevant information.[154]

7.9.2 The Use of the Law of Confidence under the Information Society

One of the underrated areas of intellectual property is the law of confidence and tradė secrets which entails valuable information and innovative ideas that form part of business strategies and methods of most organizations. Some countries have enacted statutes that address copyright, trademarks, service marks, designs and patent rights without considering the law of confidence as part of intellectual property law. Generally, the law of confidence allows a person who generates intellectual ideas or controls undisclosed information to prevent others from divulging or misusing those ideas of information. This area can be very useful in the protection of some intellectual property rights which are in the early stages and do not qualify for copyright and patent protection. The law of confidence protects information such as lists of clients and contracts. Moreover this branch of law protects information of a personal nature and even ideas which have not yet been expressed in a tangible form to qualify for copyright subsistence for instance an idea for a new dramatic play or an idea for a new computer program.[155] This means that the law of confidence can further prevent a person from divulging information, which has been given to him in confidence, on an express or implicit understanding that the information should not be disclosed to others or otherwise used by the recipient of the information.

Those authors or composers that have just formed their ideas but have not further developed their works to qualify for copyright protection, can use this branch of law to protect their ideas that have not yet been fixed or put into tangible things by entering into confidential contracts with persons that they give their ideas or information.

There is no limit on the type of information that can be protected by the law of confidence. Looking at the subsistence of protection under the law of confidence there are some legal conditions that are to be met. For information to qualify for protection under this branch there are certain basic conditions that need to be met by parties concerned. The information to be protected should not in any case be in the public domain and there should be an obligation on the imparted information. The obligation on confidentiality will be assessed based on contract, commercial relationship, employment and professional relationship.[156] Among the factors that

[154] Ibid.
[155] Ibid.
[156] Ibid.

can be considered in assessing the breach of confidence is that the information must be capable of being protected. One of the most important restrictions on information that is protected by breach of confidence is that the action will not apply to materials that are in the public domain.[157] In most cases immoral and vague information is not protected under this branch of law.

Some case laws have developed precedents on the application of the law of confidence. In *Coco v. AN Clark (Engineers) Ltd,*[158] which involved a moped engine designed by the plaintiff who entered into informal negotiations with the defendant; no contract was executed. Meggary J held that the defendant owed the plaintiff an obligation of confidence (although he doubted the confidential quality of the information). The Judge further argued that, apart from contract, an action for breach of confidence will require three elements:

- The information must have the necessary quality of confidence about it.
- The information must have been imparted in circumstances importing an obligation of confidence.
- There must be an unauthorized use of that information to the detriment of the party communicating it.

Furthermore for information to be protected by the law of confidence, it must have a quality of confidence about it. This means that where the information in hand is in common place or is common knowledge to a group of persons (for example, it is well known to computer programmers) or to the public at large, it cannot be confidential; instead, it will be considered to be in the public domain.

As discussed by David Bainbridge, the concept of confidentiality was also considered in the case of *Thomas Marshall (Export) Ltd v. Guinle,*[159] in which the defendant, who was the managing director of the plaintiff company, resigned half-way through his 10-year service contract to set up a rival business. In this case it has been stated by Bainbridge D. that the information involved sources of supply and the names of official and other contacts in Europe and the Far East. Megarry VC found for the plaintiff and he said that four elements were necessary in testing for confidential quality.

---

[157] See Bently L and Sherman B., *Intellectual Property Law* at page 928. See also *Attorney General v. Guardian News Papers [1990] AC 109*.

[158] *[1969] RPC 41.*

[159] [1976] FSR 345.

- Release of the information would injure the owner of the information or benefit others.
- The owner must believe the information to be secret and not already in the public domain.
- The owner's belief in 1 and 2 above must be reasonable.
- The information must be judged in the light of usages and practices of the particular trade or industry.[160]

In this way, the law of confidence prevents others from benefiting from the work of the person who accumulated the information in the first place. As a result, a great deal of material related to the running of a business will fall within the ambit of the law of confidence.

As noted by David Bainbridge, the vivid examples of information relevant to computers and other related technologies, which may be the subject matter of confidence, could include:

- Ideas for a new or improved computer system, hardware and software, and research and development work generally;
- Details of existing computer system as would be known by computer analysts or programmers or even users of the system (in terms of users, the system would have to be uncommon in some respect);
- Lists of customers or sub-contractors and associated information-for example, the services they perform and their credit rating. Information stored in computer databases is often confidential;
- A company's strategy for future research and development, production and marketing.[161]

Arguably, the law of confidence is very useful to employers when it comes to the matter of employer-employee relationship. Most employees tend to breach their obligations by disclosing their companies or employers information such as trade secrets, etc. by illegally accessing computer system. The question of employee-employer relationship has been highly considered and recognized by courts in some countries like UK, South Africa, etc.[162]

In *Admar Computers Pty Ltd v. Ezy Systems Pty Ltd & Ors*[163] the Federal Court was asked to examine evidence relating to a pseudocode analysis of

---

160 Op cit.

161 See Bainbridge D., *Introduction to Computer Law*, 2000 at page 91-92

162 See *Lansing Linde Ltd v. Kerr [1991] 1 WLR 251, Northern Office Microcomputer (Pty) Ltd v. Rosenstein [1982] FSR 124, and Faccenda Chicken Ltd v. Fowler [1986] 1 ALL ER 61.*

163 See White SW Computer Law, IP and Information Technology & Telecommunications lawyers at http://www.computerlaw.com.au

software on the question of copyright infringement and breach of confidentiality in circumstances where an employee left his employer and published a similar and competing product to that of the former employer. In this case, the pseudocode analysis produced evidence that the Ezy system was based upon the Admar system. However, the Court noted that copyright is intended to grant protection to the expression of an idea, not the idea itself. It was further argued that since the source code of the Admar software program had not been reproduced by Ezy, there was no infringement of copyright. According to the White SW Computer Law, IP and Information Technology & Telecommunications lawyers the pseudocode analysis evidence was found to be relevant in the claim for breach of confidence in that it suggested use of Admar's source code by a former employee in developing the Ezy source code.[164]

7.9.3 The action for breach of confidence and Remedies thereof

Case laws and some statutes from some countries provide for the remedies to those who have socially and economically suffered from the misuse of confidential information and other trade secrets. The action for breach of confidence can be used to protect certain categories of confidential information (e.g. personal or commercial information) against unauthorized disclosure or use. The most important remedy for breach of confidence is an injunction preventing the use or disclosure of the information. Computer hackers and crackers who pose serious threat to computer system can also be made accountable and liable under this branch of law.

Bainbridge in his book argues that:

> "*If the information has been divulged to sufficient people so that it can be said to be no longer confidential, an injunction will not be of any help; it would be like locking the stable door after the horse has bolted. If this has happened and the information has been used to the detriment of the person to whom it 'belongs', however, damages will be available against the person responsible and a limited injunction may be granted*"[165].

An account of profits may also be applied before the court as damage and this may be more advantageous to the plaintiff especially if the defendant has made substantial profit from the use of the information.

---

[164] Ibid.

[165] Ibid.

In *Prince Albert v. Strange*[166] the Court clearly recognized the importance of this area of law. In this case as cited by David Bainbridge by at page 91 the Queen and Prince made etchings for their own amusement intended only for their own private entertainment. Unfortunately the etchings were sent to a printer to make some impressions and someone illegally made copies and passed on to the defendant who again illegally displayed them in an exhibition in which the public could pay for admission. The plaintiffs were successful against the defendants. All in all this area is very important and useful in the protection of information in this era of cyberspace technology. Tanzania needs to effectively legislate this area taking into account the impact of digital technology.

7.10 *The Current Legal Myth on Electronic Databases*

7.10.1 Introduction

While data has been defined to mean anything that comprises information that may be stored in a computer or on a computer storage media, a database is a structured set of data that include but is not limited to lists of clients' names and addresses, or lists of employees and their details stored in a computer file.[167] In other words, it is a collection of independent works, data or any other materials arranged in a methodical way which can be accessed electronically. According to the EU Directives on Database the term database includes literary, artistic, musical or other collection of works or collection of other material such as texts, sound, images, numbers, facts, and data that can be systematically or methodically arranged and individually accessed.[168] Generally the first owner of the database is the maker of the original database who takes all initiatives in obtaining, verifying or presenting the contents of a database with exception of employee-employer relationships. A database is said to have been infringed where a person without permission of the legal owner of the right thereof extracts or reutilizes all of or a substantial part of the contents of the database.[169] It has been learnt that with the development of digital technology which has facilitated the methods of storing information electronically, databases have become commercially valuable assets.[170]

---

[166] [1849] 1 Mac & G 25.

[167] Bainbridge D. *Introduction to Computer Law* 4th Edition 2000 at page xxvi.

[168] See Article 17 of 11/3/1996, No.96/9 Directive 96/9/EC of the European Parliament and of the Council of 11 March 1996.

[169] See Bentley L. and Sherman B., *On Intellectual Property Law* at page 303. See also EU Directives on Database, UK CDPA and compare with the Copyright and Neighbouring Rights Act, 1999 of Tanzania.

[170] See Lloyd J.I., *Information Technology Law*, 2000 at pages 442-443

Copyright is the most relevant area of intellectual property that can be successfully used to protect databases structured in any form. It is possible for an owner of a database to have double rights. For instance the creative individual works in the database may be protected using copyright on their own right. Likewise, the same database can be protected on its own right.[171]

One of the challenges for domestic and international legal systems in the information age is how appropriately to deal with the needs of electronic database producers. In recent years, the electronic database industry has grown significantly. A large number of businesses rely on the value of databases they have developed for commercial exploitation. Examples of such databases include electronic libraries such as LEXIS and Westlaw that may be accessed online or via CD-ROM or other digital storage media. It is a bare fact that the digital technology database has enabled the production of more modern facilities that effectively enable easy access to vast collection of information anywhere in the world at a time.[172]

The use of computer technology in more and more areas of life in most countries including Tanzania has given rise to public concern. The new opportunities to perform cross-computations of different registers or databases already created in the public and private sector prompted the concern for privacy which ultimately led to the world's first regulation on the national level of computers and privacy.[173]

On the other hand, it is indisputable that the making of databases requires the investment of considerable human, technical and financial resources while such databases can be copied or accessed at a fraction of the cost needed to design them independently. It is possible for unauthorized people to illegally extract or reutilize the contents of a database created by others or owners who invested and used their skill, labour and judgment in creating databases. This constitutes acts which can have serious economic, legal and technical consequences.

7.10.2 Database protection at international level

There are certain legal instruments that have been developed at regional and international level for database protection. For instance at regional level, the European Union and its members has gone further in recognizing the economic significance and protection of electronic databases and other related programs produced by the computer industry. There is effective legislation that operates at regional and national level for regulating this

[171] Ibid.

[172] Ibid at pages 300-301.

[173] Law and IT Swedish Views, ICT Commission Report 2003 at page 9.

area. For instance the EU Directive on Copyright (databases),[174] recognizes that databases are vital tools in the development of an information market within the community which can be used in many other fields while the making of such databases requires the investment of considerable human, technical and financial resources. This substantiates effective protection of databases under a well designed legal framework that reflects the development of technology.

Initially databases including romantic poems were protected under copyright as literary works. As technology developed the trend of database protection in most countries has dramatically changed. For instance the European Directives[175] and the US case of *Feist Publications Inc. v. Rural Telephone Service Co Inc (supra)* influenced the UK to significantly change the legal protection of databases through the introduction of Copyright and Rights in Databases Regulations 1997. There is now dual protection of databases in the UK that is copyright in case of intellectual creation and database right where there is a substantial result of investment. Furthermore, *sui genesis* right was introduced aiming at providing short term protection for databases.[176]

Furthermore the EU Directive passed in 1996 which seems to aim at harmonizing all legislation regulating copyright in the area of databases obliges member states to recognize the importance of using *sui generis* right to protect non-original databases.

Copyright and database right are all useful to both electronic and non electronic databases.

For instance Regulation 13 of the said Directive provides that

(1) A property right (database right) subsists, in accordance with this Part, in a database if there has been a substantial investment in obtaining, verifying or presenting the contents of the database.

(2) For the purposes of paragraph (1) it is immaterial whether or not the database or any of its contents is a copyright work, within the meaning of Part I of the 1988 Act.

The said Regulation further provides for determining the author or owner of a database as follows:

"(1) Subject to paragraphs (2) to (4), the person who takes the initiative in obtaining, verifying or presenting the contents of a

[174] Directive, 11/03/1996, No.96/9 Directive 96/9/EC of the European Parliament and of the Council of 11 March 1996.

[175] (OJ [1996] L77/20).

[176] Op cit at page 57.

database and assumes the risk of investing in that obtaining, verification or presentation shall be regarded as the maker of, and as having made, the database."

Moreover the regulation provides for a situation where the database is infringed whereby a person is said to have infringed database right in a database "if, without the consent of the owner of the right, he extracts reutilizes all or a substantial part of the contents of the database."[177]

"(2) For the purposes of this Part, the repeated and systematic extraction or re-utilization of substantial parts of the contents of a database may amount to the extraction or re-utilization of a substantial part of those contents."

With regard to the term or duration of database protection under the UK, database right in a database expires at the end of the period of fifteen years from the end of the calendar year in which the making of the database was complete.[178] The owner of the database is the author or the natural persons or group of natural persons or first creator, the person whose skill, labour and judgment created an original database. Where a database is created by an employee in the execution of his duties or following the instructions given by his employer, the employer exclusively shall be entitled to exercise all economic rights in the database so created, unless otherwise provided by contract.

The model of protection adopted was to provide for a standard copyright treatment for databases requiring skill, effort or judgment in their making but, in addition, to introduce a new *sui generis* right specifically aimed at providing shorter-term protection for databases that might not meet the standard but which were, nevertheless, the result of a substantial investment which would be prejudiced if such database had no protection.[179]

The EU Directive on database as a right and *sui generic*, were designed to protect the investment in obtaining, verifying or presenting the contents of a database. The object of the *sui generis* right is to ensure protection of any investment and give the marker the option of preventing the unauthorized extraction or reutilization of the contents of the database.[180] The Directive obliges member states to provide dual protection of electronic databases which recognizes that while copyright protects the selection or arrangements of materials the database right can protect the collection and verification of the materials themselves.

---

[177] See Regulations 14 and 16.

[178] Regulation 17.

[179] See Jacquiline L., *Databases as Intellectual Property; New Legal approaches* at pages 139-140.

[180] See Articles 39, 40, 41, 42 and 48 of the Directive.

This kind of e-database protection needs to be adopted by the copyright laws in Tanzania and the entire East African Community to encourage more innovation and the use of databases. The law should give economic rights and other related rights to authors who use their labour, skill, efforts and judgment in preparing original databases. These rights should include exclusive right to reproduce, translate, adapt, arrange or alter, distribute and communicate to the public.

The EU Directive further affords an appropriate uniform level of protection for databases to secure the remuneration of the maker. The Directive seems to reflect the impact of digital technology on the misuse of databases and the legal protection of databases is provided in any form.

Article (43) stipulates as follows:

"Whereas, in the case of on-line transmission, the right to prohibit re-utilization is not exhausted either as regards the database or as regards a material copy of the database or of part thereof made by the addressee of the transmission with the consent of the right holder."

Apart from aiming to protect the copyright in the original selection or arrangement of the contents of a database, this Directive further seeks to safeguard the position of makers or databases against misappropriation of the results of the financial and professional investment made in obtaining and collecting the contents by protecting the whole or substantial parts of a database against certain acts by a user or competitor.

Our domestic laws can adopt these principles of database protection from an EU legal perspective which seems to effectively recognize the efforts of database makers and the economic benefits of these databases.

At international level there are some relevant conventions that afford protection to databases such as the WIPO Performances and Phonograms Treaty,[181] the WIPO Copyright Treaty and the TRIPS Agreement which are not technologically reflected by Intellectual Property laws in Tanzania. Article 5 of the WIPO Copyright Treaty 1996[182] provides for the protection of data and databases. The article stipulates that "compilations of data or other material, in any form, which by reason of the selection or arrangement of their contents constitute intellectual creations, are protected as such."

There are various business models for commercialising such databases. In some models, customers are charged fees for access to electronic information *per se,* as with many online libraries. There are electronic product

[181] Adopted by the Diplomatic Conference on 20 December 1996.

[182] Ibid.

catalogues that help in online shopping, such as the various catalogues of books, music, and numerous other products available through online stores such as amazon.com. Databases of information about services, such as travel, financial, legal, and/or medical services that are usually accessible online; for example, travelocity.com and expedia.com in the field of travel services are very useful.[183]

There is no legal framework that clearly provides dual protection of databases in Tanzania. It is hard to find protection of databases through database right and *sui generis* right under the Copyright Law in Tanzania. The law needs to be amended to accommodate dual protection of databases to promote innovations and investment.

Electronic database producers are not clearly protected by any law for their efforts in compiling and commercialising valuable databases. To date, the existing laws on intellectual property in most countries including Tanzania have proved lacking in this context. The reason for this is that copyright law might protect some aspects of electronic databases, but it will not protect the contents of a database per se. Copyright may protect software which is used in search engines and formatting of a database and this may be of some comfort to database producers. However, in terms of the contents of a database or compilation, copyright in most jurisdictions will only protect the original selection.

Tanzania lacks effective intellectual property laws especially copyright laws that reflect the development of technology. There is need to create a legal framework or regulation that will assure the protection of databases. This can be done through granting copyright to original databases or by introducing *sui gereis* system in non-original databases. In this way database owners are assured of the exclusive right to reproduction, adaptation, translation, distribution and access to the public.

The European Union realised that databases were not sufficiently protected in most member states and its parliament and the Council passed an effective copyright (database), Directive.[184] The other justification was based on the fact that making databases requires the investment of considerable human technical and financial resources and the vulnerability of these electronic databases. This Directive seems to be a reward for database makers. The Directive seeks to safeguard the position of makers of databases against misappropriation of the result of the financial and professional investment made in obtaining and collecting the contents by

[183] Ibid.

[184] 11/3/1996, No.96/9 Directive 96/9/EC of the European Parliament and of the Council of 11 March 1996. See also Articles 5, 8 and 9 of the above Directive.

protecting the whole or substantial part of database against certain acts by a user or competitor.

7.11 *The Legal Protection of Designs and Semiconductor Products*

Designs and semiconductors are very relevant to the products and works created using computer technology. These conducting materials such as RAM, ROM, etc. can perform different functions in computer systems as they act as brains.[185] Design law and copyright law can be useful on the protection of computer hardware and semiconductor production. It is unfortunate to see that this growing area of computer technology is not reflected by IP laws in Tanzania. While patent might be useful in the protection of innovations related to computer hardware, design law and copy right law in Tanzania do not provide for semiconductor products. Unfortunately Tanzania has not yet signed and ratified the Treaty on Intellectual Property in respect of Integrated Circuits 1989. On the other hand there are examples of laws from other jurisdictions that clearly protect design rights in semiconductor chips. For instance with the UK Copyright Act and the US Semiconductor Chips Protection Act, creators and innovators of semiconductor chips and design rights thereof can be assured of legal protection.[186]

In fact there is hardly effective legal framework that regulates the design regime in Tanzania. The only remedy in Tanzania could be the TRIPS Agreement. Article 35 of the treaty obliges members to provide protection to layout-designs (topographies) of integrated circuits (referred to in this Agreement as layout-designs) in accordance with Articles 2 through to 7 (other than paragraph 3 of Article 6), Article 12 and paragraph 3 of Article 16 of the Treaty on Intellectual Property in Respect of Integrated Circuits.

In addition to that Article 36 provides for the scope of the protection as follows:

> "Subject to the provisions of paragraph 1 of Article 37, Members shall consider unlawful the following acts if performed without the authorization of the right holder:[187] importing, selling, or otherwise distributing for commercial purposes a protected layout-design, an integrated circuit in which a protected layout-design is incorporated,

[185] See Lloyd, *Information Technology Law*, 2000 at pages 474-475.

[186] Ibid.

[187] The term "right holder" in this Section shall be understood as having the same meaning as the term "holder of the right" in the IPC Treaty.

> or an article incorporating such an integrated circuit only in so far as it continues to contain an unlawfully reproduced layout-design."

On the other hand, the main and most specific convention that regulates integrated circuits at international level is the treaty on intellectual property in respect of integrated circuits.[188]

Article 2 of the treaty defines "integrated circuit" as a product, in its final form or an intermediate form, in which the elements, at least one of which is an active element, and some or all of the interconnections are integrally formed in and/or on a piece of material and which is intended to perform an electronic function.

The very article further defines "layout-design (topography)" to mean a three-dimensional disposition, however expressed, of the elements, at least one of which is an active element, and of some or all of the interconnection of an integrated circuit, or such a three-dimensional disposition prepared for an integrated circuit intended for manufacture.

The main area of intellectual property rights that is protected is the layout-design (topography) which means a layout-design (topography) in respect of which the conditions or protection referred to in this treaty is fulfilled.

Article 8 of the treaty provides for principles for the protection of semiconductor products or integrated circuits whereby members are obliged in formulating or amending their laws and regulations, to adopt measures necessary to protect public health and nutrition, and to promote public interest in sectors of vital importance to their socio-economic and technological development, provided that such measures are consistent with the provisions of this agreement. This article seems to reflect the development of technology as far as intellectual property is concerned. The WIPO Treaty might also be useful as far as the protection of semiconductor topographies is concerned.

Having realized that CDPA has done little in this area, the UK implemented the TRIPS Agreement and EU Community Directive (Legal Protection of Topographies of Semi Conductor Products)[189] by enacting the semiconductor products (protection of topography) regulations 1987. The said regulations came out with a topography right in the layout of an integrated circuit. In 1989 these regulations were replaced by Design Right (Semiconductor Regulation) 1989 creating new rights known as

[188] The Treaty on Intellectual Property in Respect of Integrated Circuits Done at Washington, DC, on 26 May 1989 (INTEGRATED CIRCUITS TREAT).

[189] 87/54/EEC/OJ[1987] 24/36). See also Bainbridge D., *Information Technology Law* at pages 141-143.

semi conductor design rights. Most conditions for copyright subsistence and protection including remedies for infringement and exceptions apply *mutatis mutandis* to semiconductor topography. There are cross references between these regulations and CPPA 1988 meaning that all must be read together. Tanzania needs to have a comparative study of the UK legal system on this area and create an effective legal framework that will protect the emerging innovation and creative endeavors in designs and semiconductor products.

CHAPTER EIGHT

Internet Domain Names

8.1 *The Legal Myth on the Evolution of .com*

The development of technology with the evolution of e-commerce which has resulted in the sale of goods and services online has brought a new dimension of trade and service marks where traders or companies opt to use "e-trademarks" namely domain names. Domain names have been successfully used by business companies to identify themselves and establish their presence under cyberspace. Domain names have become valuable corporate assets and are becoming the most important means of identification for companies and businesses on the Internet as they facilitate communication with the company's customer base.[1] Domain names under cyberspace are among the areas brought by the development of technology that has created e-commerce. Domain names are Web or Internet addresses used by web servers, companies, organizations, etc. to identify each other on the Internet.[2] It is an alternative to a numerical Internet Protocol (IP) address. Domain names which are the text name of a numeric IP address of a computer on the Internet can be used to identify Internet sites. These Internet domain names which ordinarily begin with the prefix "www" are not the same with normal postal addresses. Unlike a postal address, a domain name can be accessed anywhere in the world and does not change when a person or owner moves from one place to another. It is the primary method by which users identify and access websites, and is matched to the IP address through the DNS system which facilitates the users' ability to navigate the Internet.[3] Each domain name is supposed to be registered on the principle of "first come first served". Each domain name must be unique to avoid unnecessary disputes. In other words domain names can be read and resolved from right to left. In some cases domain names such as Amazon.com have been registered as trademarks. The use of a trademark within a domain name allows for the easiest means of identification of a company's business for an Internet user. Trademarks facilitate identification

---

1 See Michael Handler, Internet Domain Names and Trade Mark law, University of Sydney, See also Meadows, J., Trademark Protection for Trademarks Used as Internet Domain Names (1997) 65 University of Cincinnati Law Review 1323 at 1324.

2 See Turban, E., *E-Commerce* 2002 at pages 20-23.

3 Reed, C., *Internet Law Text and Materials* 2000 at page 33.

of the sources of merchandise and are important vehicles for the creation of business goodwill in relation to particular commodities.[4]

During the last twenty-five years, the Internet has evolved from a United States government research project into a prominent international medium of communication thus facilitating international commerce and a global exchange of knowledge.[5] Throughout this evolution, the Domain Name System (DNS) has been playing a major role in the rise of Internet popularity by providing a "human friendly" method of Internet navigation. Internet domain names are very useful tools for online business transactions. The domain names might be allocated by domain name registries at country level e.g. .tz, .za and .uk or at a global level e.g. .com, .org.

8.2 *An Overview of the Domain Name Structure*

The nature and structure of most domain names seem to be related to commercial enterprises and non-profit organizations. The initial categories of domain names can be identified into two main groups; generic and country code[6] which forms three generic domain names that is

- .com
- .net and
- .org

In most countries, domain names might be associated with the nature of business. For instance in the UK domain names are registered based on some categories such as ac.uk for academic institutions, gov.uk for government departments and co.uk for commercial organizations and other categories.[7]

8.3 *National Domain Names*

In most countries national domain names are regulated and registered by both the public and the private sector. Due to the ICCAN Policy, the private sector is given a great role in registering and allocating domain names. Generally in the UK, this role is played by a non-profit making company,

---

4 Michael Handler, Internet Domain Names and Trade Mark law, University of Sydney. See also Meadows, J., Trademark Protection for Trademarks Used as Internet Domain Names (1997) 65 University of Cincinnati Law Review 1323 at 1324. See also Gabay, M., 'The Role of Trademarks in Consumer Protection and Development in Developing Countries in Ricketson, S., *And Intellectual Property: Cases, Materials and Commentary*, (Sydney: Butterworths, 1994) at pages 894-895

5 See Lisa M., Sharock, *The Future of Domain names Dispute Resolution* 2001 at page 1.

6 See Lloyd, I., *Information Technology Law*, 3rd Edition 2000 at pages 22-23.

7 Ibid.

Nominate. This means that governments have delegated the powers of the management of domain names and the allocation of IP addresses.

After some legal debate at national and international level it was ultimately, agreed to establish a body called the Internet Corporation for Assigned Names and Numbers (ICANN). ICANN was established in October 1998 and is now somehow linked to WIPO in the event of disputes over domain names and cyber-squatting.

In terms of legal status, ICANN is a company registered under the law of California. ICANN which is an American Company established under Californian law and is responsible for co-coordinating some of the technical functions relating to the Internet. While in the UK, a non-profit making company Nominet plays this role, in Tanzania there are few people or agents who facilitate registration and sale of domain names.[8]

Some scholars have argued that the situation with regard to the national domain is rather more complex, with a mix of public and private sector organizations playing a big role in the domain name registry.[9] While in Tanzania by 2004 two persons were said to be registering domain names, there is no legal framework that governs domain names in the country. Even the Trade and Service Marks Act does not mention domain names which have always been linked with trademarks.[10] Some developing countries under ASEAN such as Brunei, Cambodia, Malaysia and Viet Nam already have laws that regulate domain names. Mechanisms in resolving disputes related to domain names online have also been developed in these countries.

8.4 *The Domain Name System*

The domain name system (DNS) serves the central function of facilitating users' ability to navigate the Internet and it does so with the aid of two components. A domain name is the human friendly address of a computer that is usually in a form that is easy to remember or to identify, such as www.wipo.int.

The DNS has been administered by IANA, pursuant to principles that were described in Request for Comments (RFC) 1591 of March 1994. The DNS operates on basis of a hierarchy of names. At the top, are top-level domains, which are usually divided into two categories: the generic top-level domains (gTLDs) such as .com, .net, .org and the country code

---

8 Nominet UK derives its authority from the Internet industry in the UK and is recognised as the UK registry by the Internet Assigned Numbers Authority (IANA) in the US.

9 Lloyd, J.I., *Information Technology Law,* 3rd Edition 2000 at page 25.

10 The Trade and Service Marks Act (Act No. 12 of 1986) [CAP 326 R.E.2002].

top-level domains (ccTLDs) as .tz, .ca, .za, www.wipo.int. Generally, ccTLDs) is a TLD used in the Internet DNS to identify a country such as tz for Tanzania whereby two letters chosen for each country are derived from the ISO 3166 Standards. In this case, even the rules and policies for registering domain names in the ccTLDs vary significantly by country.

Domain names must not be confused with property rights in names, such as trademarks. A domain name is acquired through simple contract with a registry, and any right, in respect of the name, derives from that contract.

8.5 *Legal Rights in Domain Names*

Generally all activities carried out under cyberspace pose legal implications that need to be addressed and solved. The fundamental nature of domain names gives rise to an inevitable conflict between holders of legal rights to particular names. The reason for the conflict is that domain names must be absolutely unique. While trademarks are governed by the Trade and Service Act in Tanzania there is no legislation that regulates domain names in Tanzania like in other countries in East Africa. There is a high possibility of cyber-squatting and passing among companies doing business online.

A website designed to form the domain name may contain valuable information related to intellectual property rights such as designs, copyright and trademark or service marks. Information contained in a website accessed through a certain domain name might lead to infringement of intellectual property rights which in most cases will raise some legal concerns. This might raise jurisdiction problems in case of a dispute where the parties are not able to identify the country location of a particular website or domain name.

8.6 *Domain Names Disputes*

Given the increasing number of registries located throughout the world, the possibility for domain name disputes is exacerbated. Since, the registration is relatively simple, inexpensive and done on a first come first served basis, disputes and conflicts are likely to arise as cyber squatters register trademarks and famous names and later on put the domain name on auction. It is only when the actual company or person comes up for registration; they find that the same name has already been registered. As part of dispute settlement amicably out of judicial system which seems to be expensive, some remarkable policies and rules have been developed at international level. It has been noted that the dispute policy in the past appeared to create some problems for domain name holders who may have registered a domain name in good faith, only to have a large corporation demand that it be surrendered based on the similarity between the domain name and the corporation's trade mark.[11] Domain names can cause cyber-squatting, passing off, trade mark infringement, trade libel[12] and defamation. Internet Corporation for Assigned Names and Numbers (ICANN) developed new Dispute Resolution Policies which set forth the terms and conditions in connection with a dispute between a domain name holder and any party other than ICANN. According to these policies, terms and conditions, a domain name holder by registering and maintaining a registration or renewing a registration, is held to warrant that, amongst other things, to their knowledge, the registration of the domain name will not infringe upon or otherwise violate the rights of any third party; that they are not registering the domain name for an unlawful purpose; and that they will not knowingly use the domain name in violation of any applicable laws or regulations. The policy further gives responsibility to the domain name owner to fully determine whether their domain name registration infringes or violates someone else's rights.[13]

In an effort to control the problem, all registries are obliged to comply with ICANN policies regarding operation of the domain name system. Registrars must also agree to operate the ICANN Uniform Domain Name Dispute Resolution Policy. This obliges applicants to agree that any disputes will be adjudicated by an approved dispute resolution service. At present three organizations operate such services.

- The World Intellectual Property Organization
- E-Resolution
- The National Arbitration Forum

On the other hand, Christopher Reed has summarized the basic principles of domain name dispute settlement policy as follows:

- First come first served
- Any trademark proprietor who makes genuine complaint is entitled to relief
- The administrative proceedings act only where the domain name is identical or confusingly similar to the alleged trademark

---

[11] See Layers discussion in White SW Computer Law, Intellectual Property, Information Technology & Telecommunications Lawyers.

[12] See *Nissan Motor Co .v. Nissan Computer Cop ([1998] FSR 265) and Joyce v. Sengupta [1993] 1 ALL ER 897.*

[13] See Layers discussion in White SW Computer Law, Intellectual Property, Information Technology & Telecommunications Lawyers.

- Any suit against the defendant having a registered trademark is most likely to fail.

Trademark owners and domain name owners should know their legal rights under the UDRP. UDRP seems to be a strong weapon for trademark owners (including owners of unregistered marks) and a potentially big problem for owners of domain names that are the same or identical.[14] There are quite a number of instances indicating dispute between trademark and domain name holders. Rarely it might be difficult for someone to get protection on their trademark against the misuse by others as a domain name as the claimant has to convince the dispute settlement authority that there has been false and misleading or misrepresentation by the domain name holder who used it purposefully for business.[15] Generally someone can be assumed to have used a domain name in bad faith where the following circumstances are observed from the legal point of view:

- Circumstances indicating that you have registered or you have acquired the domain name primarily for the purpose of selling, renting, or otherwise transferring the domain name registration to the complainant who is the owner of the trademark or service mark,[16] or to a competitor of the complainant, for valuable consideration in excess of your documented out-of-pocket costs directly related to the domain name; or
- You have registered the domain name in order to prevent the owner of the trademark or service mark from reflecting the mark in a corresponding domain name, provided that you have engaged in a pattern of such conduct; or
- You have registered the domain name primarily for the purpose of disrupting the business of a competitor; or
- By using the domain name, you have intentionally attempted to attract, for commercial gain, Internet users to your website or other online location, by creating confusion with the complainant's mark as to the source, sponsorship, affiliation, or endorsement of your website or location or of a product on your website.[17]

---

[14] See Domain Name Law & Domain Name Disputes By Charles Runyan, Ph.D., J.D. Domain Name Law Attorney.

[15] For fuller discussion on domain names see Reed C., *Internet Law Text and Materials* 2000 at pages 46-47.

[16] See Lloyd, J.I., *Information Technology Law*, 3rd Edition, 2000.

[17] See Lisa M. Sharock, The Future of Domain Names Dispute Resolution 2001 at page 1.

8.7 *Domain Names Cyber-squatting*

Cyber-squatting has been explained as the act of registering a domain name that is the same as, or confusingly similar to, the trademark of another with the intention of selling (at a profit) the domain name to the trademark owner.[18] As noted earlier the evolution of domain names has created a new relationship with trade and service marks that has posed legal challenges and fear of legal battles among the users. The misuse of trademarks and domain names has created more conflicts and disputes among companies and organizations due to cyber-squatting. The problem with domain name cyber-squatting or piracy has been alarming over the world and is threatening domain name owners and even trademark and service holders. A study indicates that the nuisance of cyber-squatting can also be evidenced from the World Intellectual Property Organization (WIPO) whereby in 2006, cyber-squatting disputes filed increased by 25% as compared to 2005.[19] The development of technology has facilitated easy identification of companies and other business institutions or organizations while at the same time improving of business promotion by the use of trademark or service marks within a domain name.[20] There has been a quick response to solve this problem at national and international level. Some countries like the UK and the US reformed their laws to curb the whole question of cyber-squatting and dispute settlement. At international level this has necessitated the formation and establishment of (ICANN) and the system and procedures of dispute settlement out of court administered by WIPO.

It is believed that there are people who by serving and selling or licensing domain names online get more profit. The situation has always been that the domain name holder illegally registers or actually uses the domain name in bad faith or trademark holder's goods or services. This has not prevented the courts from providing a remedy to the trademark holder on various grounds, including trademark dilution, passing off and unfair competition. Indeed no one is ready to see his trademark or domain name being illegally registered in bad faith and sold for more profit.[21] The law of passing off might be very relevant in curbing this problem. The remedies available are injunction orders, account of profits and damages among other things. However under cyberspace which is boundary less a jurisdiction problem or dispute on the ownership might arise as any website say in Tanzania can have a similar domain name with the one in South Africa. Two important appellate decisions from the US illustrate the

---

18 Shine Joy, Domain Name Cybersquatting and dispute resolution at http://www.legalserviceindia.com/articles/cddisp.htm on 31 December 2008.

19 Ibid.

20 UNCTAD on Legal Aspects of E-commerce, Nairobi 2006.

21 See *Playboy Enterprises In. v. C. Publishing Inc.*

different grounds on which cyber-squatting can be restrained.[22] While trademarks must be registered, domain names might not. While trademarks and service marks can be registered under a classification according to Nice Agreement, registration of domain names based on classification is not clear under the policies and laws. The registration is rather based on categories such as top-level domains (gTLDs) and the country code top-level domains (ccTLDs).

8.8 *Judicial Consideration on Domain Name Disputes*

There are some examples of cases from various countries indicating the conflict on domain names. The case of *Card Service International Inc. v. McGee*[23] is believed to be one of the earlier cases pertaining to cyber-squatting whereby the American Court held that the domain name serves the same function as a trademark and is not merely to be construed as an address, as it identifies an Internet site to those who reach it. In the UK, the cyber-squatting issue came before the Court of Appeal in *Marks & Spencer plc and others v. One In A Million Ltd*[24] whereby the issue of cyber-squatting was clarified and the practice of domain piracy was effectively buried. The facts were very similar to the Panavision case, as the defendants had registered numerous trademarks of British companies as domain names, including Marks and Spencer (both .com and .co.uk), bt.org, britishtelecom.co.uk, Sainsbury.com, cellnet.com, and virgin.org and had offered to sell them to the plaintiffs. The Court argued that there were clear elements of cyber-squatting, passing off and trademark infringement which attracted damages such as an injunction obliging the defendant to return the domain name to the right holders. In this case, the Court further argued as follows;

> "*The history of the defendant's activities shows a deliberate practice followed over a substantial period of time of registering domain names which are chosen to resemble the names and marks of other people and are plainly intended to deceive. The threat of passing-off and trade mark infringement, and the likelihood of confusion arising from the infringement of the mark are made out beyond argument in this case, even which (sic) it is possible to imagine other cases in which the issue would be more*

---

22 See the US case of the 9th Circuit Court of Appeals decision *Panavision International LP v. Toeppen case no. 97-55467 (9th Cir, April 1998).*

23 See Shine Joy, Domain Name Cybersquatting and dispute resolution at http://www.legalserviceindia.com/articles/cddisp.htm accessed on 31 December 2008. See also *Yahoo! Inc. v. Akash Arora & Anr.*, whereby the Indian Court held that trademark law applies with equal force on the Internet as it does in the physical world.

24 [1998] FSR 265.

nicely balanced. The result is that the plaintiffs in all five actions are entitled to final injunctions."[25]

In upholding the decision of the High Court, the Court of Appeal through Lord Justice Walker developed crucial factors and criteria that can be used or considered in determining whether to grant relief or not as cited by Ian Lloyd in his book as follows;

> "*In assessing the passing off, trade mark infringement and cyber-squatting, the court should consider, the similarity of names, the intention of the defendant, the type of trade and all the surrounding circumstances. If it be the intention of the defendant to appropriate the goodwill of another or enable others to do so, I can see no reason why the court should not infer that it will happen, even if there is a possibility that such an appropriation would not take place. If taking all circumstances into account the court should conclude that the name was produced to enable passing-off, is adapted to be used for passing-off, and if used, is likely to be fraudulently used, an injunction will be appropriate.*"[26]

In 1997, the UK Court made another landmark decision as far as misuse of domain names and trademarks electronically is concerned. The decision which seems to follow the US court argument decision was made in *British Telecommunications and Ors v. One in a Million and Ors*[27] whereby the court argued that the registration of famous trademarks as domain names and their use would constitute a trademark infringement even though the marks were not used by the defendant. The relevant marks were marksandspencer.com; marksandspencer.com.uk; j-sainsbury.com; sainsburys.com; ladbrokes.com; virgin.org, bt.org; and cellnet.net. The Court ordered that One in a Million be restrained from the use or sale of the domain names in question and be compelled to assign the domain names to the plaintiffs, the trademark owners.

The above case followed the US decision that the registration of famous trademarks as domain names and their use would constitute a trade mark infringement even though the marks were not used by the defendant. The Court ordered that One in a Million be restrained from the use or sale of the domain names in question and be compelled to assign the domain names to the plaintiffs, the trademark owners.

---

25 [1998] FSR 265 at page 273, as cited by Lloyd, J.I., on his book, *Information Technology law*, 3rd Edition 2000, at page 463.

26 [1999] FSR 1 at 8.

27 As accessed through www.computerlaw.com.au on 9 August 2008.

In some cases a dispute involving multiple trademark holders might arise where more than one party has trademark rights in the same word or sign. In this situation, the dispute arises as to who controls the domain names incorporating the trademark.[28] This is echoed from *Nissan Motor Co. v. Nissan Computer Cop*[29], which is illustrative of the bitter clashes that can occur between multiple holders of identical marks in the Internet setting. In this case Nissan Motor Company filed a suit alleging both cyber-squatting and traditional infringement and granted an injunction to the right holders. The court granted a permanent injunction to prevent use or sale of the domain names, and ordered that the domain name registrations be transferred to the plaintiffs.

In *Harrods Ltd v. UK Network Services Ltd*[30] the court granted summary judgment and the defendant was ordered to release the domain name harrods.com to the plaintiff. In *Pitman Training Limited et al. v. Nominet UK* the principle of first come first served and registration in domain name dispute resolution was well illustrated.[31] What happened in this case was that the two companies with common origin used a similar name that is Pitman Training Ltd and Pitman Publishing whereby the two companies had a dispute over pitman.co.uk. The two businesses which originated from a breakup of the Pitman business both claimed they had the right to own the domain name "pitman.co.uk". Pearson was the first to register the domain name as its own. Pitman Training Limited unsuccessfully commenced legal proceedings against both Pearson and Nominet to regain control of the domain name.

Furthermore, in *MBNA v. Freeman*[32] as cited by Turban E. whereby the dispute involved a domain name mbn.co.uk and trademark for MBNA, the court granted injunction and prevented the defendant from selling the domain name. Similarly in *Easyjet Airline v. Dainty*[33] the court had no problem in holding that the domain name was a vehicle of fraud and ordered the transfer of the domain name to Easyjet.

There are a number of recent cases on domain name cyber-squatting and trade and services mark misuse electronically from the US that have been reported. A good example is the case of *Panavision International v. Toeppen* whereby Mr Toeppen was ordered to stop using the trademarks "Panavision" and "Panaflex" as domain names and to transfer the registrations of the

[28] Sharrok, M.L., in Duke L.J., 817 (2001), "The Future of Domain Name Dispute Resolution; Crafting Practical International Legal Solutions from within the UDRP Framework".

[29] 89 F.Supp 2d 1154 (C.D Cal.2000).

[30] [1997] ESRF 797] EIPR D.106. See also the citation of the Case in Bainbridge D., *Introduction to Computer Law* 2000 at page 130.

[31] [1998] FSR 265.

[32] See the full discussion Turban, E., *E-commerce* 2002 at pages 26-27.

[33] Ibid.

domain names "panavision.com" and "panaflex.com" to Panavision International. Toeppen who is a resident of Illinois was sued in a California Court as his infringement was directed at a Californian business.[34]

Cyber-squatting has increasingly been recognized as a problem, which needs to be solved, as some entrepreneurs take advantage of the reputations of others to register domain names which may attract members of the public. Of particular concern is the growing practice of registering the names of celebrities, particularly where the domain name is used for a pornography site. The US legislature has already addressed the problem of the increase in cyber-squatting in the Anti-cyber-squatting Consumer Protection Act 1999 (ACPA) which amends the US Trademark Act of 1946. It creates civil liability for bad-faith registration with intent to profit on domain names that are identical or confusingly similar to distinctive trademarks or which dilute famous trademarks. A non-exhaustive list of factors to be considered in determining whether bad faith exists includes:

- The prior bona fide use of the name in the offering of goods or services;
- The provision of material and false contact information when applying for the domain registration;
- The person's offer to sell or otherwise assign the domain name to the owner of the mark for financial gain without having used it in connection with the bona fide offering of goods and services; and
- The registration of multiple domain names, which the person knows, is identical or confusingly similar to distinctive marks or dilutes famous marks.

Identification methods online and accessing specific sites can also be simplified by the use of hyperlinks. While trademarks are governed by the Trade and Service Mark Act 1987, there is no law that governs domain names in Tanzania hence there is a great likelihood of pirates cyber-squatting domain names. While many countries have established dispute resolution policies for domain names Tanzania has not yet adopted any such policies.

In the US the *US Anti-cybersquatting Consumer Protection Act (ACPA)*[35] has been enacted for the purpose of regulating domain names.

A good example of a domain name dispute is the case of *Prince Pl v. Prince Sportswear Group Inc.*[36] The dispute involved the two companies competing for legitimate rights on prince.com domain name in different jurisdictions.[37]

---

34 As accessed through www.computerlaw.com.au on 9 August 2008.

35 1999.

36 (1998) FSR 2.

37 CH-1997-P No.2355, July 18, 1997.

The conflict concerned the use of the word prince.com as a domain name for a website. ICANN 1992 introduced UDRP which is a cheap, fast and cost effective way of resolving domain name disputes. On the other hand, the dispute on domain name cyber-squatting in *Panavision International LP v. Toppen*[38] involved the dilution of a trademark. The defendant who registered trademarks as domain names for sale was held liable.

The court's argument was based on Section 115 of the Federal Trade mark dilution Act 15 which plainly stipulates that;

> "*The owner of the famous mark shall be entitled ... to an injunction against another person's commercial use in commerce of a mark or trade name, if such use begins after the mark has become famous and causes the dilution of the distinctive quality of the mark.*"[39]

At East African level the battle over domain names is shaping up suggesting a great likelihood of domain names cyber-squatting, passing off, trademark infringement and dispute thereof. It has been argued by various experts that companies or institutions that fail to take precautions and register their domain names are likely to fall into multiple hands of extortionists.[40] In the meantime the Internet is believed to have spawned a cut-throat competition between companies with similar names over domain names and shrewd individuals have registered domain names hoping to get more money by selling them to various companies and institutions. This can make a lot of companies with trademarks to lose their goodwill if no effective legal measures are enforced. In Kenya a great likelihood of domain name dispute can be observed from two companies namely Equity Bank and Wanam Associates whereby the Equity Bank rushed to register *equitybank.co.ke* while at the same time the later company also registered the same domain name as *equitybank.co.ke* which seems to clearly deny the bank the benefit associated with its brand name.[41]

Many companies in the East African Community have not fully taken advantage of registering their domain names or websites hence they face the risk of losing the value of goodwill that their business names carry, since they are unprotected against any shrewd competitors who are greedy on cashing in on their market. Arguably the countries lack legal framework to safeguard the aggrieved parties where individuals register company names as their domain names for extortion. The current legal framework protects trademarks (passing off), patent, copyright and it is difficult to enforce

[38] Case No. 97-55467.
[39] See Reed, C., *Internet Law Text and Materials* 2000 at page 54.
[40] See the *Kenya Sunday News* dated 10 of December 2006.
[41] Ibid.

because they deal with tangible products and the registration of domain names is in the hands of the private sector. The problem seems to be as hot as counterfeit and pirating whereby cyber squatters register known trademark names as their domain names and approach the companies who own the trademarks to buy the domain names.[42]

However this is also a great challenge at international level whereby major companies have suffered at the hands of extortionists and cyber squatters as indicated in the above mentioned cases. At one time Coca-Cola Company had to pay substantial amounts of money to reclaim its name coke.

8.9 *Dispute Resolution outside the Court System*

The dispute on domain names have sometimes been solved outside court under alternative dispute resolutions using some policies and guidelines. Due to the contractual nature of the relationship between the holder of the domain name and registry, it is possible to provide in that contract for some initial dispute resolution by the registry itself. The registry has 19 directors drawn from a range of Internet interest groups. The Internet Corporation for Assigned Names and Numbers (ICANN) has produced a Dispute Resolution Policy to which all domain name registries now adhere.[43] This Uniform Domain Name Dispute Resolution Policy (the "Policy") has been adopted by the ICANN, and is incorporated by reference into your Registration Agreement, and sets forth the terms and conditions in connection with a dispute between you and any party other than the registrar over the registration and use of an Internet domain name registered by you.

The basic principles of this dispute policy can be summarized as follows:

The "first come, first served" method of allocating domain names remains fundamental; the decision of the Court in *Pitman Training Ltd v. Nominet UK*[44] supports this policy of domain names and the importance of early registration. The dispute concerned the use of the domain name www.pitman.co.uk by two competing companies.

For the complainant on domain name cyber-squatting to successfully use UDRP it is recommended to show that:

- The domain name is identical or confusingly similar to a trade mark or service mark in which the complainant has rights;

---

[42] Ibid.

[43] Uniform Domain Name Dispute Resolution Policy (as Approved by ICANN 24 October 1999), c ICANN 1999.

[44] [1997] FSR 797.

- The domain name owner has no right or legitimate interests in respect of the domain name and
- The domain name that has been registered is being used in bad faith. Use of the domain name in bad faith is established by showing that the domain name has been registered or acquired primarily for the purposes of selling, renting or otherwise transferring the domain name to the owner of the trademark or service mark or to one of its competitors for valuable consideration among other things.[45] Where someone registers a domain name incorporating a trademark then the domain name holder could be in breach of the trademark law.[46]

[45] For detailed discussion see Turban, E., *E-commerce* 2002 at pages 20-22.

[46] See Section 10 of the UK CDPA 1988.

CHAPTER NINE

CONCLUSION

9.1 *Observations*

The foregoing discussion has revealed the great impact of the development of Information and Communication Technologies in the world including Tanzania and EAC in general. There is no doubt that the digital revolution springing from IT or ICT brings fundamental changes to communication leading to development of a new digital economy under the so called information society in which we now live, whereby information in its many forms is becoming a very important commodity thus posing challenges as to how it should be properly regulated.

This technological revolution has brought great changes and impacts affecting the way business is done, the way in which goods and services are ordered, marketed and the way in which contracts are made and performed. This trend poses great challenges for the current offline laws in Tanzania and other countries which must immediately respond to these developments on e-transactions that might boost the economy. The most significant aspect of this technological revolution is the development and the use of e-commerce.

The other area which has been greatly affected by this cyber technology includes Intellectual Property and Taxation Systems. The Internet has facilitated dissemination and infringement of intellectual property rights. There is no doubt that digitized goods and services pose a great challenge as far as e-taxation is concerned given the nature of offline laws in Tanzania. The laws in Tanzania neither cover online transactions nor recognize cyberspace or electronic signatures.

One can observe that common law countries like Tanzania seem to historically rely heavily on the transfer of written, signed and authenticated documents. There are some statutory rules that require some contracts to be made or evidenced in a particular way namely: by deed, under seal and writing, be signed manually before a witness and be evidenced with original documents.

Most laws governing business transactions provide that, the contract must be in writing and duly signed or authenticated before a witness, requirements which are no longer applicable in cyberspace world hence affecting these offline laws which have to be changed and reformed to accommodate e-commerce principles.

Arguably the current offline legislation that regulates communication, storage of information and transaction in Tanzania and other countries are not in tune with technological changes. Most legislation still maintain manuscript signatures as a means of authentication of documents and identifying parties creating a discriminatory approach to e-signatures and data messages or alternatives to paper based methods under e-commerce. These laws need to be reformed to reflect the impact of computer technology and other related technologies. In addition there is need to fully regulate all activities on the Internet or cyberspace. All legal changes to reflect technology need to be harmonized at regional level such as East African Community, SADC and international level. Some Model Laws such as UNCITRAL and Commonwealth need to be considered and adopted where necessary when changing or enacting cyber laws in Tanzania.

9.2 *Government Initiatives*

The Law Reform Commission of Tanzania on its own initiative as mandated by the enabling Act [CAP 171 RE.2002][1] has made a thorough research and review on the laws that are paper based methods which provide for the requirements of writing, hand written signatures and original documents. All this was done with a view of coming up with an effective legal framework that will permit, where appropriate the use of alternative paper based methods such as data message and electronic means of authentication (digital signatures). In line with this, the government through the Parliament amended the Evidence Act 1967 to allow e-evidence to be admissible before the court.

The introduction of Computer Law at the Faculty of Law, University of Dar Es salaam can also bring more changes by having more lawyers and other academics that are conversant with the legal aspects related to ICT or cyber laws. This area of law which changes with the development of technology if well appreciated can bridge the gap between technology and laws in Tanzania.[2]

During the preparation of the final text of this book, the government through Tanzania Communications Regulatory Authority and the Ministry of Communications, Science and Technology was in the final stage of preparing a Draft Bill namely the Electronic and Postal Communications Act (EPOCA). This Bill was aimed at repealing the Tanzania Communications

1 The Law Reform Commission of Tanzania Act.

2 The Author of this book was the first lecturer to introduce and successfully teach Computer Law/Cyber/ICT Law in Tanzania in 2003.

Regulatory Authority Act,[3] The Broadcasting Services Act,[4] and the Tanzania Communications Act.[5]

The Act addresses issues related to electronic communications, dispute resolutions, registration of SIM Cards, postal communications and other related issues. The Act further highlights the offences related to electronic communications and SIM Cards including some penalties. However the proposed Act does not address issues related to electronic transactions, communication of data messages, the liability of intermediaries (ISPs/OSPs), online dispute resolution, domain names administration, domain names cyber-squatting, online consumer protection, principles of data protection, authentication means of electronic communication such as electronic signatures, cryptography providers, etc. All these issues need to be fully addressed in this Act or any other proposed law as these are key components of effective and highly assured security on electronic communications. The proposed Act should be compared with other effective cyber laws from other jurisdictions such as South Africa,[6] Mauritius, Malta, Singapore, the UK, India, Australia, etc. All in all Tanzania and other East African Countries need to have effective legal frameworks that can cope with any technological changes to assure cyber security at national, regional and international level. There is also need to consider the relevant regional and international legal instruments and see how these can be adopted, signed and ratified as cyberspace or Internet has no boundary and does not recognize geographical limitations in terms of legal enforcement and compliance as anything can happen anywhere at any time in the world.

[3] Act 12, 2003.

[4] Cap 306.

[5] Tanzania Communications Act.

[6] Compare with the South Africa Electronic Communications and Transactions Act, 2002. See also the UK Electronic Communications Act 2000 and 2003.

BIBLIOGRAPHY

1. Bainbridge D., *Introduction to Computer Law*, Longman 4th Edition 1999.
2. Bakari J.K.,"a holistic Approach for Managing ICT Security in Non-Commercial Organizations", *A Case Study in a Developing Country*, Universitetssevice US-AB, Stockholm, Sweden 2007
3. Bradgate R., *Commercial Law,* 3rd Edition Oxford: Oxford University Press 2000.
4. Bwana J., *Challenges Facing Regulation of E-commerce in Tanzania* N.C:N.P.
5. Bwana J., on *E-banking and law in Tanzania* N.C:N.P.
6. Chipeta B.D., *A Magistrates Manual on Criminal and Civil Procedures* T.M.P Book Dept. 1987.
7. Edgar T., "Multimedia Convergence and the future of copyright in Broadcasts", *The Uganda Law Journal 2003*
8. Fifoot C. & Furmston, *Law of Contract*, 4th Edition 2001 N.C:N.P.
9. Gare S. & Christie A., *Blackstone's Statute on Intellectual Property* 5th Edition 2002 N.C:N.P.
10. Goodman J., "on The Pros and Cons of online Dispute Resolution, an assessment of cyber mediation" *Duke Law and Technology Review*, 2003.
11. Kelman A., Turban E. *on E-Commerce*, 2002 N.C:N.P.
12. Jacquiline L., *"Databases as Intellectual Property: New Legal and Regulatory Approaches," in ISLAT/IASTED* Third International Conference: Law and Technology 45-53 ed. S. Lesavich 2002.
13. Latimer, P., Australian Business Law, CCH Australia Limited, North Ryde 1996.
14. Lisa M. Sharrock, The Future of Domain Name Dispute Resolution: Crafting Practical International Legal Solutions from Within the UDRP Framework, 51 Duke Law Journal p.817 (2001.
15. Lloyd J.I., *Information Technology Law,* 3rd Edition, LexisNexis Butterworth UK; 15 Aug 2000.
16. McKenzie, P. & Ren Y. 2001. China's new regulatory regime for online banking services. E-Commerce Law Report, 3(10): 28-29.

17. Mambi. A., "Peering to the New Horizon", *The New Media*, The paper was presented at the Australasian Law Reform Agencies Conference, Sydney 2006.

18. Mambi A., *Copyright Infringement on Music Industry and the impact of technology on IP in Tanzania*, Dissertation submitted at the University of Aberdeen for LLM Requirements in 2003.

19. Sarkar S., Law of evidence, 16th Edition, Volume 1, (Thoroughly Revised & Enlarged) (In India, Pakistan, Bangladesh, Burma, Ceylon, Malaysia & Singapore LexisNexis Butterworths Wadhwa Nagpur 2007

20. Sarkar S., Law of evidence 16th Edition, Volume 2, (Thoroughly Revised & Enlarged) (In India, Pakistan, Bangladesh, Burma, Ceylon, Malaysia & Singapore LexisNexis Butterworths Wadhwa Nagpur 2007.

21. Schiavetta, S. *Online Dispute Resolution, E-Government and Overcoming the Digital Divide*, Norwegian Research Centre for Computers and Law, University of Oslo 2005

22. Sherman B. and Bently, L.., *Intellectual Property Law*, Oxford, Oxford University Press 2002.

23. Singh A., *The Law of Contract*, 9th Edition, 2005, Eastern Book Company, Lucknow, India

24. Smith & Keenan's, *Company Law* 13th Edition, 2005, Pearson Longman Harlow, UK

25. Smith & Keenan's, *Law for Business 13th Edition*, 2006, Pearson Longman Harlow, UK

26. Turban E., *on E-Commerce*, 2002, Sweet and Maxwell Publishers, London

27. *The Swedish ICT Commission on Law and IT 2002*

28. *The Final Report on E-Commerce and cyber crimes by the Law Reform Commission of Tanzania 2006*

29. Wahab M.S., on "Online Disputes resolution challenging the global digital", 2005

30. Reed C., *Internet Law; Text and Materials*

31. *The UNCITRAL Model Law on E-commerce with Guide to Enactment 1996 with additional articles 5 bis as adopted in 1998*

32. *The UNCITRAL Model Law on Digital Signatures 2001*

33. Wilson, C. *Intellectual Property Law (Nutshells)*
Sweet & Maxwell; 2Rev Ed edition 2005.

Websites

34. http://www.perkinscoie.com/resource/ecomm/prc.htm website accessed 26/*02/2003*

35. www.pitman.co.uk

36. http://www.itu.int/dms_pub/itu-s/md/03/wsis/doc/S03-WSIS-DOC-0004!!MSW-E.doc

37. google.com

Case Index

G

H

I

J

L

M

N

O

P

R

S

T

U

Subject Index